In accordance with the latest syllabus prescribed by the council for the Indian Certificate of Secondary Education Examination, New Delhi.

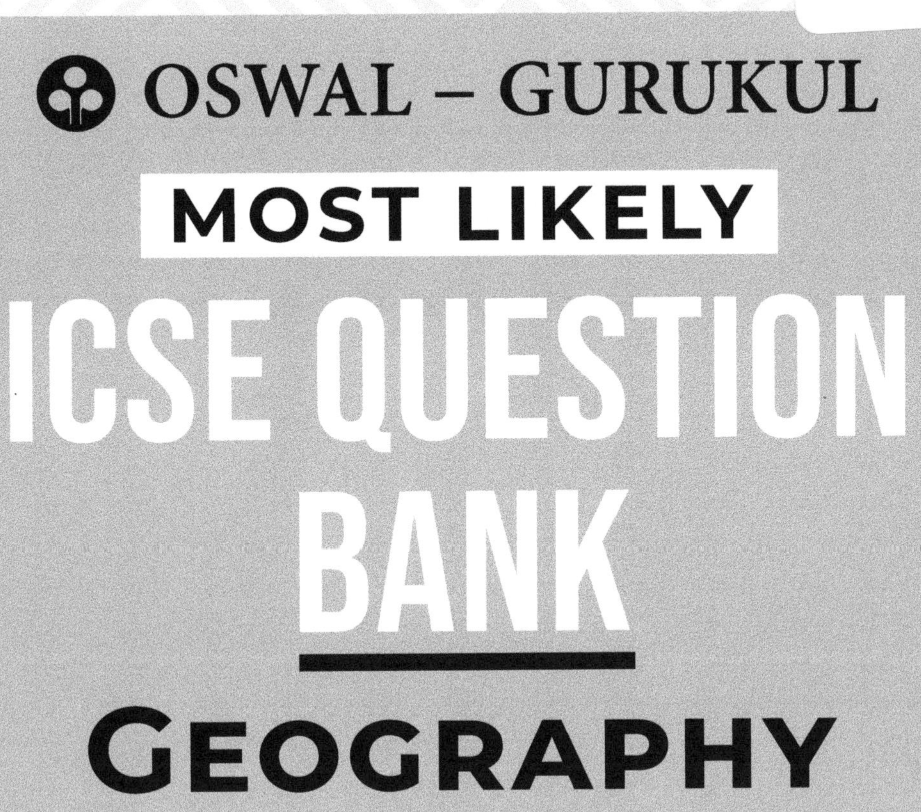

OSWAL – GURUKUL

MOST LIKELY

ICSE QUESTION BANK

GEOGRAPHY

CLASS IX

By

PANEL OF AUTHORS

EDITION : 2022

ISBN : 978-93-92563-08-9

PRICE : ₹ 265.00

PRINTED AT : Upkar Printing Unit, Agra

PUBLISHED BY

OSWAL PUBLISHERS

Head Office : 1/12, Sahitya Kunj, M.G. Road, Agra - 282 002

Phone : (0562) 2527771-4

Whatsapp : +91 74550 77222

E-mail : info@oswalpublishers.in

Website : www.oswalpublishers.com

The cover of this book has been designed using resources from Freepik.com

PREFACE

It is a matter of immense pride for us to present the 'ICSE MOST LIKELY QUESTION BANK' series, especially prepared for students appearing for Board examinations in the oncoming year.

This book has been created with the specific purpose of making the students' journey of learning, understanding and revising the concepts, effortless and simple. The topical approach with ample questions for every category is adopted to reinforce the students' understanding of each chapter. The category-wise division also allows them to peruse their progress as well as keep a check on their grasp of the theory.

Meticulous care has been taken in writing the book in simple, student-friendly language without compromising with the clarity of style.

We are confident that the book will enable the candidates to develop a better understanding of the curriculum and help them organize their learning process. This book shall definitely prove to be a fruitful tool for the students and encourage them towards scholastic excellence.

Constructive suggestions for further improvement of the book are always welcome.

—Publisher

IMPORTANT NOTE

The global outbreak of the Novel Coronavirus (COVID-19) has impacted all aspects of life including the educational life at schools. Schools across the country have been shut since March, 2020 due to the pandemic. While numbers of CISCE affiliated schools have tried to adapt to this changed scenario and have tried to keep alive the teaching learning process through online classes, there has been a significant shortening of the academic year and loss of the instructional hours.

To make up for the loss in instructional hours during the current session 2020-2021, the CISCE has worked with its subject experts, to reduce the syllabi for all major subjects at the ICSE and ISC levels. Syllabus reduction has been done, keeping in mind the linear progression across classes while ensuring that the core concepts related to the subject are retained.

The following reduced syllabi, for the current Academic Year 2020-2021 have been made available on the CISCE website www.cisce.org under 'Publications':

- ICSE Reduced Syllabus for Class IX
- ICSE Reduced Syllabus for Class X
- ISC Reduced Syllabus for Class XI
- ISC Reduced Syllabus for Class XII

Heads of CISCE affiliated schools have been asked to ensure that the concerned subject teachers at the ICSE and ISC levels transact the syllabus strictly according to sequence of topics, so as to facilitate further reduction in syllabus, if required, depending on the situation of the pandemic in the country.

We at Oswal Publishers, have developed all our books on the basis of the original syllabi with complete subjective knowledge of all the subjects, so that the students have an access to the entire syllabus. However, for the examination purpose, the students are advised to structure their preparations considering the latest alterations by the Council.

Scan this to know the recent changes in Syllabus

CONTENTS

How to choose a
GREAT CAREER

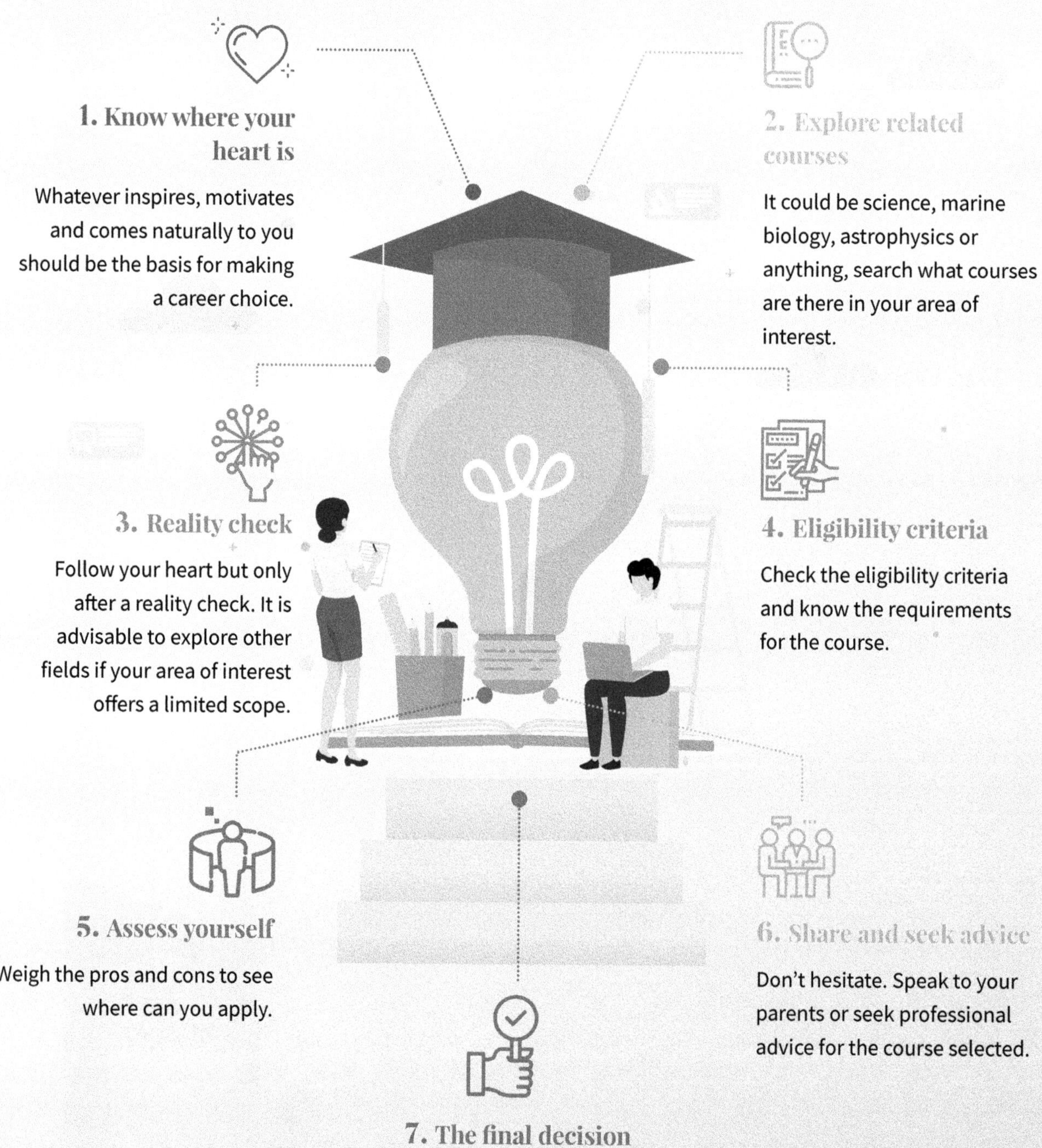

1. Know where your heart is

Whatever inspires, motivates and comes naturally to you should be the basis for making a career choice.

2. Explore related courses

It could be science, marine biology, astrophysics or anything, search what courses are there in your area of interest.

3. Reality check

Follow your heart but only after a reality check. It is advisable to explore other fields if your area of interest offers a limited scope.

4. Eligibility criteria

Check the eligibility criteria and know the requirements for the course.

5. Assess yourself

Weigh the pros and cons to see where can you apply.

6. Share and seek advice

Don't hesitate. Speak to your parents or seek professional advice for the course selected.

7. The final decision

Once you are through with all the steps, you will know where you stand and will be better placed to make the right choice.

Go where your strength is, not where your friends are.

STUDYING ONLINE IN A VIRTUAL GROUP

Virtual study groups are proven to be as effective as the conventional study groups. They are beneficial for each member as they allow individual participation, clearing doubts via meaningful discussions and most importantly provide a friendly support system.

STEPS TO CREATE AN EFFECTIVE VIRTUAL STUDY GROUP

- Before anything else, you need to choose a group of 8-10 people who have the same syllabus and goals as yours.
- Next, fix up a time table that is suitable to all the members. Each day, everyone should come prepared with the topic of discussion in the group.
- After this, you need to find a digital platform where you can organise your study session. ExamTime and Thinkbinder are two of the dedicated web-sites for this use. You can also use common text and video communication apps like WhatsApp or Skype to gather all the members at one place for the purpose of study.
- Avoid going off topic, into idle chat. After a topic has been discussed, all the members should prepare notes for revision and share them in the next session.
- In the final round, you can hold a special quiz session in which all the members can participate and assess their level of understanding of the topic.

So, when you have to prepare for your next test or exam, organise an online group study session with your friends and study smart to obtain the perfect score. You can tell us about your virtual group study experience at contact@oswalpublishers.com . All the best!

WEEKLY SCHEDULE

	MONDAY	TUESDAY	WEDNESDAY	THURSDAY	FRIDAY	SATURDAY	SUNDAY

GOALS

DON'T FORGET!

NOTES

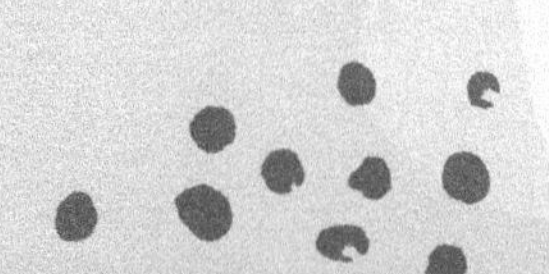

Very Short Answer Questions | Set 1 |

Chapter 1. Earth As a Planet

Q. 1. Name the closest and the farthest planet from the Sun.

Ans. Mercury is the closest and the Neptune is the farthest planet from the Sun in the Solar system.

Q. 2. State two effects of the revolution of the Earth around the Sun.

Ans. Revolution of the Earth around the Sun will result in

(i) Change in seasons.

(ii) Variation in the length of day and night.

Q. 3. What is the average distance of the Earth from the Sun?

Ans. The average distance of the Sun from the Earth is 150 million kilometres.

Q. 4. Name the major layers of the Earth.

Ans. The three major layers of the Earth are lithosphere, hydrosphere and atmosphere.

Q. 5. What is the shape of the Earth?

Ans. The shape of the Earth is not a perfect sphere. It is an oblate spheroid. It means the Earth is slightly flattened at the pole with a bulge at the equator.

Q. 6. Define the terms.

(i) Apogee

(ii) Perigee

Ans. (i) Apogee is the farthest point of the Moon from the Earth, i.e. 406,700 kilometres.

(ii) Perigee is the nearest point of the Moon from the Earth i.e. 382,500 kilometres.

Q. 7. Define water cycle.

Ans. Water cycle is the continuous movement of water through various spheres of the Earth. The cycle involves the process of evaporation of surface water and transpiration from the vegetative covers followed by condensation and finally results in various forms of precipitation such as rain, snow, hail, sleets, etc.

Q. 8. How many terrestrial planets are there in the solar system and which among them is largest?

Ans. Our Solar system has four terrestrial planets: Mercury, Venus, Earth and Mars. Earth is the largest planet among them.

Q. 9. What is the importance of the Ozone Layer?

Ans. Ozone layer in the Earths atmosphere contains relatively higher concentration of ozone (O_3) in the stratosphere that restricts 97-99% high-frequency ultra-violate rays to reach the Earth surface by absorbing them. They also help in retaining the heat radiated from the surface of the Earth.

Q. 10. Define biosphere.

Ans. The layer of the Earth that sustains life is called biosphere. It contains almost all the plants, animals, microbes, humans, insects, and everything living. From top to bottom it is a stretch of about 20 kilometres. It includes part of lithosphere, hydrosphere, atmosphere and other spheres.

Q. 11. What is the mean average temperature of the Earth and why is it important?

Ans. The mean average temperature of the Earth is 14° C. It is the ideal temperature that supports life.

Q. 12. Name the blue planet of the solar system and mention why it is called so?

Ans. The Earth is called a blue planet of the solar system. 71% of the Earth's surface is covered by liquid or frozen water which creates an impression of blue circular mass when seen from the space. This is the reason the Earth is called a blue planet.

Q. 13. How many known satellites are there in the Solar system? Name the largest satellite of Saturn.

Ans. There are 57 known satellites in the Solar system. Titan is the largest known satellite of Saturn.

Q. 14. What unit do we need to measure distances in the universe?

Ans. For measuring the distances between celestial bodies in the universe, the unit required is the light year. It is the distance travelled by light in one year, i.e. 9.4607×10^{12} km.

Q. 15. Which planets have rings around them?

Ans. Saturn, Uranus and Neptune have rings around them.

Q. 16. Why does the moon appear to be bigger than other celestial bodies even if its size is small?

Ans. Even if the size of the moon is smaller than other celestial bodies in the universe, it appears to be bigger than them due to the nearness of the moon from the Earth.

Q. 17. Which is the hottest and coldest planet of the Solar System?

Ans. Venus is the hottest and the Neptune is the coldest planet of the Solar System.

Q. 18. Which planets are known as the Twin planets in the Solar system and why?

Ans. The Venus and the Earth are called Twin Planets in the solar system because both planets have almost same size, mass and composition. Also, they are the neighbouring planets.

Q. 19. How does the earth create a magnetic field around it and how it is important to us?

Ans. The outer core of the earth consists of molten iron and flow of convection current in the molten iron develops a magnetic field around the earth. The magnetic field of the earth surface helps in keeping the cosmic rays away from the earth's atmosphere.

Q. 20. What is the orbital period of the moon and what is its average speed?

Ans. The orbital period of the moon is 27 days 7 hours 43.7 minutes and the average orbital speed is 1.022 km/s.

Q. 21. What do you mean by atmosphere?

Ans. The gaseous envelope that covers the Earth is known as atmosphere. It contains a mixture of gas, dust and water vapour. The mixture comprises of 78% of Nitrogen, 21% of oxygen and a very little amount of carbon dioxide, argon and other gases.

Q. 22. What do you mean by hydrosphere?

Ans. The part of the planet made up of water is called th hydrosphere. This includes oceans, rivers, lakes and clouds. It also includes atmospheric water vapour and the water present underground.

Q. 23. Why only one side of the moon is visible form the Earth?

Ans. The time taken by moon to complete one revolution around the Earth is almost equal to the time taken for its rotation. The situation is known as synchronous rotation, or tidal locking. This the why we can see only side of the moon.

Q. 24. Define antipodal balance between land and water.

Ans. The antipodal balance between land and ocean implies the arrangement of continents and ocean on the earth in such a way that the land on one side of the globe is balanced by the water on the other side.

Q. 25. What is the position of Earth with respect to sun?

Ans. The Earth is the third planet from the Sun and orbits at an average distance of 93 million miles.

Q. 26. Name the early mathematician who held the view that Earth was spherical in shape.

Ans. The Greek philospher and mathematician, Pythagoras stated that the earth was a perfect sphere and the statement was supported by Aristotle with several arguments.

Q. 27. What is Geoid? **[November, 2019]**

Ans. Geoid word has combination of two words 'Geo' means Earth and 'id' means like. The word Geoid means something like Earth.

Q. 28. What conditions favour life on Earth? **[February, 2020]**

Ans. Life on Earth is favoured by the following points:

(i) Moderate climate.

(ii) Availability of Water.

(iii) Availability of land to practice agriculture and build houses.

Chapter 2. Latitudes and Longitudes

Q. 1. What do you mean by a globe?

Ans. Globe is the spherical representation of the earth with a network of latitude and longitude drawn over it. The globe serves the purpose of identifying various features of the earth surface.

Q. 2. What do you mean by geographical grid?

Ans. The geographical grid is the network of latitudes and longitudes used for locating any place accurately over a map or globe.

Q. 3. What do you mean by latitude?

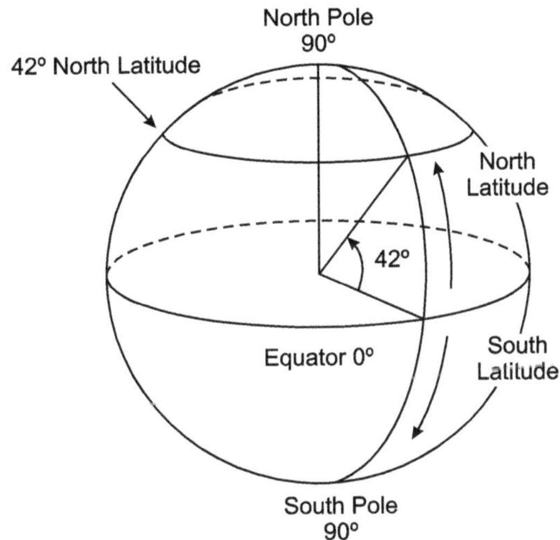

Ans. Latitude is the angular distance of a point, north or south of the equator from the centre of the Earth. It is usually measured in degree, minute and seconds.

Q. 4. What do you mean by longitude?

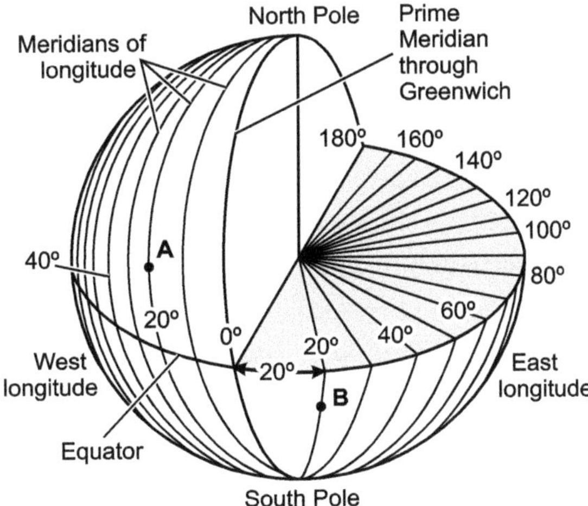

Ans. Longitude is the angular distance between the Prime meridian at Greenwhich and a point on any meridian on the surface of earth. It is the expressed in degree, minutes and seconds.

Q. 5. State the importance of pole star.

Ans. Pole star is the only star which is located directly above North Pole and this is the reason it hardly appears to move or changes its position. It helps in getting the north direction as its position remains unchanged all through the night and year.

Q. 6. Write the name of the most important latitude and longitude?

Ans. The most important latitude is equator and the most important longitude is Prime Meridian.

Q. 7. What is equator and how is it important to us?

Ans. Equator is the imaginary line that runs through the centre of the Earth horizontally and divides the Earth into two equal halves i.e. Northern Hemisphere and Southern Hemisphere.

Q. 8. What is Prime Meridian and how is it important to us?

Ans. Prime Meridian is an imaginary line that passes through the city of Greenwich, England. Like equator it also divides earth into two equal halves but vertically, i.e. Eastern and Western Hemispheres. It is also considered as the base for determining time zones of the world. It is who known as Greenwich meridian.

Q. 9. Why latitudes are also called as parallels of Latitude?

Ans. The lines of latitude run parallel to equator as well as to each other. So they are called parallels of latitude.

Q. 10. Why longitudes are also called meridians?

Ans. Meridian means 'midday'. When the Sun is overhead on certain longitude it is midday or noon for that particular longitude. Thus longitude is also known as meridians.

Q. 11. What do you mean by local time?

Ans. Local time means the time of a certain place determined on the basis of the apparent movement of the Sun. When the Sun is at its highest point or zenith, the time happens to be noon there. It varies by four minutes for every longitude.

Q. 12. What do you mean by the Standard Time?

Ans. The Standard Time is the official time of a country based on the standard meridian passing through it.

Q. 13. Which longitude is used for determining the world standard time and what is the value of it?

Ans. The value of longitude passing through Greenwhich city in London is used for determining the world standard time. The value of Greenwhich mean time is 0° longitude.

Q. 14. What do you mean by Indian Standard Time?

Ans. Indian Standard Time is the time observed through out India. i.e. GMT+ 05:30 hours. The time is determined on the basis of the Standard Meridian of India which passes through 85.5° E (82° 30′) longitude.

Q. 15. What do you mean by a time zone and why it is required?

Ans. A time zone refers to a region of the globe that follows a uniform standard time so as to satisfy social, legal and commercial purposes. Time zones are required when countries have vast east-west longitudinal extent. Practically it is impossible to have one standard time when the east west extent of a country is too large. Thus we require more than one time zone instead of only one for such countries.

Q. 16. What do you mean by the International Date Line?

Ans. The International Date Line refers to the north-south imaginary line on the surface of earth that passes through the Pacific Ocean. It is accepted internationally that a new calendar day begins at this line. One day is on the east of this line and the following day is on the west of this line.

Q. 17. What do you mean by great circle route and how they are important?

Ans. A great circle refers to any circle on the Earth's circumference whose centre coincides with the centre of the Earth. Since a great circle represents the shortest distance between two point anywhere on the Earth's surface, they are mostly followed by sailors and pilots for navigation.

Q. 18. Name a latitude which forms a Great Circle. **[November, 2019]**

Ans. Equator or 0° latitude forms Great circle.

Q. 19. What do you understand by the Standard Meridian? **[February, 2020]**

Ans. A meridian or longitude is selected as a standard time for a country on which the most important city is located or part of it is called as Standard Meridian.

Q. 20. Why it is practical to follow standard time rather than the local time? **[February, 2020]**

Ans. It is practical to follow standard time rather than the local time because following the local times in a country will create confusion for its citizens. Moreover, people travelling from one time zone to another will always direct their watched according to their location.

Q. 21. What is a time zone? How many time zones are there in the world? **[February, 2020]**

Ans. A time zone is a region on a globe that experiences similar standard time. There are total 24 time zones.

Q. 22. Which pressure belt is known as 'horse latitude'? Why? **[February, 2020]**

Ans. Subtropical high pressure belt that lies between 25° to 35° N and S is called as horse latitude. It is known as horse latitude because during ancient days sailors used to unload their horses (cargo) in the sea to make their ships lighter.

Q. 23. Name the latitudes which demarcate northern and southern limit of the torrid zone. **[February, 2020]**

Ans. The boundary of Torrid Zone has been demarcated by Tropic of Cancer (23.5° N) in the north and Tropic of Capricorn (23.5° S) in the south.

Q. 24. Calculate the time of a place located at 30° E Longitude, when it is 10 P.M. at 30° W longitude. **[February, 2020]**

Ans. The time at 30° W = 10:00 P.M.

Time difference at 30° E = 60 × 4 is 240 minutes or 4 hours

Because 30° E lies in the Eastern Hemisphere, we will add the time

Thus, the time at 30° E is = 10:00 + 4 hours

= 2:00 A.M.

Chapter 3. Rotation and Revolution

Q. 1. What do you mean by rotation of the Earth and how it is important?

Ans. The rotation of the Earth refers to its circular motion on its own axis. It takes 24 hours to complete one rotation. It results into the occurrence of day and night.

Q. 2. What do you mean by revolution of the Earth and how it is important?

Ans. The revolution of the Earth refers to the movement of the Earth around the Sun in an elliptical orbit. The Earth takes 365 days and five hours to complete one revolution. Earth revolution around the sun brings changes in the season.

Q. 3. What is the shape of the earth's orbit?

Ans. The Earth's orbit is elliptical in shape.

Q. 4. What do you mean by the axis of the Earth and what angle does it make with the plane of the orbit?

Ans. The Earth's axis is the imaginary straight line that joins two poles of the Earth. It makes an angle of 66½° with the plane of the orbit.

Q. 5. What do you mean by circle of illumination?

Ans. The circle of illumination means the imaginary line that divide the illuminated portion from the darken part of the Earth.

Q. 6. What do you mean by solar day and sidereal day?

Ans. The solar day is refers to the time taken by the Sun to return to the same position in the sky. On the other hand sidereal day refers to the time taken by the Earth to rotate on its own axis relative to the star, which is four minutes shorter than the Solar day.

Q. 7. State the reason why we do not feel the motion of the Earth.

Ans. We don't feel the motion of the Earth as we are also moving with it at the same constant speed.

Q. 8. What do you mean by solstice?

Ans. Solstice refers to the day of the year when the sun reaches to the highest position in the sky and result in the longest day of the year. For Northern Hemisphere the day is on 21st of June every year and for Southern hemisphere the day is on 23rd of September.

Q. 9. What do you mean by the term equinox? **[November, 2019]**

Ans. When the Sun is overhead at the equator, it results in equal length of day and night on the Earth surface. The day is called as equinox.

Q. 10. Which region is often called the Land of Midnight Sun and why?

Ans. Norway is often called the Land of Midnight Sun as it experience a summer in which the sun never sets for six month and a winter where the sun never rises for six months.

Q. 11. Explain the relationship between the seasons in Northern and Southern Hemisphere.

Ans. The change in seasons occur due to the revolution of the Earth around the Sun. As the Sun makes an angle of 23.5° with its orbital plane, the seasons experienced in the Northern Hemisphere is quite opposite to those experienced in the Southern Hemisphere. The Northern Hemisphere gets more hours of day light during June, Thus it experiences summer. On the other hand the Southern Hemisphere does not get minimum hours of day light and experiences winter during June.

Q. 12. What consequences would have been experienced if the axis of the earth was vertical instead of tilted?

Ans. If the earth axis was straight instead of titled, we would have experience the following changes.

(i) The length of day and night would have been equal at all the places.

(ii) There would have no seasons.

Q. 13. What do you mean by aphelion and perihelion?

Ans. The aphelion and perihelion are the two positions of the Earth which are fixed with response to the Sun.

Aphelion refers to the farthest position of the Earth with respect to the Sun in its orbit. This usually occurs during early July, nearly two weeks after June Solstice.

Perihelion refers to the nearest position of the Earth with respect to the Sun in its orbit. This usually occurs on about 3, January.

Q. 14. How seasonal impact differs in low and high latitudes?

Ans. The seasonal variation across the latitudes is distinctly felt. The low latitudes receive abundance of solar radiation and rainfall whereas the regions of the high latitudes receive comparatively less amount of solar radiation and less rainfall.

Q. 15. On which date will the North Pole have 24 hours of day light? **[November, 2019]**

Ans. The North Pole of the Earth experiences 24 hours of day light during summer solstice i.e., 21st June.

Chapter 4. Structure of the Earth and Internal Processes

Q. 1. What is the density of rock of near the surface of the earth and the average density of the earth?

Ans. The density of rock near the surface of the earth is 2.8 g/cc and the average density of the earth is 5.5 g/cc.

Q. 2. Name the layers of the earth.

Ans. Earth's layers comprise of an outer, middle and core. The outer layer is called crust which is solid. The middle layer is called mantle and it is viscous. The core is further divided into a solid core and outer liquid core.

Q. 3. What do you mean by lithosphere?

Ans. The outer layer of the Earth is also called lithosphere. The name is derived from the Greek word 'lithos', which means rocks or stones. Thus lithosphere exactly means the rocks sphere as it is primarily made up of rocks.

Q. 4. What is the average depth of the Earth's crust? How does it vary from continent to ocean?

Ans. The average depth of the Earth's Crust is around 60 km. The depth of the continental crust is about 30 kms, whereas the depth of oceanic crust varies between 25-30 kms.

Q. 5. What are the subdivision of lithosphere?

Ans. The lithosphere has two subdivisions. They are

(i) Sial

(ii) Sima

Q. 6. What do you mean Sial?

Ans. The upper layer of the crust is called Sial. This is also called the continental crust. It is made up of rocks that contain mainly silicates and aluminum, from which the name Sial is derived.

Q. 7. Why do you mean Sima?

Ans. Sima is the lower layer of the crust or lithosphere. It also refers to oceanic crust. The rocks of this layer mainly contains silicate and magnesium, from which the name Sima is derived.

Q. 8. What does the Continental Drift Theory state about Sima?

Ans. The Continental Drift Theory of Wegener states that, the original landmass of Sial or Pangaea was fractured and drifted apart to form newer separated continental landmasses.

Q. 9. What do you mean by discontinuity?

Ans. The layers of the Earth are separated by each other by thin layers, known as discontinuity. The discontinuity is a surface where the seismic waves change their velocity.

Q. 10. What do you mean by the Mohorovicic discontinuity?

Ans. The Mohorvicic Discontinuity is the layer that separates the crust from the mantle. The layer is the lower limit of the Earth's crust which is situated at an average density of 32 kilometres beneath the continental crust and the average depth decreases to 8 kilometres under the oceanic crust.

Q. 11. Define mantle. What are its main components?

Ans. Mantle is the second layer in the interior of the earth. The average thickness of the mantle is 2900 km. The layer consists of rocks that contains silicate and metals like magnesium and iron.

Q. 12. What do you mean by Asthenosphere? Why do we call it a low velocity zone?

Ans. The upper part of the mantle is known as Asthenosphere. As the velocity of earthquake wave decreases in it, it is also called low-velocity zone.

Q. 13. What do you mean by Gutenberg Discontinuity?

Ans. The Gutenberg Discontinuity is the layer that separates the mantle from the core. In this layer the velocity of the primary waves decreases, whereas the secondary waves disappears completely.

Q. 14. What do you mean by Mesosphere inside the earth's interior?

Ans. The lower part of the Mantle is called Mesosphere. It is located at a depth of approximately 750 kilometres.

Q. 15. Define core. State one of its important features?

Ans. Core is the inner most layer of the Earth's interior, which is also known as Barysphere. According to Greek terminology Bary means heavy and the name suggests it is the densest of all the layers of the earth. The layer is characterized by high temperature and pressure.

Q. 16. What do you mean by convection current?

Ans. Convection current is the flow of heat energy inside the interior of the Earth. The heat is generated due to the high temperature and pressure present within the Earth. The convection current helps in moving the molten material from the core to the crust.

Q. 17. State the theory of Plate tectonics.

Ans. The Earth's crust is divided into number of plates among which seven are major and the rest are minor plates. The theory of plate tectonics states the sliding of these plates with relation to each other over the mantle.

Q. 18. What do you mean by constructive plate margin?

Ans. Sometimes during sliding the plates drift apart from one another. These are called divergent plate and the space between them is known as constructive plate margin. As a result of the drifting the magma wells up from the interior and cools down near the surface. Thus a new landform is created. This is the reason the margin between these kinds of plates is called constructive plate margin.

Q. 19. What do you mean by destructive plate boundaries?

Ans. At time while moving over the magma layer boundaries, plates tend to move towards each other and thereby collide with each other. As a result one part of the plate is destroyed as it slides below the other. The process is called subduction.

Q. 20. What do you mean by conservative margin?

Ans. Conservative plate are also known as transform plate margin. It refers to the position where the plates slide past each other. The friction between the plates results in the occurrence of constant earthquakes.

Q. 21. Name the major plates on the earth's crust.

Ans. Major plates of the Earth are the American plates, the Pacific plates, the Eurasian Plates, the African Plate, the Indo-Australian plate and the Antarctic Plate.

Q. 22. How does the Ozone layer protect life on the Earth's surface? **[November, 2019]**

Ans. Ozone is a life protecting layer present in stratosphere. This layer absorbs the harmful incoming UV (Ultra Violet) radiations from Sun and shields life from intense, harmful form of energy.

Q. 23. What is the composition of the Earth's Crust? **[February, 2020]**

Ans. Earth's crust is composed of continental crust and oceanic crust. The continental crust consists of silicate and aluminum (SIAL). The oceanic crust is composed of silicate and magnesium (SIMA).

Q. 24. What is the composition of the core of the Earth? **[February, 2020]**

Ans. The core is made up of nickel and iron commonly known as NIFE (NI+FE).

Chapter 5. Landforms of the Earth

Q. 1. What do you mean by geomorphology?

Ans. The term geomorphology refers to the systematic study of earth's relief features. The term was derived from three words geo means the earth, morph means the form and logy means science.

Q. 2. What do you mean by topography?

Ans. The topography is a picture of various natural features on the land surface. It furnishes the detailed information of a particular area like mountains, hills, rivers, roads, lakes and valley, etc.

Q. 3. What do you mean by a terrain?

Ans. Landforms are the natural features of the earth that are created due to the internal or external force of the earth. These consolidated stretch of landforms on the surface of the earth is called terrain.

Q. 4. Define mountains.

Ans. Mountains are the landforms that rises above the surrounding land, land above 600 m is called a mountain, while land below 600 m is called a hill.

Q. 5. Write down two characteristics of Fold Mountains?

Ans. The two characteristics of Fold Mountains are:

(i) They form parallel ranges.

(ii) They are prone to sudden forces which results in volcanic eruption and earthquake.

Q. 6. What do you mean by orogenic movements?

Ans. Orogenic movement refers to the process of mountain building when the continental plates crumple towards each other thereby pushing the crust upward to form one or more mountains.

Q. 7. Name any two recently occurred mountain building processes along with the associated time period.

Ans. The two recent periods of mountain building are as follows:

(i) The Caledonian period which occurred nearly 350 million years ago.

(ii) The Hercynian period which occurred nearly 240 million years ago

Q. 8. What do you mean by syncline and anticline?

Ans. When the mountains were formed out of the folding process of continental margins, the crusts were wrinkled. The up folds or the crests were called anticlines. On the other hand, the down folds or the troughs were called synclines.

Q. 9. Which mountain range has the highest and largest mountains in the world?

Ans. The Himalayas are the world's highest and largest mountains. It stretches across mid-Asia with 281 peaks.

Q. 10. Name the highest peak of the world along with its height?

Ans. Mount Everest is the highest peak in the world with a height of 8848 m. It belongs to the continent of Asia.

Q. 11. What do you mean by rift valley?

Ans. A linear-shaped valley created due to divergence of the plates and crustal extension is called a rift valley. It is a low land between several high lands and mountain ranges, which deepens further by the force of erosion.

Q. 12. What do you mean by plateaus?

Ans. Plateaus are the highlands which usually elevated significantly above the surrounding and consist of flat terrain at the top. They are also called tablelands.

Q. 13. What do you mean by alluvial plain?

Ans. The depositional landforms created by the alluvium carried out by the rivers are known as alluvial plains. Alluvial plains can be categorised into various type based on the location of the alluvial deposits, such as piedmont plains, flood plains and deltas.

Q. 14. What do you mean by piedmont plains? Give an example.

Ans. When the rivers deposit the alluvium at the foothills of the mountains they form piedmont plains. For example, plains formed at the foothills of Himalayas, Uttarakhand and Uttar Pradesh.

Q. 15. What do you mean by a delta?

Ans. A delta is a monotonously flat landform created by a huge amount of the silt brought by rivers. For example Ganga- Brahmaputra delta, deltas of North China.

Q. 16. Give two examples of old fold mountains.

Ans. The old fold mountains were formed more than 200 million years ago. The examples of old fold mountains are the Ural mountains of Western Russia and the Appalachian mountains of Eastern North America.

Q. 17. Give examples of young fold mountains.

Ans. The young fold mountains were formed nearly 25 million years ago. For example the Rocky mountain chains of North America and the Himalayan mountain range of Asia.

Q. 18. What do you understand by geosynclines?

Ans. Geosynclines are the linear troughs created due to the subsidence of the earth's crust because of sediment accumulation.

Q. 19. Define epeirogenic movement.

Ans. Epeirogenic movement is the continental building movements which mean upheavals or depressions of land exhibiting long wavelengths and little folding apart from broad undulations.

Q. 20. Define Diastrophism.

Ans. Diastrophism refers to the deformation of the earth's crust due to folding and faulting. It leads to the formation of continents and ocean basins.

Q. 21. Name the largest and highest plateau in the world?

Ans. The Tibetan Plateau is the largest and the highest plateau in the world and thus known as the roof of the world.

Q. 22. What do you mean by karst plain?

Ans. The plain created by the erosion of limestone area by underground water is known as karst plain. These types of plains are found in Yugoslavia, Southern France and plain of Kentucky.

Q. 23. What do you mean by Lacustrine Plains?

Ans. The plains formed due to the deposition of sediments in the lake basin are called Lacustrine Plains. The Kashmir valley of India is a type of Lacustrine Plain.

Q. 24. Give an example of each of the following: **[November, 2019]**

(i) Block Mountain (ii) Structural Plain

(iii) Volcanic Plateau

Ans. (i) Examples of block mountain- Vindayas and Satpura hills in India and Sierra Nevada in USA.

(ii) Examples of structural plain-The great plains of USA and central lowlands of Australia.

(iii) Examples of Volcanic plateau- Columbian plateau of USA and The Deccan trap of India.

Q. 25. How are fold mountains formed? **[February, 2020]**

Ans. The Fold Mountains are formed due to compression forces of the Earth that crumple the layer of surface into arches and troughs.

Chapter 6. Rocks

Q. 1. Define rocks. How they are formed.What are the various types of rocks found on the Earth?

Ans. Rocks are naturally occurring solid substances having inorganic compound. They contain different types of minerals. Rocks are of three types: igneous rocks, sedimentary rocks and metamorphic rocks.

Q. 2. Mention the formation of any one type of rock.

Ans. Igneous rocks are formed from the lava released form the volcanic eruption. The molten lava come out of the vents of the volcano and spreads on the surface of the earth. Eventually the lava gets cool down and solidified to form the igneous rocks.

Q. 3. Why are igneous rocks also known as primary rocks?

Ans. The igneous rocks are directly formed from the cooling of molten lava released from volcanic activities. The formation of igneous rocks involves cooling and solidification. This is the first rock that is formed in the rock cycle. From igneous rocks sedimentary rocks are formed and finally the sedimentary rocks convert to metamorphic rocks. This is the reason igneous rocks are called primary rocks.

Q. 4. What is lithification?

Ans. The process of lithification takes place in sedimentary rocks when the loose sediments turns in to hard rocks or lith. The process involves three procedures; evaporation, compaction and cementation.

Q. 5. Name two processes that lead to the formation of sedimentary rocks.

Ans. Two processes that lead to the formation of sedimentary rocks are lithification, erosion and deposition.

Q. 6. State two differences between rocks and minerals.

Ans. (i) Rocks consists of minerals, whereas the mineral contains one or more elements.

(ii) Rocks are heterogeneous in their composition. On the other hand minerals are homogenous in their composition.

Q. 7. Name two landforms made up of igneous rocks.

Ans. The two landforms made up of igneous rocks are sills and dykes.

Q. 8. What are sills and dykes?

Ans. Sills and dykes both are types of intrusive igneous rocks. The only difference is that dykes are the horizontal intrusion whereas the sills are the vertical intrusion in another types of rock strata.

Q. 9. Which rocks are associated with ore of metals?

Ans. The igneous rocks are associated with ore of metals, as they are originated by cooling of magma into crystalline rocks which are rich in metal.

Q. 10. Which rocks are associated with fossil fuels?

Ans. Fossil fuels are associated with sedimentary rocks. The fossils are trapped between two layers of sedimentary rocks. For example–Coal.

Q. 11. How igneous rocks are formed?

Ans. The igneous rocks are formed by the solidification and crystallization of molten lava released from deep within the Earth near the active plate boundary or hot spot.

Q. 12. How sedimentary rocks are formed?

Ans. Sedimentary rocks are formed by deposition of sediments by air, water, ice and gravity. Eventually these sediments settle down one over the other and turn hard through the process of evaporation, compaction and cementation.

Q. 13. Write down any two characteristic of extrusive igneous rocks.

Ans. (i) Extrusive rocks are exposed to the outside atmosphere after releasing from the core of the Earth. Thus cools down quickly.

(ii) The process of cooling is so quick that the lava did not get time to be crystalized and thus produce finely grained rock with glassy texture and small crystals.

Q. 14. Write down any two characteristic of intrusive igneous rocks.

Ans. (i) Intrusive igneous rocks get solidified and crystalized beneath surface of the earth. The minerals comparatively takes more time to be crystalized.

(ii) It produces igneous rocks of relatively large and irregular mass.

Q. 15. Define Hypabyssal.

Ans. Hypabyssal is the igneous intrusion caused due to the cooling and solidification of rising molten lava in the crack beneath the Earth's surface.

Q. 16. What do you mean by ultra-basic rocks?

Ans. The igneous rocks which do not contain silicate in them are called the ultra-basic rocks. They primarily consist of ferrous and magnesium. For example: Carbonatites.

Q. 17. Name any three elements of earth's crust.

Ans. The elements of earth's crust are silicon, aluminum, iron, magnesium, calcium, potassium, sodium and nickel.

Q. 18. What are the important characteristics of basic igneous rocks?

Ans. Important characteristics of basic igneous rocks are as follows:

(i) These rocks contain less quantity of silica and high quantity of basic oxides like iron and magnesium.

(ii) They are darker in colour with large and dense grains of crystal.

Q. 19. Which is the most wide spread rock of the world?

Ans. The sedimentary rock is the most wide spread rocks in this world.

Q. 20. What are the agents of sediment deposition?

Ans. The agents of sediment depositions are river, wind and glaciers.

Q. 21. What are metamorphic rocks? Explain with example.

Ans. When the complete texture of rocks originated from volcanic activities and diastrophism, the metamorphic rocks are formed. For example: conversion of limestone into marble or shale into slate.

Q. 22. Based on the involvement of agencies, how many type of metamorphism are there?

Ans. Based on the involvement of agencies there are two types of metamorphism: thermal and dynamic metamorphism.

Q. 23. What do you mean by thermal metamorphism? Give example.

Ans. When the transformation of rock is caused due to the increase in the temperature, it is known as thermal metamorphism. For example: transformation of Graphite into Limestone.

Q. 24. What do you mean by dynamic metamorphism? Give example.

Ans. When the rocks are subjected to tremendous pressure, the process of metamorphism is called dynamic metamorphism. For example: Finely grained non- foliated metamorphic rock known as Hornfels.

Q. 25. State two ways in which Igneous Rocks differ from Sedimentary Rocks. **[November, 2019]**

Ans. (i) Igneous rocks are formed out of volcanic eruption. On the other hand, sedimentary rocks are form by deposition of agents of erosion.

(ii) Igneous rocks are crystalline rocks rather sedimentary rocks have layered structure.

Chapter 7. Volcanoes

Q. 1. What do you mean by a volcano?

Ans. A volcano is a conical mountain that possesses a crater or vent through which the lava fragments of rocks and gasses erupt from the earth's crust.

Q. 2. Classify the volcanoes based on the frequency of eruption.

Ans. Based on the frequency of eruption, volcanoes are of three types:

(i) Active Volcanoes

(ii) Dormant Volcanoes

(iii) Extinct Volcanoes

Q. 3. Classify the volcanoes based on types of eruptions.

Ans. Based on types of eruption, the volcanoes are of four types:

(i) Central Volcanoes

(ii) Conical Volcanoes

(iii) Shield Volcanoes

(iv) Fissure Volcanoes

Q. 4. Give an example of one active and one dormant volcano.

Ans. Mount Etna in Italy is an active volcano, and Vesuvius in Italy is a dormant volcano.

Q. 5. Name any two types of landforms made by volcanoes.

Ans. Two landforms made by volcanoes are:

(i) Cider cone

(ii) Caldera

Q. 6. What do you mean by composite cones?

Ans. Composite cones are the aggregation of several cinder cones or parasite cones, which are made up of alternating layers of lava and ash. These are presumed to be the most significant and highest volcanic cones in the world. For example, Mount Fuji in Japan and Mount Vesuvius in Italy.

Q. 7. What do you mean by a cinder cone?

Ans. The cinder cones are the steep slope hills of the loose pyroclastic fragment that built around the volcanic vent. The pyroclastic materials like clinkers and ashes are thrown out to the air and deposited around the vent as a cone.

Q. 8. What do you mean by a fissure?

Ans. A fissure refers to the long narrow opening or line of the opening created due to the cracking and splitting of the rocks or the earth.

Q. 9. What is a caldera?

Ans. A large basin-shaped volcanic depression formed due to the collapse of subsidence of the mouth of the vent during an eruption.

Q. 10. What do you mean by dykes?

Ans. Dykes are the vertical arrangement of solidified lava in the vertical cracks. They pierce through the bedding planes.

Q. 11. What do you mean by Sills?

Ans. Sills are the horizontal solidification of lava deposits in the horizontal planes. They accumulated around the bedding planes of sedimentary rocks.

Q. 12. What do you mean by phacoliths?

Ans. When magma is deposited on the crest of an anticline or at the base of a syncline, it is known as Phacoliths. These are generally acidic. These are dome-shaped landforms.

Q. 13. What do you mean by Lapoliths?

Ans. Lapoliths refer to the saucer-type formation created due to the solidification of lava in the shallow basins.

Q. 14. Define Laccoliths?

Ans. When the intrusive acidic lava solidifies to produce dome-shaped structures, they are called laccoliths.

Q. 15. What do you mean by Batholiths?

Ans. When large masses of magma cool down deep below the earth's surface, they form Batholiths. These dome shape structures contain rocks with large grains produced from the slow cooling of magma.

Q. 16. What do you mean by Geysers?

Ans. Geysers refer to the intermittent jets of streams that are produced by the heating of underground water by coming in contact with magma. When the water under the ground surface gets extremely hot they are converted into steams and come out to the surface with tremendous pressure.

Q. 17. What do you mean by Hot spring?

Ans. The hot springs are the geo-thermally heated groundwater that emerges on to the surface of the earth, and there is a continuous flow of heated water to the spring.

Q. 18. How volcanic landforms are formed? Give an example of anyone volcanic landform.

Ans. The volcanic landforms are created when the pyroclastic material ejected out of the volcanoes are accumulated on the surface of the earth. One of such landforms is a cinder cone.

Q. 19. What is the difference between magma and lava?

Ans. When the molten materials are moving under the earth's crust, it is known as magma. When the magma is ejected to the earth's surface, it is called lava.

Q. 20. Name four extrusive landforms.

Ans. The extrusive landforms are calderas, lava shield, composite cones, and craters.

Q. 21. Name four intrusive landforms.

Ans. The intrusive landforms are dykes, sills, lapoliths, batholiths.

Q. 22. Name two important volcanic belts of the World.

Ans. The important volcanic belts of the World are:

(i) Circum-Pacific Belt

(ii) Mid-World Mountain Belt

Q. 23. What do you mean by the Magma chamber of a volcano?

Ans. The large pool of liquid magma beneath the surface of the earth is called Magma Chamber. The molten magma in such a chamber has tremendous pressure which gradually fracture the rock around it, creating a way for the magma to more upward.

Q. 24. Mention two constructive effects of volcanoes. **[November, 2019]**

Ans. After the eruption of volcano, the ash containing nutrients increases the fertility of soil. Secondly, volcanoes bring out the mineral deposits closer to the surface which makes it easier for geologist to do mining.

Chapter 8. Earthquakes

Q. 1. Explain the following terms: (i) Seismology (ii) Epicenter.

Ans. (i) Seismology: The science that deals with study of seismic waves is called as seismology.

(ii) Epicenter: The point on the surface of the earth exactly vertically above the origin point of earth quake or focus.

Q. 2. (i) What is Richter scale?

(ii) State its use

Ans. (i) Richter scale or Richter magnitude scale was developed Charles F. Richter in the year 1935. This scale measures the intensity of earth by the energy freed from rocks.

(ii) It's a scale used for the measurement of earthquake intensity.

Q. 3. Define the following terms: (i) Seismic waves (ii) Richter scale.

Ans. (i) Seismic waves: The waves generated by an earthquake are called as seismic waves. These waves are of three types: P-wave, S-wave and L-wave or surface wave.

(ii) Richter Scale: It is a device to measure the intensity of earthquakes. The intensity of earthquake is expressed by numbers based upon logarithmic system.

Q. 4. (i) What is the term used to describe the point on the earth's surface where the intensity of earthquake is maximum?

(ii) Name the origin point of earthquake.

Ans. (i) Epicenter is the point on the earth surface where the intensity of the earthquake is maximum.

(ii) The point where energy is released or the point of origin of earth is called as focus.

Q. 5. (i) Name the instrument used to record the intensity of seismic waves.

(ii) Give one natural cause of earthquakes.

Ans. (i) The instrument used to record the intensity of seimic wave is called as Seismograph or seismometer.

(ii) Earthquakes are also caused by natural reasons like movement of lithospheric plates.

Q. 6. Mention two anthropogenic causes that lead to earthquake.

Ans. Two prime anthropogenic causes behind the earthquakes are:

(i) Mining

(ii) Dam Building

Q. 7. Name two earthquake prone zones of the world.

Ans. The two earthquake prone zones in the world are:

(i) Circum-Pacific Belt

(ii) Mid Atlantic Belt

Q. 8. Name three types of earthquake waves.

Ans. Three types of seismic waves are:

(i) P-waves

(ii) S-waves

(iii) Surface waves or L-waves

Q. 9. (i) What does PTWC stands for?

(ii) Where is it located?

Ans. (i) PTWC stands for—Pacific tsunami warning center.

(ii) It is located in Hawaii group of islands.

Q. 10. Give three examples of earthquakes. Indicate two major belts of earthquake.

Ans. Three examples of earthquake are: Bhuj, India (2001), Nepal earthquake 2015 and Indonesia 2004. Two major earthquake belts are: Circum Pacific Belt and Mid Atlantic Belt.

Q. 11. What is the term used to describe the point on the Earth's surface where the intensity of Earthquakes is maximum? **[November, 2019]**

Ans. Epicenter is the point on the Earth surface where the intensity of the Earthquake is maximum.

Chapter 9. Weathering

Q. 1. Define the following terms: (i) Weathering (ii) Denudation.

Ans. (i) Weathering: It is the mechanical fracturing and chemical decomposition of rocks, in situ, by natural agents at the surface of the earth.

(ii) Denudation: It is a long term sum of processes that cause the wearing away of the Earth's surface leading to the reduction in elevation and landscape.

Q. 2. In which landform exfoliation is common?

Ans. Exfoliation is common in desert region. It is due the reason that in deserts the range of temperature is very high. Higher is the range of temperature higher is the impact of exfoliation.

Q. 3. How weathering is essential in the formation of soil?

Ans. Bio-diversity on our planet is based on natural vegetation or forest. Weathering helps in the disintegration of rocks and formation of forests and natural ecosystems.

Q. 4. (i) What is denudation?

(ii) Name the process involved in it.

Ans. (i) The word 'denude' means to uncover or strip off something. Thus denudation means the process of removing something.

(ii) Denudation includes weathering, mass movement, erosion, etc.

Q. 5. What is the role of plants in accelerating the biological weathering?

Ans. The roots of the plants and trees exert tremendous pressure on the rocks. This pressure of the roots mechanically breaks the rocks apart and exposes the rocks to weathering.

Q. 6. How is mass wasting different from the erosion process?

Ans. Mass wasting is a down slope movement of debris under the great influence of gravity. On the other hand erosion is physical removal and transportation of weathered rock by the agents like wind, river or ice, etc.

Q. 7. Explain the following terms: (i) Permeable rock (ii) River menders.

Ans. (i) Permeable rock: A rock that allows water to seep through its pores, spaces and joints. Permeability is basically a property of a rock.

(ii) River meanders: When a river flows in a plain on very non-similar rock course. The river forms S-shape depositional loops. These loops are called as river meander. In simple language, the zig-zag path of a river is called as river Meander.

Q. 8. Explain the process of formation if river meander.

Ans. Meanders are formed when propensity of water flowing over very gentle gradient and unconsolidated alluvial deposits make the river bank irregular.

Q. 9. (i) Name a feature formed by deposition work of a river.

(ii) How it is useful for mankind?

Ans. (i) The depositional feature of river is called delta.

(ii) Delta provides extensive new alluvium, which is perfect landform to do farming.

Q. 10. Explain the formation process of sand dunes.

Ans. When an obstruction (generally a boulder or turf of shrubs) obstruct the direction of wind in arid area. These obstructions obstruct the speed of the wind and cause the deposition of sand particles and forms sand dunes.

Q. 11. (i) What do you mean by Delta?

(ii) Which agent of denudation is associated with delta?

Ans. (i) During its old stage, when a river meets a sea or a lake, it deposits its sediments roughly in a triangular form. This depositional landform at the mouth of a river is called Delta.

(ii) The agent of denudation related to delta is river.

Q. 12. Mention one landform associated with young and mature stage of a river.

Ans. Landform associated with young stage of a river is called as valley. Land form associated with mature stage of a river is called as river meander.

Q. 13. Use one word for the following statements:

(i) The plains formed by the deposition work of river or stream.

(ii) A permeable stratum or zone below the earth's surface through which groundwater moves.

Ans. (i) Alluvial plains

(ii) Aquifer

Q. 14. What is hydration?

Ans. Hydration is the process when minerals incorporate water into their molecular structure. The volume of certain minerals increases due to hydration.

Q. 15. Describe the work of plants as agent of erosion.

Ans. The roots of plants and trees enter the cracks and joints. These roots exert pressure on the rock and widen the cracks. These cracks further widen more and finally the rock split into parts.

Q. 16. How is a water fall formed?

Ans. When the two rock of different hardness are horizontally layered. The underlying soft rock is eroded rapidly. As a result, the water falls vertically from a certain height from the edge of hard rock. This is how water fall forms. For. e.g. Dhuandar falls are formed by river Narmada.

Q. 17. Name the different process of chemical weathering.

Ans. The different processes of chemical weathering are: solution, hydration, oxidation, reduction and carbonation.

Q. 18. Name the major types of weathering. Name the two processes involved in gradation.

Ans. There are three types of weatherings. These are physical or mechanical weathering, chemical weathering and biological weathering. Two process involved in gradation are degradation and aggradation.

Chapter 10. Hydrosphere

Q. 1. Define the following terms: (i) Hydrosphere (ii) Neap tide.

Ans. (i) Hydrosphere: The water mass present on the Earth is referred a hydrosphere. Hydrosphere includes all the water bodies such as lakes, seas, ponds, etc. It is one of the four realms of the Earth.

(ii) Neap tide: When the earth, sun and the moon are not in straight line, the force exerted is least and the difference between high and low tide is less. These tides are called as Neap tides.

Q. 2. Define the following terms: (i) Spring tide (ii) Ocean current.

Ans. (i) Spring tide: When the earth, moon and the sun are in one straight line, the force exerted is maximum. This leads to the creation of high tide called as spring tide.

(ii) Ocean current: It is a movement of stream of water in a fixed direction. Ocean currents move generally at a speed of 2-10 kms.

Q. 3. Name a few important ocean currents of Pacific Ocean.

Ans. Kuroshio Current, North Equatorial Current, South Equatorial Current and Peru Current or Humboldt Current.

Q. 4. Mention the factors affecting ocean currents and their circulation.

Or

Mention two factors that effect the circulation of ocean current? **[February, 2020]**

Ans. The factors that affect the ocean currents and its circulation are:

(i) Planetary winds

(ii) Variation in ocean temperature

(iii) Variation in ocean salinity

(iv) Rotation of the Earth

(v) Shape of coastline

Q. 5. Why ocean currents do not move in a fixed direction?

Ans. The ocean currents do not move in a fixed direction because of the following reasons:

(i) Due to variation in ocean water salinity.

(ii) Due to difference in heating of ocean water- by solar energy.

Q. 6. "Our planet earth is called as Blue Planet or watery planet". Give reason.

Ans. Planet earth is called as Blue or watery planet because 71% of its surface is occupied by water mass and only 29% of its surface is land. If we look at the Earth from space it looks blue because of more water composition.

Q. 7. What is the antipodal arrangement of land and water on Earth?

Ans. Antipodal arrangement of land and water on Earth means that if on the one section of the earth is land and exactly opposite of this section would be the Water mass because of the rough distribution of land and water on our planet.

Q. 8. Define the term "Tidal Range"?

Ans. Tidal Range is the difference between high and low tide. The tidal range depends upon position of Sun and the Moon.

Q. 9. Discuss the role of hydrosphere in making the Earth habitable space.

Ans. The role of hydrosphere in making the Earth hapitable space are:

(i) Hydrosphere helps in maintaining the temperature of the earth.

(ii) Hydrosphere is the sources of water to us.

(iii) Hydrosphere is the source of water for atmosphere.

Q. 10. (i) Where does Gulf Stream current originates?

(ii) How it forms dense fog at the coast of New Foundland?

Ans. (i) Gulf stream current originates in the Gulf of Mexico around 20°N.

(ii) The convergence of this warm current with Labrador Current near Newfoundland results in heavy fog.

Q. 11. In what ways warm ocean currents are different from cold ocean current?

Ans. Warm ocean currents are those currents which flow from the low latitudes in the tropical zone towards the high latitudes.

Cold currents are those ocean water currents which flow from the high latitudes towards the low latitudes.

Q. 12. List two prime impacts of tides.

Ans. (i) Tides help in making the rivers navigable and also cleans the mouth of the river or estuaries.

(ii) Tides carrying salty water to the cold countries and retard the process of freezing of the coast.

Q. 13. (i) What is the percentage share of hydrosphere on earth?

(ii) Why it is important?

Ans. (i) Hydrosphere covers 71% of Earth's surface.

(ii) The world's oceans generate half of the oxygen on Earth, are the primary regulator of global climate, and provide economic and environmental services to billions around the globe.

Q. 14. (i) What do you mean by surface winds?

(ii) How are they caused?

Ans. (i) These currents are the water movements that take place on the top layer of the ocean and make up about 10% of the ocean currents.

(ii) They are caused primarily by winds, which create a friction as they move over the water.

Q. 15. Mention the time difference between two tides.

Ans. Every place on the earth experiences tides twice a day. Tides occur at an interval of 12 hours and 26 minutes instead of difference of exact 12 hours.

Q. 16. Why does ocean differs in their salinity?

Ans. The level of salinity of ocean water depends on rainfall and rate of evaporation. Places where rainfall is higher, the salinity level is low and places where evaporation is higher the level of salinity will be higher.

Q. 17. Name the two movements of Ocean water.

Ans. The two movement of ocean water are tides and currents.

Q. 18. How the movement of ocean current is influenced by the prevailing winds?

Ans. The friction between the wind and the water surface affects the movement of the water body in its course. The Easterly ocean currents on the either side of the equator are associated with trade winds.

Q. 19. Why the ocean currents of Southern ocean follow the general pattern?

Ans. Because the southern ocean is not affected by the movement of monsoonal winds. These winds move northward from the equator. Thus, the southern Indian Ocean remains unaffected and its currents follow the general pattern of flow.

Q. 20. Name the important ocean currents of atlantic ocean.

Ans. The important ocean currents of Atlantic ocean are:

(i) Gulf Stream Current. (Warm current)

(ii) Labrador Current. (Cold current)

(iii) Canary Current. (Cold current)

(iv) North and South Equatorial Currents.(Warm current)

(v) Falkland Current. (Cold current)

Q. 21. What do you understand by the term 'Coriollis effect'?

Ans. Due to the rotation of the earth, the ocean currents does not move in a straight line rather tend to deflect in the right direction in the Northern Hemisphere and left in the Southern Hemisphere. This deflection force caused by rotation of the earth is called as 'Coriolis effect'.

Q. 22. State two differences between oceans and seas.

Ans. The differences between oceans and seas are as following:

(i) Size: In term of size, oceans are larger in size as compared seas.

(ii) Depth: In term of depth, oceans are deeper than seas.

Q. 23. Discuss the economical uses of tides.

Ans. The economical benefits of tides are as under:

(i) Tides are used to generate energy i.e. tidal energy.

(ii) High tides carry salty water to the low lying areas, which is used for preparing common salt.

(iii) Major cities like Kolkata and London have been developed as tidal port cities.

Q. 24. What is sea water salinity? How is it measured?

Ans. Sea water is salty in taste. Salinity of sea water is a term used to define the total content of dissolved salts in sea water. It is measured as the amount of salt (in gm) dissolved in 1kg of sea water. It is expressed as parts per thousand.

Q. 25. What do you understand by hydrosphere? **[November, 2019]**

Ans. Hydrosphere is the water mass present over the Earth. The word hydrosphere is the combination of two words 'Hydro' means water and 'sphere' means zone. The various forms of water mass present over earth are oceans, seas, lakes, rivers, ponds, etc.

Q. 26. Name a cold ocean current which affects fishing industry of Japan. **[February, 2020]**

Ans. Oyashio current of Japan favours its fishing industry.

Q. 27. (i) What is the importance of hydrosphere? **[February, 2020]**

(ii) What percentage of the Earth is covered by the Hydrosphere?

Ans. (i) Hydrosphere is an important realm of the Earth because it maintains the temperature of our planet and also hydrosphere is the main source of moisture in the atmosphere.

(ii) Hydrosphere has covered 71% of total area of Earth.

Chapter 11. Atmosphere

Q. 1. Define the term C.F.C.

Ans. C.F.C- Stands for chlorofluorocarbons. This is a combination of gaseous compounds like carbons, chlorine, fluorine and sometimes hydrogen also.

Q. 2. Define the term normal lapse rate.

Ans. Normal lapse rate: Normal lapse rate is a rate at which the atmospheric temperature decreases with rise in altitude. In general condition is 6.5 °C per kilometer.

Q. 3. Name two prime elements of weather and climate.

Ans. The two prime elements of weather and climate are:

(i) Temperature

(ii) Air Pressure.

Q. 4. What type of solid particles is present in the atmosphere? State their significance.

Ans. Solid particles present in our atmosphere are dust particles, salt particles, pollens or volcanic ashes, etc. These solid particles help in scattering of solar radiation.

Q. 5. What is Green house effect?

Ans. Green house effect is basically a heat trap in the Earth's atmosphere which makes the earth's atmosphere warm.

Q. 6. What are the causes of Green house effect?

Ans. Green house effect is caused by the release of green house gases like water vapour, methane and carbon dioxide.

Q. 7. What is the role of ozone in atmosphere?

Ans. Ozone gas protects the humans from the harmful ultra violets rays released by the sun. This gas absorbs the UV rays which can cause many types of skin diseases and eye related diseases to us.

Q. 8. (i) What is the composition of CO_2 in our atmosphere?

(ii) Why are we worried about the increase of CO_2 in atmosphere.?

Ans. (i) The percentage of CO_2 is only 0.036% in our atmosphere.

(ii) The percentage of CO_2 is only 0.036%. because CO_2 is transparent to incoming solar radiations but opaque to outgoing terrestrial radiations. Thus, this gas is responsible for green house effect. This means little increase in the composition of CO_2 may leads to global warming.

Q. 9. (i) In which atmospheric layer the amount of water vapours is highest?

(ii) What is the source of water vapours present in atmosphere?

Ans. (i) The highest amount of water vapour is present in the troposphere.

(ii) The source of water vapour in the troposphere is the evaporation from the water masses like oceans, seas, lakes, ponds or river, etc.

Q. 10. (i) What is water vapour?

(ii) How water vapour is added to atmosphere?

Ans. (i) Due to increase in temperature, water changes its form from liquid to gaseous state. This gaseous form is water vapour.

(ii) Heat from the Sun evaporates water from the water masses like seas, oceans, lakes, rivers or ponds. This evaporation is the biggest source of water vapour in our atmosphere.

Q. 11. (i) In which atmospheric layer ozone gas is found?

(ii) What is the purpose of ozone gas?

Ans. (i) Ozone layer is found in the upper part of Stratosphere.

(ii) Ozone layer is of high significance for human beings, because it protects us from harmful ultra-violet rays emitted by the Sun.

Q. 12. Mention two ways to save ozone depletion.

Ans. To protect the ozone layer, the following steps can be taken:

(i) Minimize the use of automobiles or prefer car pooling.

(ii) Depending more on renewable sources of energy than fossil fuels like coal and crude oil.

Q. 13. Discuss the source of carbon dioxide in our atmosphere.

Ans. The source of carbon dioxide in our atmosphere is burning of fossil fuels, solid wastes, trees and other biological materials.

Q. 14. State two prime properties of Ionosphere.

Ans. Two properties of Ionosphere are:

(i) Ionosphere is located between 80 kms to 400 kms above the surface.

(ii) This atmospheric layer contains electrically charged particles called as ions, which helps in radio wave transmission.

Q. 15. Why don't jet aircrafts fly in the troposphere?

Ans. Jets don't fly in the troposphere because the troposphere is the zone of mixing of atmospheric elements like temperature variations, air pressure variations, moisture, rainfall and lapse rate. Thus, these conditions are not safe for the aircrafts to fly.

Q. 16. Name the atmospheric layer which helps in long distance communication and why.

Ans. Ionosphere helps in long distance communication because it has electrically charged ions. This layer reflects back the radio waves transmitted by the earth.

Q. 17. How ozone depletion is harmful to us?

Ans. Depletion of ozone gas causes increased UV radiation on the earth surface. This ultra violet radiation causes various health issues like skin diseases, eye cataract, and immune disorders and may cause skin cancer.

Q. 18. In what ways argon is used commercially?

Ans. The commercial uses of argon are:

Argon has high commercial and industrial uses. It is use for manufacturing of light bulbs, welding equipment and lasers.

Q. 19. What is the proportion of argon in our atmosphere?

Ans. The proportion of argon in our atmosphere is 0.93%.

Q. 20. Discuss the extent of troposphere and tropopause.

Ans. Troposphere is the lowest layer of atmosphere. The height of troposphere varies from equator towards the poles. The troposphere extend at 18 kms near the equator and just 8 kms over the poles. Tropopause starts immediately after the troposphere. Tropopause is about 1.5 kms thick.

Q. 21. What is the role of troposphere in atmosphere?

Ans. Troposphere is the most crucial layer of the atmosphere. It contains 90% of the total air in the atmosphere. Troposphere has the entire weather phenomenon like formation of clouds, moving of wind, dust particles. Thus, it provides ideal condition to support life on earth.

Q. 22. What do you mean by carbon sink? Name the major carbon sinks.

Ans. Carbon sinks are the natural sources that stores carbon containing chemical compound more than it releases. Major carbon sinks of earth are plants, soil and oceans.

Q. 23. (i) Name the gas found in abundance in atmosphere.

(ii) What is its proportion in atmosphere?

(iii) What role does this gas play in our atmosphere?

Ans. (i) The main gases present in our atmosphere is Nitrogen.

(ii) Its proportion is 78% in our atmosphere.

(iii) Nitrogen plays an important role in growth of plant. It helps to make chlorophyll in plants, which is used in photosynthesis to make their food.

Q. 24. (i) In which layer of the atmosphere do we find ozone? **[February, 2020]**

(ii) Why is the Ozone layer very significant in the atmosphere?

Ans. (i) Ozone layer is found in the upper part of Stratosphere.

(ii) Ozone layer is of high significance for human beings, because it protects us from harmful ultra-violet rays emitted by the Sun.

Chapter 12. Insolation

Q. 1. Why in India the maximum temperature is experienced in the month of May but not after summer solstice?

Ans. Because after summer solstice the monsoon winds become active throughout India and it is experienced in the month of May.

Q. 2. Explain the role of nature of soil in determining the temperature of place.

Ans. Different soils react differently to the heat. The soil with more moisture (loamy and clayey soil), react slowly to the heat and also looses heat slowly as compared to arid or semi-arid soils (sandy and desert soil). The dark colored soil absorbs more heat than the light colored soil.

Q. 3. Explain the following terms:

(i) Isothern

(ii) Normal lapse rate.

Ans. (i) Isotherm: These are the lines drawn on weather map to show areas having same temperature.

(ii) Normal lapse rate: The loss of heat with increase in height is called as normal lapse rate. In normal condition it is 1^0C with every 165 m increase in height.

Q. 4. Name three heat zones of the Earth.

Ans. Three heat zones of the earth are:

(i) Torrid Zone

(ii) Temperate zone

(iii) Frigid zone

Q. 5. Name the three process by which earth's atmosphere is heated.

Ans. Three processes by which earth's atmosphere get heated are:

(i) Convection

(ii) Conduction

(iii) Radiation

Q. 6. What do you mean by insolation?

Ans. The energy received by the earth is known as a incoming solar radiation which in short termed as insolation.

Q. 7. Give its two importances of insolation.

Ans. The two importance of Insolation are:

(i) The insolation causes the movement of air and ocean currents.

(ii) Due to insolation, the hydrological cycle happens on the earth. This cycle includes evaporation and precipitation.

Q. 8. What is the location of Frigid Zone in Northern Hemisphere? Mention its one significance.

Ans. Frigid Zone lies between Arctic Circle and the North Pole in the Northern Hemisphere. Frigid Zone receives oblique sun rays throughout the year. This results in very low temperature.

Q. 9. Explain the impact of length of the day on the amount of insolation received.

Ans. Length of the day has direct relation with insolation received at a place. Higher is the length of a day higher is the amount of insolation received at a place.

Q. 10. Discuss in short two processes by which the atmosphere get heated up.

Ans. (i) Conduction: The lower atmospheric layers get heated up by the transfer of heat from the surface. In this case the heat transfer from the hotter body to the cooler body.

(ii) Convection: When air gets heat up due to conduction, it rises up and creates a vacuum near the surface, which is filled by the cold air which descend down. The cold air also gets heated up and the circulatory motion begins, called as convection.

Q. 11. Explain the following terms:

(i) Heat budget

(ii) Albedo

Ans. (i) Heat budget: The balance of heat maintained by the earth between insolation and terrestrial radiation is called a heat budget.

(ii) Albedo: The amount of radiation reflected back to space by the earth surface is called albedo of the earth.

Q. 12. What is the major source of atmospheric heat? How it works?

Ans. The major source of atmospheric heat is conduction. The lowest layer of air is heated due to its contact with the hot surface. The heat from the lower layer is warmer than the upper layers of atmosphere.

Q. 13. Define the following terms:

(i) Insolation rate

(ii) Freezing pair.

Ans. (i) Insolation rate: Insolation rate is the amount of solar energy heating the surface at per unit time.

(ii) Freezing point: Freezing point is a temperature at which the liquids start converted into solids.

Q. 14. What is the temperature at the surface of Sun? How Sun transfer its heat?

Ans. The temperature of the surface of the Sun is about 6000° C. The Sun transfers its heat in form of short waves. The heat that reaches the earth surface is called as Insolation.

Q. 15. What do you mean of diurnal range of temperature?

Ans. The difference between the maximum and the minimum temperature of a day is called as diurnal range of temperature.

Q. 16. Why deserts have higher range of temperature than coastal areas?

Ans. Deserts have higher range of temperature because of lack of water masses and more availability of land mass. We know that the land gets heated up faster than the water mass and also cooled down faster than water mass.

Q. 17. Give one example of continental and maritime climate.

Ans. (i) Continental type of climate - New Delhi

(ii) Maritime type of climate - Mumbai

Q. 18. What do you mean by temperature?

Ans. Temperature is the degree of hotness and coldness of any substance or a body.

Q. 19. Name the instrument to measure the temperature.

Ans. Temperature is recorded with the help of a thermometer.

Q. 20. What is the unit to denote temperature?

Ans. Temperature is denoted in Degree Celsius (°C) or degree Fahrenheit (°F)

Q. 21. What do you understand by terrestrial radiation? **[November, 2019]**

Ans. During the day time Earth heats up by solar radiation. After that heated Earth becomes a radiating body and sends the energy back to the atmosphere in long waves. This process is called as terrestrial radiation. This process heats up the lower part of the atmosphere.

Chapter 13. Pressure Belts and Winds

Q. 1. The coriollis force is directly proportional to the angle of latitude.

Ans. Because coriollis effect is zero at the equator (0° latitude) and highest at the poles (90° latitude).

Q. 2. Explain the Isobar term.

Ans. Isobars: These are the lines drawn on weather map to show areas having same atmospheric pressure.

Q. 3. Explain the terms ITCZ.

Ans. ITCZ: It stands for inter tropical convergence zone. This is a zone which lies between tropic of cancer and tropic of Capricorn where trade winds (North Eastern and South Eastern) meet.

Q. 4. In which category of winds, does 'Chinook Wind' fall and why?

Ans. Chinook wind comes in the category of warm and dry wind.

Q. 5. Why Chinook wind is called 'Snow Eater'?

Ans. After rising from Pacific Ocean, the wind ascend the Canadian Rockies as a cool wind but as it starts descending Eastern slope it becomes warm and melts the frozen snow. That is why Chinook wind is called as 'snow eater'.

Q. 6. Why trade winds are called so?

Ans. In ancient times, the maximum trade use to happen by ordinary ships. The sailors used to take advantage of trade winds particularly between Europe and America.

Q. 7. Name the cold wind that prevails over North-West of Mediterranean Sea.

Ans. The cold wind that prevails over North-West of Mediterranean Sea is called as Mistral wind.

Q. 8. In which seasons does cold wind flow?

Ans. Cold wind flows in the winter season.

Q. 9. Why does monsoon wind come in the category of seasonal winds?

Ans. Monsoon winds are seasonal winds because monsoon winds change their direction. Once in a year they flow as a sea breeze and once in a year they blow as a land breeze.

Q. 10. What are pressure belts?

Ans. Pressure belts represent an area with her high pressure or with low pressure zone.

Q. 11. Why do places have difference in pressure belts?

Ans. The variation in pressure belts are found because of variation in distribution of temperature zones. The places with high temperature experiences low pressure and vice-versa.

Q. 12. What is ITCZ stands for?

Ans. ITCZ stands for Inter Tropical Convergence Zone. It is a zone of high temperature and low atmospheric pressure. ITCZ is a zone where trade winds from Sub- tropical high pressure zone meets.

Q. 13. What is shifting of ITCZ?

Ans. ITCZ does not remain stagnant rather it keeps shifting from equator towards sub-tropical region in Northern Hemisphere and same in Southern Hemisphere because of earth's revolution.

Q. 14. Why Equatorial low pressure belt is also called as 'Doldrums'?

Ans. Equatorial low pressure belt is a zone of convergence, where trade winds meet. This zone experiences extremely calm air movement. Thus, it is called as 'Doldrum'.

Q. 15. Mention a characteristic of 'Doldrums'.

Ans. Doldrums are calm and light winds.

Q. 16. Name the instrument of measuring atmospheric pressure?

Ans. Barometer.

Q. 17. In which unit the atmosphere pressure is measured?

Ans. Atmospheric pressure is measure in millibars (mb).

Q. 18. Name the instrument used for measuring direction of a wind.

Ans. The instrument used for measuring the direction of a wind is called as wind–vane.

Q. 19. How does wind-vane function?

Ans. Wind-vane is marked with an arrow and has direction mentioned on it. When wind blows the wind-vane turns and reflects the direction from which the wind is coming.

Q. 20. Name the three major pressure belts.

Ans. Three pressure belts are:

(i) Equatorial low pressure belt

(ii) Sub-tropical high pressure belt

(iii) Sub-polar low pressure belt.

Q. 21. State the Ferrel's law.

Ans. Ferrel's law states that al the moving objects are deflected to right in the Northern Hemisphere and in the Southern Hemisphere the objects will be directed towards their left. This happens due to rotation of the Earth.

Q. 22. Give three ways in which an anticyclone affects the weather conditions.

Ans. (i) Anticyclones lead to dry and calm weather conditions.

(ii) Anticyclone may leads to formation of fog and frost during winter season.

(iii) With the anticyclones there is extensive rainfall.

Q. 23. Name an area where typhoons are experienced.

Ans. Most of the typhoons are experienced in North-West pacific region. This region is also called as typhoon alley.

Q. 24. Between which latitudes are winds referred to as 'Roaring'?

Ans. Roaring forties is another name of westerlies at 40° S latitude.

Q. 25. How does coriollis force vary from low to higher latitudes? **[November, 2019]**

Ans. Coriollis force varies from high to lower based on latitudes because as the latitude increases, the speed of the earth's rotation decreases. The deflection is highest at the poles and decreases to zero at the poles.

Q. 26. What is the meaning of the term pressure gradient? **[November, 2019]**

Ans. The variation in the heat distribution of the Earth leads to variation in air pressure at different places. This variation in air pressure is called as pressure Gradient.

Q. 27. (i) Mention two factors that affect atmospheric pressure. **[February, 2020]**

(ii) Give one way in which Monsoon is similar to and one way in which it is different from Land and Sea breezes?

Ans. (i) Two factors that affect the atmospheric pressure of a place are:

1. Location of a place in term of latitudinal.
2. Height from the mean sea level.

(ii) Monsoon is similar to land and sea breeze in a way that monsoon changes its direction twice a year according to the pressure variation over land and sea.

Monsoon wind is different from land and sea breeze in a way that the general flow tendency of land and sea breeze is day and night respectively, but monsoon winds move in summers (sea to land) and in winters (land to sea).

Chapter 14. Precipitation

Q. 1. What do you mean by condensation? Name two forms of condensations.

Ans. The process in which the water vapour changes into liquid is called condensation.

Two forms of condensation are dew and fog.

Q. 2. Name three types of rainfall. Which one is most common in equatorial regions?

Ans. Three types of rainfall are convection rainfall, orographic rainfall and frontal rainfall.

The most common rainfall in equatorial region is convection rainfall.

Q. 3. Why does Polar Region receives less rainfall?

Ans. Poles receive low rainfall because of the following reasons:

(i) Most of the water found in poles is in frozen form, which supports least evaporation.

(ii) Poles receive slanting or solar radiation which minimizes the chance of evaporation.

Q. 4. Explain the process of cloud formation.

Ans. The clouds are formed when warm and moist air rises up. Due to increase in altitude it loses its temperature and condensation happens. The water vapours turn into minute water droplets, which are the basis for the formation of clouds.

Q. 5. (i) What is absolute humidity?

(ii) How it is expressed?

Ans. (i) The actual amount of the water vapour present in the air is called absolute humidity.

(ii) Absolute humidity is expressed in gram per cubic meter (g/m^3).

Q. 6. Why frontal rainfall is common in mid-latitudes?

Ans. Reason being mid-latitudes are the meeting point of cold polar air mass and hot sub-tropical air mass. This condition provides suitable condition for frontal rainfall in mid-latitudes.

Q. 7. Explain land and sea breezes.

Ans. During summer season the continents experience low pressure but pressure over ocean or seas are higher, thus wind move from water to land is called Sea breeze. The vice versa condition prevails in winters which resulted into movement of wind from continents to water masses called land breeze.

Q. 8. (i) Define the term absolute humidity.

(ii) How it is measured?

Ans. (i) Absolute humidity is the amount of water vapour present in the certain volume of air.

(ii) It is always expressed in grains per cubic or grams per cubic centimeter.

Q. 9. Name a region where cyclonic rainfall occurs.

Ans. This rainfall is linked with temperate and tropical cyclones, when two extensive air masses of different physical properties meet. The warm air mass rises and after cooling at saturated point it gets condensed and cause rainfall.

Q. 10. Why the rate of evaporation level is least at poles?

Ans. The rate of evaporation level is least at poles due to two big reasons:

(i) The sun rays does not fall straight, thus the temperature does not rises to the evaporation level.

(ii) The water bodies present there remains at freezing level, which supports least evaporation.

Q. 11. Why the rainfall distribution is not same everywhere?

Ans. It is true that rainfall distribution is not same everywhere because rainfall depends upon the following factors. As these factors changes place to place the distribution of rainfall too varies:

(i) Location in term of latitude

(ii) Height from mean sea level.

(iii) Distance from the sea

Q. 12. The southern slope of Himalayas is greener than northern. Why?

Ans. The Himalayas cause obstruction to the monsoon winds (sea breeze) and leads to orographic rainfall from its southern slope. Thus southern slope of Himalayas is a windward slope which remains greener than northern slope.

Q. 13. What happens when cold air mass meets warm air mass?

Ans. When two air mass of different temperature meet, it's always warm air rises up. Because cold air mass is heavy and warm air mass is lighter in weight. While rising upward the warm air mass gets condensed and cause frontal rainfall.

Q. 14. What is the meaning of rain shadow? Name a part of India sub-continent that experiences rain shadow.

Ans. Rain shadow is the other name of leeward side of a mountain. This is a slope of mountain that remains rain free. In India eastern slope of Western Ghats is a rain shadow zone.

Q. 15. What are the different forms of precipitation?

Ans. The common forms of precipitation are rainfall, snowfall, hailstorm, etc.

Q. 16. Name the different forms of condensation.

Ans. Different forms of condensation are dew, fog, mist, frost and clouds.

Q. 17. Give one similarity between clouds and fog.

Ans. Similarity between cloud and fog: Both are the form of condensation that happens when water vapor condenses or freezes to form tiny droplets or crystals in the air.

Q. 18. Mention the geographical conditions required for dew.

Ans. Geographical conditions required for dew are:

(i) Cloudless sky: The clear sky allows the terrestrial radiation to pass and helps in reduction of surface temperature.

(ii) Presence of vegetation: The vegetation cover increases the humidity level through transpiration.

Q. 19. Explain the following terms: **[November, 2019]**

(i) Humidity (ii) Condensation

Ans. (i) The presence of water vapour in the air is called Humidity. Water vapours are the gaseous state of water.

(ii) Condensation is the transformation of water vapours (gaseous form) into water (liquid form). It is caused by loss of heat.

Chapter 15. Pollution and Environment

Q. 1. Define Pollution.

Ans. Any activity that violates the original character of the nature and leads to its degradation is called pollution.

Q. 2. What are the causes of pollution?

Ans. With the increasing urbanization and industrialization, constant exposure to radiation and noise, the earth and its environment are polluted.

Q. 3. Why are trees grown in and around the industries?

Ans. Tree planting around the factories absorbes carbon-dioxide and it also can arrest dust and fly-ash from the factories.

Q. 4. Which gas is emitted from refrigerators and air-conditioners?

Ans. CFC or chlorofluorocarbons is the gas emitted form the refrigerators and air-conditioners.

Q. 5. What is oil-spill?

Ans. Spread of mineral oil or crude oil in the sea or ocean is called oil spill.

Q. 6. What is meant by radiation?

Ans. Radiation is the emission or highly charged particles and electromagnetic rays entering the earth's atmosphere from outer space. It is also the cause of pollution.

Q. 7. What kind of pollution is produced by Brick kilns?

Ans. Brick kilns use coal to burn the bricks which in turn given out huge quantity of carbon-dioxide and particulate matter such as smoke and dust. This causes air pollution which is harmful to the environment.

Q. 8. How is thermal pollution caused?

Ans. Thermal power plants release the recycled hot water into the rivers or sea causing water pollution. The hot water raises the temperature of the water body affecting the acquatic life.

Q. 9. How does increase in carbon-dioxide affect atmosphere?

Ans. Increase carbon dioxide leads to global warming *i.e.*, the temperature of the Earth's atmosphere increases due to increase in CO_2. This in the long run causes climatic change, globally.

Q. 10. Why is it necessary to grow plants in the neighbouring areas of cement industries?

Ans. Cement industry emits plenty of dust which is very, harmful for plants, animals and humans.

Q. 11. Why do people in cities suffer from viral fever, allergies, etc?

Ans. Long-term exposure to hazardous materials in the air, causes asthma and allergies to the people.

Q. 12. What are the sources of noise pollution?

Ans. The sources of noise pollution are:

(i) Trains

(ii) Automobiles

(iii) Jet Aeroplanes

(iv) Radio, T.V., Loud speakers, musical bands.

Q. 13. What is Methemoglobinemia?

Ans. This is a water borne disease. Infants are most susceptible to nitrate content. High nitrate content of water is associated with Methemoglobinemia.

Q. 14. What is Minamata disease? Explain.

Ans. Minamata disease is a form of mercury poisoning. Methyl mercury damages the nervous system, leading to insomnia, tremors, bleeding of gums, etc.

Q. 15. What are the effects of arsenic poisoning?

Ans. Arsenic in mild doses cause nausea, vomiting and stomach burns. In lethel dose it many cause death due to shock and vascular failure.

Q. 16. When did the Bhopal gas tragedy happen?

Ans. The Bhopal gas tragedy happened in the early hours of December 3rd 1984.

Q. 17. What was the main cause of the accident?

Ans. The main cause of accident was release of 40 tonnes of methyl isocyanate into the atmosphere from the Union Carbide pesticide factory in Bhopal.

Q. 18. What were the short term effects due to the accident?

Ans. The initial effects of exposure were coughing, vomiting, severe eye irritation and feeling of suffocation.

Q. 19. When did the chernobyl disaster occur?

Ans. Chernobyl disaster occurred on April 26th 1986.

Q. 20. Where did the disaster happened?

Ans. The disaster happened at the Chernobyl nuclear power plant in ukraine.

Q. 21. What was responsible for the disaster?

Ans. The design of the plant was defective. So the reactor exploded during the experiment throwing toxic radioactive gases. The safety measures were poorly designed.

Q. 22. What were the effects of Chernobyl disaster?

Ans. Thousands of people became exposed to Chernobyl radiation, affecting living organisms, The orgnism affected by radiation suffered from genetic disorders, variety of cancers and lukaemia.

Q. 23. Why are farmers encouraged to use manure instead of chemical fertilizers? **[November, 2019]**

Ans. Farmers are advised to use manures because of the following reasons:

1. Manure has organic content. Thus, it does not harm the crop.
2. Unlike chemical fertilizers it does not contain harmful chemicals which further dissolve in water and spoil it.

Q. 24. (i) How does excessive use of chemical fertilizers harm the environment?

(ii) What may be done to reduce such pollution? **[November, 2019]**

Ans. (i) The chemical fertilizer harm the environment in following ways:

1. Chemical fertilizers changes the pH level of soil.
2. These agricultural inputs harm not only soil health but water resources (leaching) and micro organisms too.

(ii) 1. Instead of using chemical fertilizers, organic manures should be used.

2. Fields should be left vacant regularly to regain its fertility naturally.

Q. 25. (i) How are automobiles responsible for creating air pollution?

(ii) What may be done to reduce the pollution caused by vehicles? **[November, 2019]**

Ans. (i) 1. Automobiles release toxic pollutants like hydrocarbons and nitrogen oxides.

2. At present most of the automobile units run on non–renewable sources of energy like petrol and diesel.

(ii) 1. More and more automobiles should be run on renewable sources of energy like solar energy.

2. More emphasis should be given on public transportation rather than personal transportation.

Q. 26. Mention any two steps that an individual can take to reduce noise pollution. **[February, 2020]**

Ans. (i) Individuals can prohibit blowing the car pressure horns.

(ii) The volume of music systems or loudspeakers should be in a control level during special events.

Q. 27. What do you understand by 'SMOG'? Why is it dangerous? **[February, 2020]**

Ans. Smog is a combined word of smoke and fog. Smog is formed during winters when the condensation happens on the suspended air pollutants in the air. Smog is harmful as it causes breathing problems and reduces the visibility.

Chapter 16. Natural Regions of the World

Q. 1. What is a Climatic region?

Ans. A natural region is one in which the natural environment consisting of physical and biological components is relatively uniform.

Q. 2. What is the purpose of dividing the world into major climatic regions?

Ans. The aim of dividing the world into major climatic regions is to provide a simple frame of reference. It gives a generalised idea of associated aspects like vegetation, animal life, soil and human adaptation.

Q. 3. How are the limits of a climatic region fixed?

Ans. There are no fixed or well defined boundaries between the major types of climatic regions. All boundaries are transitional in nature, across which the characteristic of one climatic type gradually merge into its neighbouring type.

Q. 4. Where is the equatorial region located?

Ans. The broad band around the earth between 10° N and 10° S of the equator forms the equatorial region.

Q. 5. Why are the diurnal and annual range of temperature very low in this region?

Ans. The Sun is overhead throughout the year and the area experience equal day and equal night. There is very little variation in the Sun's angle.

Q. 6. Give the other names by which Equatorial Regions are also popular.

Ans. Tropical wet climate or Tropical Rain forest climate are the other names by which equatorial region is popular.

Q. 7. Which parts of Asia are included in Equatorial Region?

Ans. Malaysia, Indonesia, South Philippines and New Guinea island in the South East Asia.

Q. 8. What type of Rainfall occurs in the Equatorial Regions and why?

Ans. Rainfall is a convectional type. It occurs daily in the late afternoon after intense heating of the ground during the day.

Q. 9. Name a few important trees found in Equatorial Region. How important are these trees?

Ans. Mahagony, Ebony, Rosewood and Cinchona. Chinchona is of medicinal value. Others are used for making expensive furniture.

Q. 10. What are the Equatorial Rainforest called in South America?

Ans. The Equatorial rainforest called as selvas in South America.

Q. 11. Why are the Equatorial Rainforest called 'Lungs of the Earth'?

Ans. Large quantity of oxygen is supplied by vegetation so they are often referred to as lungs of the earth.

Q. 12. What are the main occupations of the people in the Equatorial Rain forest?

Ans. The main occupation of the people are shifting agriculture, primitive hunting and food gathering.

Q. 13. What are the different names these grasslands are known by?

Ans. The grasslands are known as Compos in Brazil, Llanos in the Orinocow, river basin in S. America, Savanna in Africa.

Q. 14. What are the main occupations of the tribes living in the region?

Ans. Agriculture is not a important occupation other then in Nigeria by the Hansa Tribe. Most native people are either herdsmen or pastoratists.

Q. 15. What are the seasons experienced by the tropical monsoon region?

Ans. Three distinct seasons can be identified:

(i) Cool dry season. (Nov. - Feb.)

(ii) Hot dry season (March - May)

(iii) Hot wet season (June - Sept. - Oct.)

Q. 16. What is the role of the western cyclonic disturbances?

Ans. In winter, Punjab and the adjoining areas get light rain from the western cyclonic disturbances which originate in the mediterranean sea. The rain is good for the wheat crop.

Q. 17. What are the main occupation of the people of monsoon region?

Ans. Farming has been the dominant occupation of the people of mansoon region for thousands of years.

Q. 18. What type of natural vegetation in found in hot desert?

Ans. Vegetation in hot desert is scanty, mostly xerophytic. e.g. cacti, bulbons, thorny bushes, acacias, etc.

Q. 19. Who are Tuareg? Where do they live? What is their occupation?

Ans. Tuareg people are nomads. They live in the Sahara desert. They one pastoralists and traders.

Q. 20. What are the occupations of the Bedouins?

Ans. Bedouins of Sahara desert are primarily camel raisers, sheep and goat, herders, artisans and entertainers.

Q. 21. Name the important trees which grow in the region.

Ans. Olive, cork, oak, fig, laurel and lavender.

Q. 22. What are the main fruits grown here?

Ans. Oranges, lemons, grape, lime, apricots, peaches, cherries, etc.

Q. 23. How does it get its name?

Ans. A large part of China (Eastern and Southern) falls within this region. So the climatic region gets its name from the country.

Q. 24. Where are the temperate grasslands located?

Ans. Temperate grasslands are located in the interior parts of the continents between 35° to 55° latitudes in both the hemispheres.

Q. 25. What are the temperate grassland known as in South America and South Africa?

Ans. Temperate grasslands are known as Pampas in South America and Veldt in South Africa.

Q. 26. Why are the winters very cold in the temperate grasslands?

Ans. As the region is located in the interior of the continents mainly in the Northern Hemisphere and due to the influence of the cold ocean currents, the winters are very cold.

Q. 27. Name four common trees of the coniferous forest.

Ans. Pine, fir, spruce, larch.

Q. 28. Name the type of natural vegetation found in the Taiga region. **[November, 2019]**

Ans. Coniferous vegetation is predominantly found in Taiga region.

Q. 29. (i) Name the type of rainfall that occurs in the Amazon basin.

(ii) Mention one important characteristic feature of the climate of the Amazon basin. **[November, 2019]**

Ans. (i) Amazon basin experiences equatorial rain or convectional rain.

(ii) Amazon basin experiences high temperature and high humidity level.

Q. 30. (i) What is Campos?

(ii) Name the most important economic activity practised in this region. **[November, 2019]**

Ans. (i) Campos are the grasslands of South American continent cover mainly Brazil, Argentina and Uruguay.

(ii) The prime economic activity in these grasslands is rearing of animals and pasturing.

Q. 31. To which natural regions of the world are the following associated? **[February, 2020]**

(i) Conical-shaped soft wood trees.

(ii) 4 O'clock rains.

Ans. (i) Conical shaped soft wood is found in Taiga region.

(ii) 4 O'clock rainfall is related to Equatorial region.

Q. 32. Mention two features of the natural vegetation found in the Equatorial region. **[February, 2020]**

Ans. Two features of natural vegetation in equatorial region are:

(i) All the trees are tall with broad leaves and are evergreen.

(ii) The forests are extremely dense and form canopy which does not allow the Sun rays to penetrate.

Q. 33. Mention any two ways by which the natural vegetation in tropical deserts adapt to the arid conditions. **[February, 2020]**

Ans. The adaptations of natural vegetation in arid tropical regions are:

(i) The roots of the plants are very deep, so that they can fetch water from the deep.

(ii) The leaves are thick and needle shaped to control transpiration.

❐

Short Answer Questions | Set 2 |

Chapter 1. Earth As a Planet

Q. 1. Mention three important features of the Earth that supports life.

Ans. The features that support life on Earth are as follows:

(i) Earth's Atmosphere: The Earth is surrounded by an atmosphere which contains valuable gases such as nitrogen, oxygen and traces of other gases essential for living. The atmosphere helps the Earth to maintain a mean average temperature of 14°C that supports life.

(ii) The distance from the sun: The distance of the Earth from the Sun is neither too far or too near. It is at such a distance that it receives the right amount of heat which is conducive for life.

(iii) Presence of ozone in the atmosphere: The stratosphere around the earth contains the ozone which absorbs the high-frequency ultra-violate rays that are harmful to us. It also retains the heat radiated from the surface of Earth.

Q. 2. Write a brief note about the Solar systems.

Ans. (i) The solar system consists of 8 planets, revolving around the Sun. It also consists of satellites which revolve around planets, asteroids, comets, gases and dust.

(ii) Based on the distance from the Sun the planets are Mercury, Venus, Mars, Earth, Jupiter, Saturn, Uranus and Neptune.

(iii) The planets of the solar systems are divided into two groups: inner and outer planets. The group of planets close to the Sun are known as inner planets such as Mercury, Venus, Mars and Earth. The group of planets which are far away from the Sun are known as outer planets such as Jupiter, Saturn, Uranus and Neptune. The inner group of planets are made of rocks whereas the outer planets are made of large balls of gases.

Q. 3. Provide three pieces of evidence which prove the Earth is spherical in the shape.

Ans. The three pieces of evidence that prove the Earth is flat are as follows:

(i) Variation in the sunrise and sunset: If the Earth would have been flat then all the places of the world would have experience day and night at the same time. The variation is the result of the earth's spherical shape.

(ii) The behaviour of the ship approaching the harbour: A ship approaching the harbour is quite good evidence of the fact that the earth is not flat but a sphere. Only the mast of an approaching ship is visible from the harbour first and slowly the whole hull will come into the sight of the viewer at the harbour.

(iii) Shadow of Earth during lunar eclipse: The shape of curved shadow of the earth on the moon during lunar eclipse proves that the shape of Earth is spherical.

Q. 4. Why does the earth have optimum temperature condition?

Ans. The Earth is the only planet is the solar system, which has an optimum temperature that sustains life on it. The significant reason are as follows:

(i) The planet is situated neither too close nor too far from the Sun. The distance is just too right to maintain an average temperature of 14ºC on the Earth surface. The Zone of the optimum range is called the Goldilocks Zone.

(ii) The second most important reason is the atmospheric blanket that covers the Earth. The atmosphere protects us from the Sun's excessive heat and harmful radiation. It also helps in trapping the heat that radiates back from the Earth and keeps it warm.

Q. 5. State how the atmosphere of the Earth is different from those of the other planet.

Ans. The atmospheric blanket of Earth contains 78 percent of nitrogen and 21% of oxygen along with a minimal percentage of water and carbon dioxide. The mixture is quite different to that of the atmosphere of other planet in the solar system. Jupiter and satum are dominated by hydrogen and helium whereas the Venus and the Mars contain 96 percent of carbon dioxide and only 3% nitrogen. The atmosphere of mercury contains a large percentage of hydrogen, helium and oxygen and a small percentage of potassium, sodium, calcium and magnesium.

Q. 6. State three importance of atmosphere.

Ans. The atmosphere is essential for us because:

(i) It is indispensable for the sustenance of living beings, as it contains oxygen and other necessary gases.

(ii) It plays a vital role in the water cycle, as most of the process is being carried out in the lower atmosphere.

(iii) It prevents excess heat and harmful radiation from reaching the surface of the earth.

Q. 7. Write three importance of lithosphere.

Ans. The lithosphere is important to us because:

(i) It is the hard crust where all the activities of animal and plant kingdom take place.

(ii) It contains various minerals and nutrients which are essential for the sustence of life.

(iii) It contains huge water bodies which satisfy our demand for water and energy supply.

Q. 8. Name three factors which have made earth a habitable?

Ans. The factors that made the earth habitable are:

(i) The distance from the Sun is just optimum and thus it helps in maintaining the average surface temperature of 14°C.

(ii) The gaseous envelop known as the atmosphere that contains the important gases such as oxygen which facilitates life. It also protects the surface from the heat and harmful radiations.

(iii) It provides necessary nutrients for the growth and sustenance of life.

Q. 9. What do you understand antipodal balance between land and water?

Ans. (i) There is an antipodal balance between land and water on directly opposite side of the Earth. Land and one side of the globe is balanced by water on the other side of the Earth. For instance North Pole Artic Ocean is opposite to the continent of Antarctica.

(ii) The Northern Hemisphere is girdled by the large land masses of North America and Eurasia.

(iii) In the South Hemisphere are the continents of South America, Africa and Australia.

(iv) The landmass of Antarctica had three Prominent protroding area one towards South America, another towards South Africa and third towards Australia.

Q. 10. How the position of the pole star gives indication that the earth was spherical in shape.

Ans. The Pole star appears vertically overhead at the North pole. If the earth was flat, the pole star would be overhead at all places on the earth.

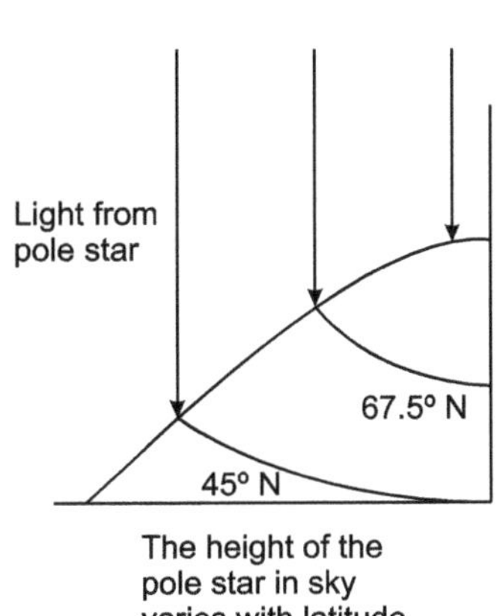

The height of the pole star in sky varies with latitude

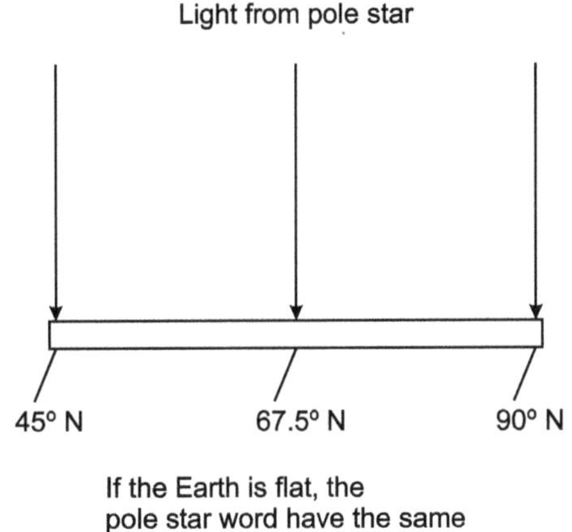

If the Earth is flat, the pole star word have the same height for all latitudes.

This a not the case. The angle of elevation of the pole star is about 40° at London and 0° at Singapore. this a only possible if earth is spherical is shape.

Chapter 2. Latitudes and Longitudes

Q. 1. State three important features of parallels of latitudes?

Ans. Three important features of parallels of latitudes are as follows:

(i) Latitudes are the angular distances of places north and south of the equator.

(ii) Each parallel of latitude is a circle.

(iii) The distance between two latitudes is equal throughout the globe.

Q. 2. State the three important characteristics of meridian of longitude.

Ans. Two important characteristics of meridians of longitude are follows:

(i) All the meridians of longitudes meet at one point i.e. pole.

(ii) The distance between two meridians decreases when we go from equator towards pole.

(iii) The distance between two longitude is maximum at the equator.

Q. 3. What do you mean by Zenith and Zenith Distance? Explain with a diagram.

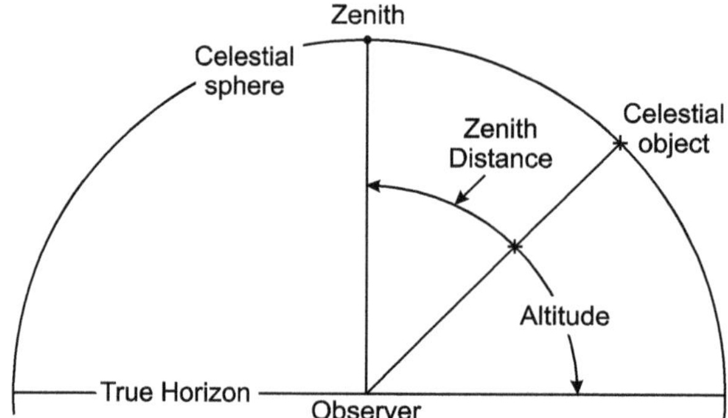

Ans. Zenith is an imaginary point direct above the observer and Zenith Distance is an angular distance of any celestial body from Zenith. It is measured by the arc of the vertical circle intercepted between the object and the Zenith.

Q. 4. Why do we call the latitudes as parallels of latitude? Name the important parallels of latitudes.

Ans. The lines of latitude run parallel to equator as well as to each other. Thus they are called parallels of Latitude.

The important parallels of latitude are:

(i) The 0° latitude or the equator which runs from east to west through the centre of the Earth and divides the Earth into Northern and Sothern Hemisphere.

(ii) 23.5° North and 23.5° South latitudes are known as the Tropic of Cancer and the Tropic of Capricorn respectively.

(iii) 66.5° North and 66.5° South latitudes are known as the Arctic and Antarctic Circle respectively.

(iv) 90° North and 90° South are known as the North and South poles respectively.

Q. 5. Explain the heat zones of the Earth.

Ans. The Earth is divided into three heat zones on the basis of difference in the insolation. They are as follows:

(i) Torrid Zone: The zone that extends between 23.5° North to 23.5° South is called torrid zone, i.e. from Tropic of Cancer to Tropic of Capricorn. The zone receives direct sun light and thus it is the hottest zone of all. This zone is also called Tropical Zone.

(ii) Temperate Zones: The zones extend from 23.5° to 66.5° in both the hemisphere i.e. from the Tropic of Cancer to the Arctic Circle in Northern Hemisphere and from the Tropic of Capricorn to the Antarctic Circle in Southern Hemisphere. These zones receive slanting rays of the sun and thus experience moderate climate. The Temperate Zone is also known as Extra-tropical zone.

(iii) Frigid Zones: These Zones extend from 66.5° to 90° in both the hemisphere i.e. from the Arctic Circle to North Pole in Northern Hemisphere and from the Antarctic Circle to South Pole in Southern Hemisphere. The zones receives the least amount of heat from the Sun and thus remain frozen throughout the year.

Q. 6. Longitude determines the time of a particular area. Explain how?

Ans. Longitude plays a major role in determining time. As the Earth is spherical in shape, it has total 360 longitudes at 1° interval.

Earth takes 24 hours to complete one rotation on its own axis.

It means in 24 hours the Earth travels 360° and in 1 hour it completes 360° ÷ 24 = 15°

For travelling 15° it takes 1 hour or 60 minutes.

So to cover 1° the Earth will take 60 ÷ 15 = 4 minutes.

This is how longitude is determinant of time of a particular place.

Q. 7. When it is 12 noon at Greenwich, what is the local time in Allahabad?

Ans. To calculate the time at Allahabad, we must be aware of the longitude that passes through it.

The longitude that passes through Allahabad is 82.5°E latitude.

That means the time of Allahabad will be ahead of Greenwich Mean Time as it is located in the eastern side of the globe.

The longitudinal difference between the two locations will be 82.5° – 0°= 82.5°.

1° difference in longitude will cause 4 minute difference in time.

82.5° difference will cause 82.5 × 4 = 330 minutes or 5 hours 30 minute.

Thus when it is 12 noon at Greenwich, the time at Allahabad will be 12 + 5 h 30 min = 17 h 30 min that is 5:30 PM.

Q. 8. GMT of Point A is 12 noon. At the same time Point B has the local time as 10 PM. What is the longitude of the point B?

Ans. The GMT is at point A is 12 hours.

As the time at Point B is 22 hours, it implies the place will be located in the Eastern Hemisphere.

The difference in time between two places will be

22 hrs – 12 hrs = 10 hrs or 600 mins.

For 4′ difference, the longitude difference is 1°.

For 600 minutes – difference the difference will be = $\frac{1}{4} \times 600 = 150°$.

As the local time is ahead of the GMT the longitude will be 150° E.

Q. 9. When it is 9 AM at 71° W (Quebec), what is the time at 120°E (Amur Blast)?

Ans. As the points are located in two different hemisphere the difference will be calculated as 71° + 120° = 191°.

For travelling 1° longitude we require 4 min.

So to cover 191° we require 191°×4 = 764 min ÷ 60 min

= 12 hr 45 min

As Amur Blast is located to the east of Quebec the time at this place will be = 9 AM + 12 hr 45 min = 21 hr 45 min which is equal to 9:45 PM.

Q. 10. Briefly decribe the three major latitudes.

Ans. The three major latitudes are as follows:

(i) **The Artic circle:** It is located at approximately 66.50° N Latitude or 66.5° N of equator. This circle of latitude stretched through eight countries.

(ii) **The Tropic of Cancer:** It is located opproximately 23.5° N latitude or 23.5° N of the equator. This line of latitude is the Northern boundary of the area referred to as the tropic or torriod zone.

(iii) **The Equator:** It is the imaginary line on the Earths surface that is equidistant from the North Pole and the South Pole, dividing the Earth into Northern Hemisphere and Southern Hemisphere.

Q. 11. Why Indian Standard Time (IST) is important for us?

Ans. Indian Standard Time (IST) is important for us due to the following reasons:

(i) India is a large country and has a large East-West extent. There is a difference of two hours between Gujarat in the West and Assam in the East.

(ii) IST helps us is organising a uniform schedule for transport like railways and air ways.

(iii) IST provides the standard time for the entire country so that the local time difference can be managed easily.

Q. 12. Why do we have different time zones on the Earth?

Ans. We have different time zones on the earth due to the following reasons:

(i) As the Earth rotates on its axis, the different part of the Earth reeceives sunlight or darkness giving us day an night.

(ii) It we have one single time zone for the earth, noon world be the middle of the day in some places but it would be mornings evening and middle of the night at other places. Since different Part of Earth experience daylight at different times we need different time zones.

(iii) For example, as the earth rotates on its axis, it moves about 15° every 60 minutes. After 24 hours it completes the full circle rotation of 360°, So each time zone of 15° of longitude wide.

Q. 13. The distance between two consecutive latitudes is always the same, but it is not in case of longitudes. Explain why this is so? **[November, 2019]**

Ans. The distance between two consecutive longitudes can never be same because longitudes are meridians and they start and merge at one point. This is because of the Geoid shape of the Earth so, the distance between two consecutive longitudes would be maximum at equator and minimum at poles.

Chapter 3. Rotation and Revolution

Q. 1. Mention two effects of rotation of the Earth?

Ans. The rotation of Earth on its own axis gives rise to two prominent phenomena:

(i) Occurrence of day and night

(ii) Development of centrifugal force that causes flattened top at the poles and bulge near the equator

Q. 2. Mention two effects of revolution.

Ans. The revolution of the Earth around the Sun results into two prominent feature:

(i) Changes in seasons

(ii) Creation of heat zones.

Q. 3. Define rotation of the Earth. Also mention two effects associated with it.

Ans. Rotation is the spinning of the Earth around its own axis, which takes nearly 24 hours to complete.

The two effects of rotation of the Earth are as follows:

(i) Occurrence of day and night

(ii) Development of centrifugal force that causes flattened top at the poles and bulge near the equator.

Q. 4. Define Revolution? Also mention two effects associated with it?

Ans. Revolution of the Earth refers to the movement of the Earth around the Sun in an elliptical orbit, which takes around 365 days to complete.

The revolution of the Earth results into the following phenomena:

(i) Seasonal changes on the earth

(ii) Creation of heat zones across latitudes.

Q. 5. Describe the two important functions that occurs only at the poles?

Ans. The poles are the two extreme location where the sun rays become extremely slanting. The two important event that occurs only at the poles are:

(i) Occurrence of alternate period of six months of day light and six months of darkness.

(ii) Production of bright lights near the pole caused by the collision of electrically charged particles coming from the sun. The phenomenon occurs during the dark phase of the poles and known as Aurora Borealis at North Pole and Aurora Australis at South Pole.

Q. 6. Explain Summer Solstice and phenomena associated with it.

Ans. Summer Solstice is the phenomenon when the Earth's North Pole has its maximum tilt towards the Sun. The phenomena occurs on 21st of June every year. It results in:

(i) The longest day and shortest night in the Northern Hemisphere.

(ii) The Northern Hemisphere receives maximum heat from the Sun and thus experiences summer.

(iii) The Sun is directly over 23° N latitude i.e. over the Tropic of Cancer.

(iv) On the other hand the Southern Hemisphere receives the least amount of solar energy as it inclines away from the sun.

Q. 7. Explain Winter Solstice and associated phenomena associated with it.

Ans. Winter Solstice is the phenomenon when the Earth's South Pole has its maximum tilt towards the Sun. The phenomena occurs on 22nd of December every year. It results in:

(i) The longest day and shortest night in the Southern Hemisphere.

(ii) The Southern Hemisphere receives maximum heat from the Sun and thus experiences summer.

(iii) The Sun is directly over 23° S latitude i.e. over the Tropic of Capricorn.

(iv) The Northern Hemisphere receives the least amount of heat and thus experience winter season.

Q. 8. What do you mean by Equinox? Explain the phenomena associated with it.

Ans. Equinox refers to that day of the year when both the Northern and Southern Hemisphere experience nearly equal length of day and night:

(i) This phenomena occurs due to the apparent movement of the Sun either towards the equator or the Tropic of Cancer.

(ii) On 23rd September and 21st of March the Sun is vertically over the equator. The former is known as Autumnal Equinox and the latter is called spring or Vernal Equinox.

Q. 9. Define the following.

(i) Dawn

(ii) Dusk

(iii) Twilight

Ans. (i) Dawn: The first appearance of light when the Sun is about to rise.

(ii) Dusk: The stage before night or the period after sunset.

(iii) Twilight: The diffused light which come when the sun is below the horizon. It is visible due to the scattering of sunlight.

Q. 10. Explain the concept of leap year?

Ans. The earth takes 365.242 days (approximately 365.25 days) to complete one revolution around the Sun. But we consider a year has a 365 day. This turns in to one extra day in the fourth year where the year has 366 days. The extra days is added to the smallest month of the year February. This is called a leap year. On the other hand Leap year refers to that year when the month of February has 29 days. It comes in every four years.

Q. 11. What do you mean by Coriolis force? How is it affected by the rotation of the earth?

Ans.

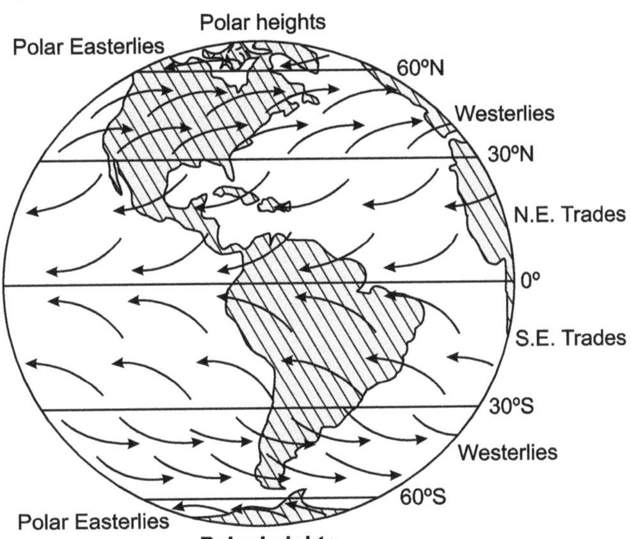

Coriolis force refers to the force experienced by a rotating object which is perpendicular to its direction of motion along with the axis of rotation. As the Earth rotates on its own axis, the objects on the Northern Hemisphere tend to deflect towards right and the objects on the Southern Hemisphere tend to deflect towards left. It can be clearly observed in global wind pattern.

Q. 12. What is midnight sun? Why does midnight sun occurs?

Ans. Midnight sun is a natural phenomenon where one can see the earth even at mid night. This phenomenon occurs near the Arctic and Antarctic circles.

As the Earth completes one rotation around the sun in every 24 hours it causes the change between day an night. The Earth has a tilt of 23.5° on its axis. Due to this axial tilt, the sun does not set in the Artic circle region and North Pole during summer solstice. At the time of winter solstice, the Artic circle region and the South Pole experience the same condition.

Q. 13. A complete revolution of the Earth makes a calender year. In this context answer the following questions.

(i) How much time is taken by the Earth to complete one revolution?

(ii) What is a leap year?

(iii) When do we have on extra day in the calender?

Ans. (i) The Earth takes 365.25 days to complete one revolution. This is roughly taken as 365 days which is a calender year or Earth year.

(ii) The year with extra day is known as the leap year. In a leap year there are total 366 days.

(iii) Since the time take by the Earth to complete its one revolution is $1/4^{th}$ day more than a calender year of 365 days. Thus after every four years an extra day is added to the calender year. This extra day is added to the month of february.

Q. 14. What are the effects of the speed of rotation?

Ans. The effect of the speed of rotation are as follows:

(i) Due to the Earth's rotation the ocean currents and the air is deflected towards the right in the North Hemisphere and toward left in the Southern Hemisphere. This effect is known as coriolis effects.

(ii) Due to the speed of the rotation, atmospheric changes occur which is due to the deflection of the cyclone and anticyclone in both the hemisphere.

(iii) A centrifugal force is created due to the rotation of the Earth which makes the Earth bulge at the equator and flattened at the poles.

Chapter 4. Structure of the Earth and Internal Processes

Q. 1. How does the temperature inside the interior of the Earth vary?

Ans. The three important properties of the matter of the Earth are temperature, pressure and density.

The temperature inside the interior of the Earth increases at a rate of 1 °C per every 32 m depth. The temperature increases rapidly up to a few kilometres and then the rate of increase in temperature reduces. When the depth descents up to 48 km down the surface, the temperature is predicted to be between 1200 °C to 2000° C. No metal can with stand such a higher temperature and thus they change their form from solid to liquid state. Near the core the temperature is calculated to be more than 4000 °C.

Q. 2. State the characteristics features of crust.

Ans. The crust or the lithosphere is the outer most layer of the earth. It is derived from the Greek word lithos, which means the rocks. Thus it can also be called rock sphere. The major characteristics of the crust or lithosphere are as follows:

(i) The rocks of this layer contain important minerals.

(ii) The average depth of this layer is about 60 km. Under the continent it is spread up to a depth of 30 km whereas under ocean the depth varies from 25-30 km.

(iii) The crust has two subdivisions Sial and Sima.

Q. 3. Write three major characteristics of Sial.

Ans. The major characteristics of sial are as follows:

(i) The sial is the upper layer of the crust which is also called as continental crust.

(ii) The layer consists of granite rocks which are rich in silicate and aluminum.

(iii) The thickness of the rock is nearly 25 kilometres.

(iv) The average density of the rock is about 2.7 gm/cm^3.

(v) The granite rocks are light in colour and less dense. Thus it floats on a denser sea of sima.

(vi) The rocks are acidic in nature.

(vii) The structure of this layer is discontinuous.

N.B: Though there are seven points mentioned here, the students can write any three of them.

Q. 4. Write down any three important features of Sima.

Ans. The important features of the layer sima are as follows:

(i) The lower layer of the crust is called sima or the oceanic crust.

(ii) The layer is made up of rocks which are rich in silicate and magnesium.

(iii) The average thickness of sima ranges from 25 km to 30 km below the ocean.

(iv) The average density of the rock is 3.0 gm/ cm^3.

(v) The layer mainly consists of basaltic rocks which are comparatively denser.

(vi) These rocks are more basic in nature.

(vii) As the layer is denser they constitute the ocean floor and continue beneath the continents.

N.B: Though there are seven points mentioned here, the students can write any three of them.

Q. 5. Discuss the important characteristics of mantle.

Ans. The second layer of the earth's interior is known as mantle. Major characteristics of this layer are as follows:

(i) The thickness of this layer is nearly 2900 km.

(ii) The rocks are made up of silicates and metal like iron and magnesium.

(iii) The average density of the layer varies between 3 and 5.5 gm/cm^3.

(iv) The upper mantle consists of molten ultrabasic rocks and known as asthenosphere. It comprises primarily of silica and iron.

(v) The lower mantle is called mesosphere and consists of solid ultrabasic rocks. The rocks mainly contain iron ad silica.

(vi) The temperature of this layer varies between 800° C - 2200° C.

N.B: Though there are six points mentioned here, the students can write any three of them.

Q. 6. Explain the characters of the core.

Ans. The core is also called Barysphere. The word is derived from the Greek word Bary which means heavy:

(i) The core is the innermost layer of the interior of the earth.

(ii) The core has high temperature and pressure.

(iii) It is the densest layer of the earth's interior.

(iv) Primarily the layer contains nickel (Ni) and iron (Fe). Hence it is called Nife.

(v) The core also has two layers the inner and the outer core.

(vi) The outer core is liquid and does not allow any kind of seismic waves to pass through it. The density of outer core is about 9-12 gm/cm^3.

(vii) The inner core is solid inner core has immense pressure. The density of the layer varies between 13-15 gm/cm^3.

(viii) The layer has an average temperature of about 5500° C.

(ix) The layer is the source of Earth's magnetic field because of the presence of iron, which generates electricity.

N.B: Though there are nine points mentioned here, the students can write any three of them.

Q. 7. Brief about the theories of plate movements.

Ans. The theory of plate movement was governed by the movement of convection current. The theory was given by German Meteorologist in 1912, which was previously known as continental drift. According to the theory around 250 million years ago the landmasses were joined together to form the one large landmass, which was surrounded by a large water bodies. Gradually the fracture started developing and the land mass parted into great slabs of rocks, which are otherwise known as tectonic plates. After getting separated from the largest landmass, the plate started moving apart and they formed the present day continents. So as to justify the drifting of these huge landmass, the theory of plate tectonics postulated in 1968. It implies that the lithosphere or the crust of the Earth is divided into seven major and number of minor plates, which slide over the mantle. The force that slide these huge landmass is generated by convection currents, which is originated from the intense pressure of rocks inside earth's core.

Q. 8. State and explain the plate tectonic theory.

Ans. The theory of plate tectonics was given by German Meteorologist Alfred Wegener in 1968, which state lithosphere or the crust of the Earth is divided into seven major and number of minor plates, which slide over the mantle. The plates move in response to convection in the upper mantle. The movements of plates are not always uniform. The movements of plates result into the formation of various landform building process depending upon the direction of the plate movement. The moving plates are either converge or diverge or slide past each other.

Q. 9. Discuss the important features of destructive margins of plates.

Ans. (i) When two plates move towards each other and collide, they are known as convergent plates.

(ii) The heavier of them goes underneath the lighter one and as a result it loses some of its part. The process is known as subduction.The collision and subsequent subduction occurs when one of the plate is oceanic and the other is continental plate, oceanic plate being the heavier one. The processes give rise to land forms like deep sea trenches and island arcs.

(iii) When both the plates are continental plates neither of the two sink and they force each other to form Fold Mountains.

Q. 10. Discuss any three important features of constructive plate boundaries.

Ans. (i) When two plates drift apart from each other they are called divergent plates.

(ii) When divergent plates move apart, the magma rises up to fill the gap and thus creates land forms like volcanoes or oceanic ridges.

(iii) The divergent plates are mostly found under ocean.

Q. 11. Explain the properties of conservative plate boundaries?

Ans. (i) When two tectonic plates slide past each other they form conservative plate boundaries or transform plates.

(ii) The plate moves either in opposite direction or in the same direction with varying speed.

(iii) The friction between the plates produce shockwaves which eventually cause major earthquakes.

Q. 12. What is Mohorovicic Discontinuity?

Ans. It is the boundary between the crust and the mantle. The Mohorovicic Discontinuity was discovered in 1909 by Andrija Mohorovicc a croation seismologist. He realised that the velocity of seismic waves is related to the density of material that it is moving through. He interpreted the acceleration of seismic wave observed within the earths outer shell as a compositional change within the Earth. The acceleration is caused by the higher density material being present at the depth. The lower density material present between the surface is called as crust and the higher density material present below the crust is known as mantle.

Q. 13. Define asthenosphere and mesosphere.

Ans. **Asthenosphere:** It is the upper mantle layer that extends from Mohorovicic Discontinuity to the depth of 700 km. It is made up of solid rocks and has an average temperature of 1100 °C.

Mesosphere: It is lower mantle layer that extends from 700 k.m. to 2900 k.m. It is made up of semi-molten rocks and has an average temperature of 1900 °C.

Q. 14. Breifly explain the chemical composition of the crust or lithosphere.

Ans. The outermost layer of the Earth is known as crust or lithosphere. It is made up of mostly solid silicate rocks like bsalt and granite. The crust is divided into two categories i.e. SiAl and SiMa.

SiAl stands for Silica (Si) and Aluminium (Al) which is known as continental crust and SiMa stands for Silica (Si) and Magnesium (Mg) which is known as oceanic crust. The SiAl floats over SiMa due to its density. The upper continental layer consists of silica and aluminium and it is comparatively lighter.

Chapter 5. Landforms of the Earth

Q. 1. What are the major classifications of mountains on the basis of mode of formation?

Ans. Mountains are classified into the following categories

(i) Mountains of deformation: Fold mountains, Fault mountains and Dome mountains.

(ii) Mountains of accumulation: Volcanic and sand dune

(iii) Relict Mountains: Formed from sculpturing and denudation

Q. 2. How are Fold Mountains formed?

Ans. The Fold Mountains are formed when two crustal plate moves towards each other and collide. During collision near compressing boundaries, rocks and debris are warped and folded into rocky outcrops, hills, mountains, and entire mountain ranges. The movements responsible for creating these folds are known as orogenic movements.

Q. 3. Write down the major characteristics of Fold Mountains.

Ans. The major characteristics of Fold Mountains are as follows:

(i) They consist of a series of parallel range.

(ii) They have snow-covered high peaks.

(iii) They also have intermontane plateaus.

(iv) They are prone to volcanoes and earthquakes.

(v) They are also characterised by gorges, canyons and waterfalls.

Q. 4. How are the Block Mountains formed?

Ans. When the tensional or compressional force acts between the crustal plates, cracks and faulting develop. These forces either lengthen or shorten the earth's crust causing a portion of it either subside or rise above the surrounding level. The process results in the formation of block mountains.

Q. 5. Why mountains are important to us?

Ans. The reasons why mountains are important to us are as follows:

(i) Mountains play an important role in protecting countries from bitterly cold winds.

(ii) They also act as a natural barrier for safeguarding the country from a defence point of view.

(iii) Mountains are the storehouse of minerals like coal, copper, iron ore, gold, gypsum and lead, etc.

(iv) Mountains are the source of rivers, which create rich alluvial plains.

(v) Mountains are the storehouse of natural vegetation. They are the source of raw materials for the forest-based industries.

(vi) Mountains have steep slopes and thus characterized by rapids, waterfalls and swift-running rivers which can be tapped for hydroelectricity.

Q. 6. What are mountains and how they are formed?

Ans. Mountains are the high rising steep lands which are elevated up to several hundred metres over the land surrounding it.

Mountains are formed by a number of ways. Most important of them are:

(i) Earth Movements which implies volcanic eruption, erosion and deposition, upliftment and subsidence of earth's crust.

(ii) Plate tectonics which refers to the movement of crustal plates and the associated actions of convergence and divergence between them.

(iii) Horizontal compression which refers to the deformation of crustal strata causing folds and wrinkles.

Q. 7. What do you mean by plateau? How they are formed?

Ans. Plateaus are the highlands which usually elevated significantly above the surrounding and consist of flat terrain at the top. They are also called tablelands.

Plateaus were formed through various processes. They are as follows:

(i) The upliftment of magma without any breakage in between could be the cause of plateau formation.

(ii) The erosional activity of wind and water on the land might result in the formation of a plateau.

Q. 8. What is the major classification of plateaus?

Ans. The plateaus are mainly classified into the following types:

(i) Intermontane Plateau: When the plateaus are enclosed by the mountains originated from tectonic upliftment, they are called intermontane plateaus. For example the Altiplano plateau in the Andes.

(ii) Continental plateaus: The plateaus which are bordered from all sides either by plains or seas and formed away from mountains are called continental plateaus. For example, the canyon of Colorado Plateau.

(iii) Piedmont plateau: The plateaus formed at the foothills of mountains are called piedmont plateaus. For example, Plateaus formed at the foothills of the Appalachian Mountains.

(iv) Volcanic plateaus: The plateaus formed due to the solidification of a successive sheet of lava released from volcanic activities are called volcanic plateaus. For example, the Deccan Trap of Maharashtra in India.

(v) Dissected Plateaus. The plateaus developed from erosional activities of river and winds are called dissected plateaus. They are broken by deep narrow valleys. For example, Brazilian plateau.

Q. 9. Write down the significance of plateaus?

Ans. Plateaus have the following significance:

(i) They are climatically the zones of comfort, because they remain cool due to their higher elevation.

(ii) They are the storehouse of minerals.

(iii) They also facilitate agriculture due to the presence of basaltic soil.

(iv) They also facilitate the production of hydroelectricity due to the presence of swift-moving rivers.

Q. 10. What do you mean by plains and how are they formed?

Ans. The extensive area of land with relatively low relief and a flat or gentle rolling surface is known as a plain.

The plains can be formed through a number of ways, such as:

(i) Washing away of a standing landform by a sudden heavy downpour and filling up depression to form a plain.

(ii) Extensive lava flows from the volcanoes and their solidification over an extensive plain will also result in the formation of the plain.

(iii) By the process of erosion and deposition of alluvium by water and wind will also result in the formation of plains.

Q. 11. Write down the major characteristics of plains?

Ans. The major characteristics of the plains are as follows:

(i) Low relief

(ii) Flatland

(iii) Very less slope

(iv) Lowlands are underlain by horizontal strata

(v) Heights are always less than 500 ft.

Q. 12. What do you mean by structural plains?

Ans. The plains created due to the upliftment of continental shelves are called structural plains. These plains are always bordered by the continents. These are structurally the most depressed areas of the world. For example, The Malabar coast of India is an uplifted plain, whereas the Russian plain is the structurally depressed plain.

Q. 13. What do you mean erosional plains? What are the major categories of erosional plains?

Ans. The plains formed due to the denudation of elevated landforms like hills and mountains by various agents such as river, winds and glaciers. These agents erode the high lands to a smooth surface and convert them into plains. These are also called destructional plains.

The erosional plains can be categorized into various types such as peneplain, pediplain, karst plain and glacial plain.

Q. 14. What do you mean by depositional plains? What are the major categories of depositional plains?

Ans. The plains which are formed by the deposition of material brought down by various agents of transportation are called depositional plains. The agents of deposition can be a river, winds, waves and glaciers. These plains are also called constructional plains. These are economically very important as they are fertile in nature and can be used for agricultural productivity. There are various types of depositional plains, such as alluvial plains, lava plains, lacustrine plains, drift plains, etc.

Q. 15. How plains are important to us?

Ans. Plains are important to us in a number of ways:

(i) As a levelled and fertile low land, a plain can be utilized for agricultural productivity.

(ii) It is easier to construct road and railway networks on plains as compared to the plateau and mountain. Thus plains facilitate better transport network.

(iii) The enhanced agricultural production and better transport network help in setting up of both agro-based and mineral-based industries on the plain and thus attracts a large number of populations.

Q. 16. (i) Name two agents responsible for the formation of Depositional Plains. **[November, 2019]**

(ii) Give an example of each type.

Ans. Two agents responsible for the formation of depositional plains are river and wind.

1. River forms alluvial plains.
2. Wind forms loess and sand dunes.

Chapter 6. Rocks

Q. 1. Define and explain rock cycle.

Ans. The process in which old rocks are transformed into new rocks is called rock cycle:

(i) The igneous rocks are primary or parent rocks formed due to the tectonic activities and eventually subjected to denudation by, wind, glaciers and ground water, etc. and thus disintegrate into sediments.

(ii) These sediments get deposited layer after layer and form sedimentary rocks through the process of lithification.

(iii) Both igneous and sedimentary rocks under tremendous heat and pressure, transforms into metamorphic rocks. These metamorphic rocks may denude to form sedimentary rocks or may melt as magma and solidifies to form igneous rocks.

In this way all the three types of rocks interchange their types from one to the other under the combined effect of heat from the interior of the earth and the solar energy.

Q. 2. Write down the important characteristics of igneous rocks.

Ans. The important characteristics of igneous rocks are as follows:

(i) The rocks are not permeable since they are very compact, hard and massive in structure. They don't have pores in them.

(ii) They have crystals in them.

(iii) As originated from volcanic activities, these rocks are loaded with minerals.

(iv) They don't have any sign of fossils because the temperature inside the interior of the earth is quiet high.

Q. 3. Write down the important characteristics of sedimentary rocks.

Ans. The important characteristics of sedimentary rocks are as follows:

(i) They are also known as stratified rocks as the sediments are deposited in layers.

(ii) They also have ripple marks on them.

(iii) The porosity of these rocks is quiet high and thus they allow water to pass through them.

(iv) They are soft in nature and thus subjected to weathering and erosion very often.

(v) Usually these types of rocks have the signs of fossils in them.

Q. 4. Write down the important characteristics of metamorphic rocks.

Ans. The important characteristics of metamorphic rocks are as follows:

(i) Since these rocks are very hard, they are more resistant to weathering and erosion.

(ii) These rocks have closely-banded interlocking structures of crystal in them.

(iii) Rocks always metamorphose in their own category. For example limestone converts into marbles and shale transforms into slates.

Q. 5. What are plutonic rocks? Give one example of plutonic rocks.

Ans. These are types of intrusive igneous rocks which are formed when the magma gets solidified and crystalized beneath the surface of the Earth. The slow cooling of magma forms relatively large crystalline course gain rocks. Laccoliths and batholiths are the example of plutonic rocks. For example pumice, obsidian and basalt.

Q. 6. What do you mean by volcanic rock? Give example.

Ans. These are types of extrusive igneous rocks. These are formed when the lava comes out from the surface of the earth on to its surface through its fissures and cracks. The lava cools down quickly and solidifies immediately after getting exposed to the normal temperature of the outer atmosphere. As a result of quick cooling the crystals created are relatively small and thus the rocks formed are fine- grained and glassy in texture.

Q. 7. Name any three types of sedimentary rocks based on the agents of formation.

Ans. On the basis of agents of formation the sedimentary rocks are divided into:

(i) Riverine rocks: The rocks formed from the deposition of sediments by the river water are called riverine rocks. They are mostly found in the river basin.

(ii) Lacustrine rocks: These types of sedimentary deposits are formed in the bottoms of ancient rocks.

(iii) Aeolian rocks: These types of rocks are formed due to the deposition of sediments or sand particles by the physical agent like wind. These rocks are mostly found in deserts.

(iv) Glacial rocks: These rocks are formed by the debris eroded from the sides and surfaces of the valley by the glaciers. The debris are left behind in the form of moraines when the glaciers melt and results in the formation of glacial rocks like boulders, gravels, etc.

(v) Marine rocks are formed when the sediments brought by the rivers scattered on the continental shelves and become thick with due course of time.

Q. 8. Explain the terms:

Ans. (i) Extrusive igneous rocks: The rocks which are formed when the lava comes out of the volcanic craters and spread on the surface outside the volcanic dome. The magma cools down and solidifies to form extrusive igneous rocks.

(ii) Laccoliths: These are the type of intrusive igneous rocks which are formed beneath the surface of the earth, thereby uplifting the crustal dome and form a lens shaped structure.

(iii) Batholiths: These are extensive and massive rocks of intrusive igneous origin that are formed deep under the earth's crust due to the cooling of magma.

Q. 9. Classify igneous rocks on the basis of mode of occurrence.

Ans. On the basis of mode of occurrence the igneous rocks are divided into:

(i) Extrusive igneous rocks: These rocks are formed near the volcanic dome due to the cooling and solidification of magma after its release from interior of the earth. The process takes place at a faster rate when the magma comes in contact with the atmosphere, on reaching the ground.
These rocks are fine-grained, less crystalised rocks as they do not get enough time for cooling.

(ii) Intrusive igneous rocks: These rocks are formed, when the magma does not come out and starts cooling inside the earth's crust. The process of cooling takes place very slowly within the crust.
As the magma gets enough time to cool down these rocks have comparative larger crystals with a course texture.

Q. 10. Classify igneous rocks on their chemical composition.

Ans. On the basis of chemical composition the igneous rocks are classified as follows.

Acidic igneous rocks:

(i) These rocks have high percentage of silica and lesser percentage of basic oxides.

(ii) They are coarse textured, light coloured rocks.

(iii) They are very hard.

(iv) They contain large crystals. For example: quartz, feldspar and mica

Basic igneous rocks:

(i) They contain lesser amount of silica and higher percentage of basic oxides, like iron and magnesium. For example, Gabbros.

(ii) When the rock does not have any sign of silica in it and only basic oxides like iron and magnesium are present, the rocks are called ultra-basic rocks.

(iii) They are dark and dense in colour.

(iv) They are fine-textured and smooth rocks.

(v) The best quality basic rock is basalt.

Q. 11. Classify the process of metamorphism on the basis of agency involved.

Ans. On the basis of agency involved in the process of metamorphism is of two types:

(i) Thermal metamorphism: As the name reflects, this process of metamorphism involves a high temperature in which the rocks transforms into a new type of rocks. For example, sandstone changes into quartzite, shale changes to slate and coal changes to graphite.

(ii) Dynamic metamorphism: The process of metamorphism which involves tremendous pressure to transform one type of rock into another is known as dynamic metamorphism. For example, transformation of clay into schist and granite into gneiss.

Q. 12. Write down the types of metamorphism based on the location.

Ans. On the basis location the types of metamorphism is classified into:

(i) Contact metamorphism: When the existing igneous rocks come under the influence of newly released lava, the process of metamorphism starts which involves tremendous heat over a smaller areal extent.

(ii) Regional metamorphism: When the process of metamorphism involves a large area due to the movement of earth, it is called regional metamorphism.

Q. 13. Classify the types of metamorphic rocks.

Ans. The metamorphic rocks are classified into the following types:

(i) Foliated rocks: These types of rocks are the result of dynamic metamorphism, where minerals within the rocks continue to squeeze and elongated until they are aligned. The rocks develop a platy or sheet like structure. For example, shale, schist, slate and gneiss, etc.

(ii) Non-foliated rocks: Unlike foliated rocks, the non-foliated rocks do not have any sign of banded or layered appearances. For example hornfels, marble, quartzite, and novaculite.

Q. 14. Why rocks are important to us? Write any three points.

Ans. The rocks are important to us because:

(i) They are the source of raw material for various industries as they provide a wide variety of minerals. For example, limestone and gypsum for cement industries; iron ore, dolomite, manganese and chromium for iron and steel industries, etc.

(ii) Rocks disintegrate into smaller particles during the process of denudation and transform to soil which are fertile. The soil can be used for agricultural purpose.

(iii) Rocks also provide precious metals like gold, silver, diamond, platinum, etc.

Q. 15. (i) What are fossils? In which type of rocks do we find fossils? **[February, 2020]**

(ii) What do you understand by 'ROCK CYCLE'?

Ans. (i) Fossils are the remains or traces of plants or animal life from ancient geological age. Fossils are found in sedimentary rock.

(ii) The transformation of one type of rock into another type under different conditions is called as 'Rock Cycle'.

Q. 16. (i) How is metamorphic rock formed? **[February, 2020]**

(ii) Classify the following rocks into igneous, sedimentary and metamorphic rocks:

1. Granite
2. Limestone
3. Basalt
4. Marble

Ans. (i) Metamorphic rock is formed as a result of changes in temperature, pressure or the composition of igneous, sedimentary or previous metamorphic rock to such an extent that the diagnostic features of the original rocks are modified.

(ii) Classification of rocks :

1. Granite – Igneous rock
2. Limestone – Sedimentary rock
3. Basalt – Igneous rock
4. Marble – Metamorphic rock

Chapter 7. Volcanoes

Q. 1. What do you mean by an active volcano? Give an example.

Ans. (i) Active volcanoes refer to those volcanoes which still erupt lava, gases, ashes, cinder, pumice, etc. at frequent intervals or have erupted in the recent past.

(ii) The World has more than 500 active volcanoes.

(iii) Mauna Loa in Hawaii is considered to be World's biggest active volcano.

Q. 2. What do you mean by a dormant volcano? Give an example.

Ans. (i) These are the volcanoes that were active in the past 2000 years, but now their status is sleeping or inactive.

(ii) Maybe in the future, the eruption will start.

(iii) The barren island of Hawaii is an example of this type of volcano.

Q. 3. What do you mean by an extinct volcano? Give an example.

Ans. (i) The volcanoes which have not erupted for a pretty long period, i.e., more than 10000 years.

(ii) They have no probability of eruption even.

(iii) Mount Kilimanjaro is one of the examples of an extinct volcano.

Q. 4. What do you mean by shield volcano?

Ans. When large quantities of magma erupt and spread over a large area, they get solidified to form a thick sheet of lava. They eventually accumulate in layers to create a plateau. The Deccan Plateau is one of such kind. The eruption always takes place along a long narrow fissure.

Q. 5. State and explain the various products of a volcano.

Ans. The important products that come from the interior of the earth form the vents are as follows:

(i) Volcanic Gas: It mainly contains a mixture of steam, carbon dioxides, and compounds of sulphur and chlorine. It comes out along with the lava during an eruption.

(ii) Lava flows: These are the streams of molten rocks.

(iii) Pyroclasts are the high-speed avalanches of hot ash, rock fragments, and gases, which flow down to the sides of the volcano.

Q. 6. Write any three causes of volcanic eruption?

Ans. The important causes of volcanic eruptions are as follows:

(i) The rocks are found in the molten state at greater depth under the earth's crust. When the pressure increases inside the earth, the lava comes out with the sudden force.

(ii) The crustal dislocation owing to earthquake leads to the formation of the fault, and the pressure from within the earth is released with the magma.

(iii) Subduction of a heavier oceanic plate under the lighter continental plates, which eventually results in the melting of the plates. This molten lava of continental crust comes out of a sudden force and cause an earthquake.

Q. 7. Mention three important constructive effects of volcanoes.

Ans. The significant constructive effects of volcanoes are:

(i) They are the source of clean and renewable geothermal energy.

(ii) They create rich and fertile soil, which facilitates growth in agricultural production.

(iii) The geyser and hot springs originating from volcanoes have medicinal value.

Q. 8. Mention three important destructive effects of volcanoes.

Ans. The significant destructive effects of volcanoes are:

(i) They destroy lives and properties.

(ii) The spread of volcanic ashes and dust can cause severe respiratory ailments and even cause death due to the loss of breath.

(iii) Dangerous gases like sulphur dioxides and carbon dioxides have a hazardous effect on the settlement nearer to the volcano.

Q. 9. Give a brief about the Circum-Pacific Belt.

Ans. The Circum-Pacific Belt stretch extends from New Zealand to the west coast of South America along the eastern edge of Asia, across the Aleutian Islands of Alaska and along the western coast of North America. The belt consists of nearly 75% of the active and dormant volcanoes of the World. The belt is also called Rings of Fires. The belt is created due to the subduction of the Pacific plate underneath other plates. The belt has developed over a zone of subduction.

Mid-World mountain belt. The belt consists of numerous islands towards the eastern coast of Asia, and these islands are formed from volcanic activities.

Q. 10. Answer the following questions.

(i) Volcanic eruption is associated with water.

(ii) Valcanic activity leads to earthquakes.

(iii) Tectonic plates responsible for volcanic activity.

Ans. (i) Volcanic eruption is associated with water because when water comes in contact with magma, it dissolves and crystallises which makes the dissolved water free. At high temperature and pressure free wate escapes out through many holes and thus causes explosion.

(ii) Most earthquakes are caused by the movement of magma. The magma exert pressure on rocks until it cracks the rock. Then the magma squirts into the cracks and start building pressures again. Every time rock cracks, it makes a small earthquake.

(iii) The tectonic plates in the lithosphere causes the movement in the Earth which results in the earthquake. The movement of these plates also results in the eruption of the volcanoes.

Q. 11. Describe the structure of a volcano.

Ans. The structure of the volcano can be described as:

(i) Vent: It is a narrow opening in the volcano that allows hot magma and ash to escape. It is usually pipe shaped.

(ii) Crater: The upper part of the vent that is a bowl shaped depression is known as the crater of the volcano. It is the highest point of volcano.

(iii) Cinder: The solid rocks that are ejected from the volcanoes is known as cinder.

(iv) Caldera: If forms when gets hollow and then collapses on itself. A caldera could look like a large indentation at the side of the volcano or it could happen at the very top.

(v) Magma Chamber: The large underground pool of molten rocks found beneath the surface of the Earth is called as magma chamber.

Chapter 8. Earthquakes

Q. 1. Expain three major impacts of earthquake.

Ans. Earthquakes are very disastrous for nature and for humans:

(i) Landslide: The vibrations caused by earthquake in the hilly and mountainous region can cause huge instability. This further leads to landslides, which can damage the natural ecosystem and human settlements and transport network.

(ii) Loss of manmade structure: Earthquakes can cause huge damage to residential set up, transport and communication network and infrastructure of a place.

(iii) Tsunami: When seismic waves originate under the sea, cause high velocity sea waves which are called tsunami.

Q. 2. Give a detail account on Tsunami and its cause.

Ans. Tsunami is the large wave that is generated when the sea floor is deformed by the seismic activities vertically displacing the overlying water in the ocean. The velocity of tsunami waves can reach upto 800 km/hour.

Tsunami is caused primarily due to plate tectonic movement. These plate moves relative to one another, at an average speed of few inches a year and earthquakes or volcanic eruption happens when these plates move and collide at their boundaries. When these plate movements occur under the ocean this lead to generation of high velocity waves called Tsunami.

Q. 3. Mention the prime earthquake zones in India.

Ans. India has three commonly known earthquake zone, which are as follows:

(i) Himalayan zone: Himalayas are the young fold mountains. Due to the folding movement the Indian plate is moving northward 5 cm/year. This folding movement develops tremors in this zone and Himalayas fall in the zone of high intensity.

(ii) The peninsular zone: The peninsular landmass is a stable landmass, but few earthquakes like Bhuj (2001), Latur (1993) and Jalabalpur (1997) have raised the question about its stability. This zone falls in the category of low intensity zone.

(iii) Indo-Gangetic Plains: This is a zone of medium intensity. Most of the earthquakes experience in this zone is of 5-6 on Richter scale. Due to high population density earthquake cause huge destruction in this zone.

Q. 4. Mention some prime factors on which intensity of an earthquake depends.

Ans. The intensity of an earthquake depends upon the following factors:

(i) Total amount of energy released.

(ii) Distance from epicenter.

(iii) Types of rocks.

Q. 5. Distinguish between seismic focus and epicentre.

Ans. Seismic focus is the origin point of seismic waves or earthquake deep inside the earth surface. The depth of seismic focus may vary from 700 kms to 30 kms.

Epicentre: It is the point on earth surface vertically above the seismic focus. The intensity is always highest near the epicentre.

Chapter 9. Weathering

Q. 1. How humans play an important role in biological weathering?

Ans. Humans play an important role in biological weathering. The following activities of human speed up the rate of biological weathering:

Human beings by disturbing vegetation, Ploughing and cultivation of soil, help in mixing and creating new contacts between air, water and minerals.

Q. 2. Discuss three factors highly responsible for mechanical weathering.

Ans. The prime factors responsible for mechanical weathering are as follows:

(i) Temperature variation: In arid and semi arid region the daily range of temperature is very high. Thus, rocks are exposed to very high temperature during day and very low temperature during night resulting into disintegration of rocks.

(ii) Wind erosion: The abrasion process of the wind acts as a tool for eroding the rock. The small fragments of dust and sand present in the wind strike the rock and disintegrate it.

(iii) Nature and structure of the rock: This factor plays an important role in mechanical weathering of the rock. Whether the rock is soft or hard, soluble or insoluble vertically arranged or horizontally arranged.

Q. 3. (i) Explain the process of mechanical weathering.

(ii) Why it is highly effective in desert region?

Ans. (i) Physical and mechanical weathering is the disintegration of rocks due to temperature variations, frost action, wind action, etc.

(ii) Temperature variation is an important aspect of physical weathering. Particularly in deserts the temperature variation is highest and moreover in desert due to less population and vegetation cover, wind also plays an important role in mechanical weathering.

Q. 4. Discuss the Characteristics of Weathering.

Ans. The characteristics of weathering are as under:

(i) It involves disintegration or decay of solid rock.

(ii) It depends on climatic conditions.

(iii) It is affected by the chemical composition, hardness, texture and permeability of rocks.

(iv) It affects the surface of the Earth.

(v) It helps in the formation of soil.

Q. 5. Define the term mass movement. Also explain its types.

Ans. When weathered material of the rocks moves down the slope under the influence of gravity is termed as mass movement. There are many types of mass movements like Earth flow, rock fall, debris slide, etc.

(i) Earth flow: When the weathered material is saturated with water and lies below the mantle rock material. The sediment saturated matter flows down slope.

(ii) Rock fall: From the steep slopes of cliffs rock fragments get a free fall and accumulate at the foot of the cliff.

(iii) Debris slide: On the slopes weathering causes a layer of weathered rocks in an unconsolidated form. This debris moves down the slope and called as debris slide.

Q. 6. Explain the three stages of the Journey of the river.

Ans. (i) Upper Course: It is also known as mountain course. It begins at the source of the rivers near the watershed, generally at the crust of the mountain range. The predominant action here is vertical erosion.

(ii) Lower Course: In the lower course of the river the river water moves downstream across a broad and leveled plain which is full of debris brought down from the upper course. The lateral erosion continues to carry on to erode its bank further.

(iii) Middle Course: In this lateral erosion tends to replace vertical erosion i.e. active erosion of the river bank which widens the V-shaped valley.

Q. 7. How does the wind a river act as a agent of denudation?

Ans. The running water, wind and ice act as a chief agent of denudation. The action of running water is considered as most important agent of denudation. The wind through not the most effective agent of erosion but it is the great agent of transportation. It may transport large quantities of fine particles of sand and dust, as it is very dominent in the arid and semi arid regions. Through the process of abrasion, deflation and attrition wind engaged itself in the process of denudation.

Q. 8. Explain how landform is formed through the process of deposition.

Ans. The landform is formed through the process of deposition in delta. A river is formed through the deposition of sediments carried by a river, as it enters slow moving or standing water. This occurs where a river enters into an ocean, sea, estuary, lake, reservioir that cannot transport away the supplied sediments.

Q. 9. What is block disintegration?

Ans. Repeated expansion and contraction of rocks due to changes in rempreature caused the weakening and breaking of rocks. for example in desert region, the high range of temperature causes the splitting of rocks. Under this process the well jointed and bedded rocks tend to split along the joints and the cracks, by breaking up into rectangular blocks.

Q. 10. (i) Name a feature formed by the depositional work of a river. **[November, 2019]**

(ii) How is it useful to man?

Ans. (i) The depositional feature of river is called delta.

(ii) Delta provides extensive new alluvium, which is perfect landform to do farming.

Chapter 10. Hydrosphere

Q. 1. Define the terms:

(i) Surface current,

(ii) Deep water current.

Ans. (i) Surface ocean currents

Surface currents refer to movement of the top layer of ocean water. Examples of surface ocean currents are California Current in the Pacific Ocean basin and the Canary Current in the Atlantic ocean basin.

(ii) Deep ocean currents

Deep-water currents describe water movement patterns far below the ocean's surface and the influence of the wind. Some examples are gulf stream, Lima, Peru, etc.

Q. 2. What happens when cold and warm current meet? How it is important for fisheries? Give one example.

Ans. At the place where warm and cold current meet, it happens to be a foggy place. The meeting point of warm and cold current is ideal for fishing because it helps in the growth of planktons *i.e.*, food for the fishing. New foundland in North American Continent is an epitome of this phenomenon.

Q. 3. Define the following terms:

(i) Coriollis effect

(ii) Thermo cline

(iii) Gyre.

Ans. (i) Coriollis effect: It is generated due to rotation of the earth. This movement causes a deflection in the direction of ocean currents. For e.g. the currents in the Northern Hemisphere deflects to their right and currents in the Southern Hemisphere deflects to their left.

(ii) Thermo cline: It is a layer deep inside the ocean beyond which the temperature decreases rapidly with increasing depth.

(iii) Gyre-These are circulatory ocean currents which are formed due to coriollis effect and wind movement.

Q. 4. Define the following terms:

(i) Planktoon

(ii) Amplitude of tides

(iii) Isohaline

(iv) Lunar tide.

Ans. (i) Planktoon: These are the microscopic algae found in the oceans. These planktons are the food of fishes in the ocean.

(ii) Amplitude of tides: The elevation of tidal high water above mean sea level is called as amplitude of tide.

(iii) Isohaline: It is an imaginary line drawn on the map to show the places having equal salinity.

(iv) Lunar tide: The tide caused by the gravitational pull of the moon in the sea. This tide is also called as moon tide.

Q. 5. Why does Alaskan coast remain ice-free in winters?

Ans. The Alaskan cost remain ice-free in winters because the north Atlantic current which is a warm ocean current makes the Alaskan coast hot. The heat of ocean water transfer to the land.

Q. 6. The ocean current of Indian Ocean does not follow the pattern of currents in the Atlantic and Pacific Ocean.

Ans. The ocean current of Indian ocean does not follow the pattern of currents in the Atlantic and Pacific ocean because the ocean currents of North Indian Ocean are largely controlled by the monsoon winds which changes its direction twice a year and also due to the shape of the landmass.

Q. 7. How the salinity variations of an ocean affect the ocean currents?

Ans. The areas with greater salinity have greater density than the areas with lower salinity. Thus, the ocean currents are generated from the areas of lesser salinity to the areas of greater salinity. Because the dense water tends to sink down and the fresh water takes its place and cause circulation.

Q. 8. Explain the effect of ocean currents on: Climate, Navigation and Economic activities.

Ans. (i) Climate: The climate of the coasts become warm or cools on the basis of the current washing. Thus, ocean currents regulate global climate, helping to counteract the uneven distribution of solar radiation reaching Earth's surface.

(ii) Navigation: An ocean current has a well defined path and momentum. This momentum helps or obstructs the navigation of ships. The ships sailing in the same direction of the current makes little effort to sail and save the fuel. On the other hand the ships sailing in the opposite direction consumes more fuel.

(iii) Economic activities: Ocean currents sweep a large refuge off the coast which is the food of planktons. As the population of plankton rise, the number of fish also increases. Thus it makes the coastal areas fit for fishing activities.

Q. 9. How are various elements of hydrological cycle interrelated?

Ans. The hydrological cycle means the movement of water on, above and in the earth. All the elements of hydrological cycle is interrelated because this is a never ending process of movement of water from the oceans to the atmosphere through the process of evaporation, condensation and precipitation. Thus it also connects the realms of earth i.e. lithosphere, atmosphere and hydrosphere.

Q. 10. Discuss the factors that influence the temperature distribution of the ocean.

Ans. The factors which affect the distribution of temperature of ocean water are:

(i) Latitude: The temperature of surface water decreases from the equator towards the poles because the amount of insolation decreases pole ward.

(ii) Unequal distribution of land and water: The oceans in the Northern Hemisphere receive more heat due to their contact with larger extent of land than the oceans in the Southern Hemisphere.

(iii) Prevailing wind: The winds blowing from the land towards the oceans drive warm surface water away from the coast resulting in the upwelling of cold water from below. It results into the longitudinal variation in the temperature and vice-versa.

Q. 11. (i) How are tides caused? **[November, 2019]**

(ii) What is the time lag between two high tides?

Ans. (i) Tides are caused by the gravitational pull of the Moon and the Sun. The Moon exerts large pull than the Sun because it is closer to the Earth. During the revolution of Earth, The Earth makes various positions in respect to the Sun and the Moon. These positions cause the rise and fall of the ocean water, we call it tides.

(ii) The time lag between two consecutive high tides is 12 hours because Earth rotates through two tidal bulges in a day (24 hours).

Q. 12. What is the influence of the following ocean currents on the coastal area where they flow? **[November, 2019]**

(i) North atlantic drift (ii) Labrador current

(iii) Oyashio current.

Ans. (i) The North Atlantic Drift current keeps the North Western Europe climate comparatively warmer as it should be at this latitude. Especially, the winters of Western Europe and Norway are not freezing cold because of warm North Atlantic Drift current.

(ii) The Labrador current is a cold current. This current brings the icebergs from Greenland and makes the Newfoundland in Canada extremely cold.

(iii) The Cold and nutrient rich Oyashio current when meets the warm Kuroshio Current at the eastern coast of Japan, form the best fishing site.

Chapter 11. Atmosphere

Q. 1. Define the following terminology: (i) Inosphere, (ii), Greenhouse effect, (iii) Aurora or Polar lights

Ans. (i) Ionosphere: It is actually the lower part of thermosphere. This zone contains electrically charged particles called ions.

(ii) Greenhouse effect: It is the result of heat trap in earth's atmosphere due to increase amount of carbon dioxide.

(iii) Aurora or polar lights: It is the result of collision of solar radiation with atmospheric oxygen and nitrogen. These lights can be around the magnetic poles of Northern and Southern Hemisphere.

Q. 2. Name the five layers of atmosphere. What are their main characteristics?

Ans. Five layers of atmosphere are:

(i) Troposphere: It is the lowest layer and its average height is 13 kms. This layer contains all the weather phenomenons.

(ii) Stratosphere: This layer is found above troposphere and extends upto 50 kms. This layer contains ozone gas.

(iii) Mesosphere: Meso means middle. This layer extend upto 80 kms and in this layer temperature decreases with height and dips down to -100°C.

(iv) Thermosphere: The temperature starts increasing in this layer and reaches upto 1500°C. This layer also contains ions that helps for radio connectivity.

Q. 3. What do you mean by global warming? Discuss two ways to control global warming.

Ans. Continuous increase in the average earth's surface and atmospheric temperature is called as global warming. Global warming can be reduced by following the steps mentioned below:

(i) Less use of vehicles or by adopting car pooling.

(ii) Using renewable resources or by adopting 3R process.

Q. 4. Define the term 'global warming'. Mention two harmful impacts of global warming.

Ans. Global warming is the increase in temperature of the whole world. The temperature of the world keeps increasing. Two harmful impacts of global warming are:

(i) The glaciers are melting at a high rate.

(ii) The coastal areas are submerging because of rise of sea level.

Q. 5. Discuss three significances of atmosphere.

Ans. (i) The atmosphere filters the harmful rays radiated by the Sun.

(ii) Atmosphere maintains the moderate temperature over the earth.

(iii) Life on earth is possible due to the perfect combination of gases present in our atmosphere.

Q. 6. Discuss the main role of presence of oxygen, carbon dioxide and Ozone in the atmosphere.

Ans. (i) Role of Oxygen: Oxygen is the most important gas in our atmosphere as all the living beings need oxygen for their survival. Apart from this, oxygen is helpful in combustion process.

(ii) Role of carbon dioxide: This gas is used by the plants for the process of photosynthesis. Carbon dioxide also plays an important role in the greenhouse effect of the Earth.

(iii) Role of Ozone: Ozone is a life saving gas in the atmosphere as it filters the harmful ultra violet gas radiated by the Sun.

Q. 7. Why the layer of the atmosphere becomes thinner with altitude?

Ans. This happens because the gravitational force cause more pressure of atmosphere closer to the surface. As the pressure of air is higher towards the surface, the air become denser too. On the other hand, the air at heights is thinner because of less pressure and less density.

Q. 8. Answer the following questions.

(i) Temperature decreases with increasing height in the proposphere.

(ii) Temperature increases with increase in height in stratosphere.

Ans. (i) The reason was that the gases in the toposphere absorbs very little solar radiation. Instead, the ground surface absorbes this radiations and then heats the tropospheric air by conduction and convection. Since this heating is most effective near the ground, the temperature in the troposphere gradually increases.

(ii) The reason for this flactuation is that ozone layer absorbs ultraviolet radiations in the lower atmosphere. Once it is absorbed, it is radiated at different wave lengths thereby warming the stratosphere.

Q. 9. What is Chloroflurocarbons (CFC)?

Ans. CFC plays a major role in the depletion of ozone layer in the atmosphere. It is man-made synthetic industrial chemical compound containing chlorine, fluorine and carbon atoms. CFC is widely used as cooling fluid in the refrigerators and air-conditioners.

Q. 10. What is the composition of Earth's atmosphere? **[November, 2019]**

Ans. The earth's atmosphere consists of major and minor gases. The major gases are Nitrogen (78.08%) and Oxygen (20.9%). The minor gases are Argon (0.9%), Carbon dioxide (0.036%), Neon (0.002%), etc.

Q. 11. Why is the height of tropopause over the Equator more than over the poles? **[February, 2020]**

Ans. The height of tropopause over the equator more than over the poles because the equator is warm and poles are cold. The heat variation between equator and poles leads to the convection currents flow from equator to poles. As the thickness increases the height over the equator also increases.

Chapter 12. Insolation

Q. 1. What do you mean by terrestrial radiation? How it is helpful in maintaining temperature of the Earth?

Ans. Earth after being heated up, become a radiating body and transmit its energy through long waves. This process is called as terrestrial radiation or Earth radiation. The amount of heat received from the Sun during day time is returned by the Earth during night time. Thus the temperature is maintained on a daily basis.

Q. 2. What is inversion of temperature? Mention two conditions required for it.

Ans. The reversal of lapse rate is inversion of temperature which means the temperature in troposphere increases with height. In such condition the surface temperature is far less than the temperature at certain height.

The two conditions required for it is:

(i) The nights should be longer than the day time.

(ii) The sky during the nights should be clear.

Q. 3. Mention two prime factors that affect the temperature of a place.

Ans. Two prime factors that affect the temperature of a place are as under:

(i) Latitudinal location: As we know places situated closed to the equator experiences hot temperature and as we move towards poles the distribution of temperature starts decreasing.

(ii) Altitude: In normal conditions in troposphere, the temperature starts decreasing as we attain the height (Normal lapse rate). Places situated at higher altitude have less temperature as compared to low altitude.

Q. 4. Why landmass and Watermass have different heating capacity?

Ans. Land being opaque gets heated up faster than water because water is transparent to one extent and takes time to get heated up. Similarly land re-radiated more energy as compared water. Thus it becomes cooler faster than water mass.

Q. 5. Why New Delhi is hotter in summers than Mumbai?

Ans. New Delhi is situated far from Mumbai, which is a coastal city. Thus, New Delhi experiences continental type of climate. It means it get hotter in summers and colder in winters. On the other hand, Mumbai experiences maritime type of climate which means moderate type.

Q. 6. In what ways the slope of mountain affect the temperature?

Ans. The slope of a mountain facing the sun received more insolation than the leeward side of it. This happens because of inclination of sun rays on such slopes. In Northern Hemisphere the south facing slopes are warmer than the north facing slopes and vice-versa in the Southern Hemisphere.

Q. 7. What is the effect of cloudiness on temperature?

Ans. Clouds play's an important role in determining the temperature of a place. Clouds lead to precipitation and moderate the temperature of a place. Clouds also prevents insolation from reaching the surface of the earth and it also restricts the terrestrial radiation to pass out of earth's atmosphere, this results in heat trap in earth's atmosphere.

Q. 8. State the main differences between heating of landmass and oceans.

Ans. The landmass and the oceans react differently to the insolation. The landmass gets rapidly and intensely heated by the isolation. On the contrary, the oceans react slowly and take longer time to get heated up because of more transparent nature than the land.

The landmass also loses the heat quickly and gets cool down rapidly. But the oceans take time to release the heat and gets cool down slowly as compared to landmass.

Q. 9. State the importance of insolation.

Ans. The importances of insolation are as under:

(i) The insolation causes the movement of air and ocean currents.

(ii) Due to insolation, the hydrological cycle happens on the earth. This cycle includes evaporation and precipitation.

(iii) Insolation is the prime factor behind the process of photosynthesis. Due to which the plants prepare their food.

Q. 10. Justify the spatial distribution of insolation at the earth's surface with three points.

Ans. The spatial distribution of earth surface varies:

(i) Maximum insolation is received over the subtropical areas than equator. This happens because of more cloud cover over the equatorial region.

(ii) The amount of insolation received is higher over the continents than over the oceans at the same latitude.

(iii) In winter, the middle latitude and the higher latitudes receives less radiation than in summers.

Q. 11. What do you mean by continental type of climate? How is it different from maritime conditions?

Ans. Continental type of climate means the areas is far from the sea or the ocean or lie in the interiors of the continent experience extreme temperature during winters and the summers. This climatic condition is called as continental type of climate.

In maritime conditions the temperature remains moderate and its impact on watermass is high. On the other hand the continental type of climate has no impact on the water mass and experiences huge range of temperature.

Q. 12. Discuss the factors on which insolation of a place depends.

Ans. The factor on which isolation of a place depends:

(i) The angle of inclination of the sun rays.

(ii) The length of day and night.

(ii) Distance from the sea.

(iii) Transparency of the atmosphere.

(iv) The distance between the Sun and the Earth.

Q. 13. Explain the heat balance of the Earth.

Ans. Assume that Earth receives 100 units of insolation out of which:

(i) 35 units are reflected back by the atmosphere without reaching the surface (27 units by clouds, 2 units by ice sheets and 6 units by dust particles in the atmosphere).

(ii) Out of 65 units 14 units are absorbed by the atmosphere and 51 units by the Earth surface.

51 units received by the Earth are radiated back in form of long waves. Out of which:

(i) 17 units are radiated back to space directly.

(ii) 34 units are absorbed by the atmosphere (19 units by the process of condensation, 9 units by convection and 6 units absorbed by atmosphere).

Q. 14. Discuss the impact of ocean currents, distance from the sea over the temperature of a place.

Ans. Impact of ocean currents: The places which come under the influence of warm ocean current record higher temperature and the places located on the coast where cold current flows experiences lower temperature.

Impact of distance from the sea: The places located near the coast comes under the influence of sea and experience moderate temperature while areas located far from the sea experiences huge variation in temperature.

Chapter 13. Pressure Belts and Winds

Q. 1. Define the following terms:

(i) Isobars

(ii) Loo

Ans. (i) Isobars: These are the imaginary lines drawn on thematic maps to mark the areas having same atmospheric pressure

(ii) Loo: It is a hot and dry wind that prevails over northern part on Indian sub continent during the months of May and early June before the onset of monsoon.

Q. 2. What do you mean by the term 'wind'? Why do we name the winds Easterly and Westerly?

Ans. Moving air is called 'wind'. Wind always moves from high pressure areas to low pressure areas. Under the category of permanent winds, winds are divided into Easterly and Westerly as per their direction so are they called by the names Easterly and Westerly.

Q. 3. Name two tropical cyclones and specify the region where it experienced.

Ans. There are two types of cyclones:

(i) Mid latitude cyclones (Tropical cyclones)

(ii) Temperate cyclones.

Mid latitude cyclones are found in with in the tropics.

Temperate cyclones are found within the circles and tropics in both the hemispheres.

Q. 4. (i) What is the meaning of the term pressure gradient?

(ii) How does it affect the velocity of the wind?

Ans. (i) The variation in the heat distribution of the earth leads to variation in air pressure at different places. This variation in air pressure is called as pressure gradient.

(ii) As we know the wind moves from high pressure areas to the low pressure areas. Higher and closer the pressure gradient, higher would be the velocity of the wind

Q. 5. (i) Define the term 'jet stream'.

(ii) Why jet Stream is called so?

Ans. (i) Jet stream is a very fast moving strong wind that flows in boundary between troposphere and stratosphere i.e. tropopause. Jet stream flows in the boundary between hot and cold mass.

(ii) Jet stream flows at the height where most of the planes fly. Planes flying from west to east receives boost from jet stream and planes flying in a opposite direction generally changes its height. Because of this huge influence of jets/planes, this wind is named as jet stream.

Q. 6. Why westerlies are also called as anti-trade winds?

Ans. The westerlies are called anti-trade winds because westerlies move in opposite direction. The direction of trade winds in Northern Hemisphere is North-East and South-East in Southern Hemisphere. On the other hand, the westerlies move South West in Northern Hemisphere and North-West in Southern Hemisphere.

Q. 7. Why the winds blowing from sea to land are warm and carry moisture? Give one example.

Ans. While winds move over the sea or the ocean it carries moisture. Reason being the oceans and seas releases the moisture to the atmosphere by evaporation. Similarly when the winds move it transport the same moisture to its destination.

Example of this type of wind is sea breeze or monsoon wind.

Q. 8. Discuss the weather conditions associated with anti-cyclones.

Ans. Anti-cyclones are the areas of high air pressure which have diverging system of surface winds. The weather conditions associated with anti-cyclones are:

(i) The weather remains fine and stable.

(ii) The sky remains clear.

Q. 9. Pressure belts shift with revolution of the Earth. Why this is so?

Ans. Pressure belts of the Earth are directly linked with the temperature of that particular place and so are with revolution. As Earth revolves around the Sun it comes across various positions like summer solstice, winter solstice and equinoxes. During these positions the temperature distribution in both the hemisphere changes and it also changes the pressure belts.

Q. 10. State the major features of trade wind.

Ans. (i) Trade winds blow from 30°N to 30°S in both hemispheres.

(ii) This wind falls in the category of permanent wind.

(iii) In Northern Hemisphere it is called North-East trade wind and in Southern Hemisphere it is called south east trade wind because of its direction.

(iv) These winds blow from cooler towards hotter areas.

(v) At their convergence point (close to equator), N-E and S-E trade winds rises up and cause rainfall.

Q. 11. (i) Name the four main pressure belts of the world. **[February, 2020]**

(ii) What is a front?

Ans. (i) The four pressure belts are:

1. Equatorial low pressure belt.
2. Sub-tropical high pressure belt
3. Sub-polar low pressure belt
4. Polar high pressure belt

(ii) A front is a weather system that is the boundary separating two different types of air i.e., a denser air and lighter air with different temperature and levels of humidity.

Q. 12. (i) Name two types of variable winds. **[February, 2020]**

(ii) Why are they known as variable winds?

(iii) What is the importance of Jet streams in the climate of India?

Ans. (i) Two types of variable winds are:

1. Cyclones
2. Anticyclones

(ii) These winds are called as variable winds as they flow over a small region and are affected by the pressure system. These winds do not flow in definite direction.

(iii) Jet streams are responsible for bringing westerly cyclonic disturbances to the northwest part of India. Jet stream causes rainfall during winter season in this part of India.

Chapter 14. Precipitation

Q. 1. Explain the following terms:

(i) Latent Heat of Vapourisation

(ii) Rain Gauge

Ans. (i) Latent Heat of Vapourisation: It is the temperature at which evaporation takes place.

(ii) Rain Gauge: It is a scientific instrument to collect and measure the rainfall of a place.

Q. 2. (i) What is humidity?

(ii) How relative humidity and absolute humidity are different?

Ans. (i) The presence of amount of water vapours in the air is called humidity.

(ii) Absolute humidity is the amount of water vapours present in a certain volume of air. On the other hand, relative humidity is the capacity of the air to hold moisture that depends on its temperature.

(iii) The absolute humidity is shown in grains per cubic centimeter while the relative humidity is expresses in percentage.

Q. 3. Explain the following terms. (i) Isohyet or Isohyetal line (ii) Lapse rate.

Ans. (i) Isohyet or Isohyetal line: It is a line joining points of equal rainfall on a map in a given period. A map with isohyets is called an isohyetal map.

(ii) Lapse rate: It is a rate at which temperature which increases in height decreases. In normal conditions lapse rate is 6.5 °C with increase of 1 km.

Q. 4. Give one way in which monsoon is similar to and one way in which monsoon is different from land and sea breeze.

Ans. Monsoon is similar to land and sea breeze in a way that monsoon changes its direction twice a year according to the pressure variation over land and sea.

Monsoon wind is different from land and sea breeze in a way that the general flow tendency of land and sea breeze is day and night respectively, but monsoon winds move in summers (sea to land) and in winters (land to sea).

Q. 5. (i) The Himalayan Mountains are linked with which type of rainfall.

(ii) Discuss its one characteristic.

Ans. (i) The Himalayan mountains are linked with orographic rainfall. As the monsoon wind from Indian Ocean prevails and strikes with Himalayas, it causes orographic rainfall.

(ii) The southern side of the Himalayas that faces the monsoon winds, become its windward side and the northern slope of the Himalayas remain dry (leeward slope) and causes the cold dry Tibetan desert.

Q. 6. Explain the following terms:

(i) Transpiration

(ii) Frost

(iii) Sublimation

Ans. (i) Transpiration: It is the process where plants absorb water through the roots and then give off water vapour through pores in their leaves.

(ii) Frost: During winter season, due to sudden decrease in temperature the moisture in air condenses directly into ice crystals. These tiny ice crystals are called frost.

(iii) Sublimation: It is a process when the excess water vapour condenses directly from gaseous form to solid form instead of liquid form.

Q. 7. Discuss one adverse and favorable effect of fog for humans.

Ans. The adverse effect of fog is it reduces the visibility that cause road accidents, delayed or cancellation of train and flights.

The climatic fog is also used for 'fog harvesting'. It means collection of fog water for domestic and agriculture use.

Q. 8. Discuss the horizontal distribution of humidity on Earth's surface.

Ans. The horizontal distribution of humidity is as under:

(i) The equatorial region is characterized by highest level of humidity because of high temperature and rainfall.

(ii) Relative humidity decreases toward the tropical high pressure belts.

(iii) From the tropical high pressure belt the relative humidity level again starts rising towards the polar region.

Q. 9. (i) Mention two basic requirements for orographic rainfall.

(ii) In which part of India orographic rainfall is experienced?

Ans. (i) The basic requirements for orographic rainfall are:

(a) Direction of the winds should be towards mountain range (not parallel).

(b) Sufficient amount of moisture for condensation.

(ii) Regions of orographic rain are Western Ghats of India and Himalayan region.

Q. 10. (i) What do you mean by precipitation?

(ii) Mention two geographical conditions required for precipitation.

Ans. (i) Precipitation: The release of moisture from atmosphere is called Precipitation. Precipitation in form of liquid is rain and in form fine flakes is called snow fall.

(ii) Two geographical conditions required for precipitation are:

(a) Dew point: The point of temperature at which particular mass of air gets saturated.

(b) Condensation: It is the transformation of water vapours into liquid form.

Q. 11. State four characteristics of main type of rainfall that is experienced in equatorial region.

Ans. The main type of rainfall experienced in equatorial region is conventional rainfall. The characteristics are:

(i) This rainfall comes in form of heavy downpour.

(ii) This rainfall is always associated with lightning and thunder.

(iii) This rainfall comes for a short duration of time.

(iii) The sky is overcast during mid day, causes darkness and heavy rain.

Q. 12. Give a reason for each of the following: **[November, 2019]**

(i) The rain shadow areas are generally dry.

(ii) Convectional rainfall occurs almost daily in the Equatorial region.

(iii) Humidity in the air decreases with height from the Earth's surface.

Ans. (i) Before the air mass reaches the leeward side or rain shadow zone, it has already poured it moisture on the windward side.

(ii) Conventional rainfall occurs almost daily in the equatorial region because the equatorial region experiences high temperature that leads to high evaporation level and followed by condensation and precipitation. Thus, conventional rainfall happens every day.

(iii) Humidity in the air decreases with height from the Earth's surface because humid air has more water content thus, its weight increase and it starts decent down and more humid air is found closer to the surface.

Chapter 15. Pollution and Environment

Q. 1. State the effects of fresh water pollution.

Ans. Chemicals release from different industries enter the fresh water bodies like river and ponds, etc. This destroy aquatic life, increase bacterial growth, depleting dissolve - oxygen for acquatic life. Sewage, which flows into the fresh water bodies increases the water borne diseases like cholera, typhoid, etc.

Q. 2. How do agricultural wastes harm the environment?

Ans. Agriculture including commercial live-stock and poultry farming is a source of many organic and inorganic pollutants in surface water.

(i) The pesticides from agricultural run-off are also the major source of water pollution, causing eutrophication.

(ii) Agricultural waste when decomposes releases harmful gas like methane and carbon-dioxide.

Q. 3. How is oil-pill caused?

Ans. (i) Waste oil from city-drains, tankers, and leakage from oil-wells cause the oil to seep into the sea and pollute the water.

(ii) Collision of sea going vessels containing oil also cause oil-spill in the sea and ocean.

Q. 4. Explain the following terms:
(i) Smog
(ii) Pollutant
(iii) CFC
(iv) Eutrophication

Ans. (i) Smog: Smog is caused due to chemical interaction between the atmospheric components and primary pollutant like, suspended particulate matter (SPM), dust, smoke, ash, sulpher dioxide radio active components, etc.
(ii) Pollutants: Any substance, gas or tiny particles that make the environment dirty or contaminated is called pollutant.
(iii) CFC: CFC is the short form of chlorofluorocarbon, typically used gas in refrigerators, air conditioner, aerosol, and propellants. This gas is harmful to the ozone layer.
(iv) Eutrophication: The process by which a body of water becomes enriched in dissolved nutrients, that stimulate the growth of algae or other aquatic plants resulting in the depletion of dissolved oxygen.

Q. 5. How do water bodies get contaminated by the effluents from the industries?

Ans. Most of the industries release chemicals like chlorides, sulphides, carbonates, nitrates, and metals like zinc, mercury, copper, cromium, etc. in the rivers or the water sources, causing water contamination. Lead, mercury and manganese are most harmful for human, plants and animals.

Q. 6. How does urbanization caused air pollution.

Ans. Urbanization leads to industrialization. All industries release harmful gases like ammonia hydrocarbons, sulphur oxides, carbon dioxide, dust, smoke, etc. These are the harmful gases that causes air pollution.

Q. 7. Name any three human activities which cause pollution of air.

Ans. Three activities are:
(i) Deforestation
(ii) Use of motor vehicles: Exhaust from the vehicles causing air pollution.
(iii) Oil refineries discharge harmful gases like ammonia, hydrocarbon and sulphur oxide. Aluminum plants release fluoride, dust, etc. Cement industries emit plenty of dust which are very harmful.

Q. 8. How is ozone layer depleted?

Ans. Chloroflurocarbon, a synthetic chemical compound, used in refrigerators, air conditioners, fire extinguishing fluids. The release of CFC molecules into the stratosphere where intense ultraviolet rays split them. Its reaction with ozone causes depletion of ozone.

Q. 9. What is meant by global warming?

Ans. When the temperature of the Earth increases due to increase of carbon dioxide as a result of burning of fossil fuels and depletion of vegetation cover from the Earths surface. Global warming may cause havoc on Earth due to climatic changes.

Q. 10. How does soil pollution affect human life?

Ans. Chemical fertilisers do damage when they are washed into waterways, lakes and underground aquifers, and kill aquatic life. Chemical fertilizers destroy the soil's natural balance, leaving it lacking in nutrients. Soil pollution can also cause neuromuscular blockage as well as depression of the central nervous system, headaches, nausea, fatigue, eye irritation and skin rash.

Q. 11. How does oil spill affect sea birds and marine life?

Ans. The oil spread on the sea water acts as an insulating layer between air and water, causing deficiency in dissolved oxygen in water, killing varieties of sea animal. The sea birds that catch fish by dipping into the sea water are unable to fly due to the oiling of their wings.

Q. 12. What causes central and peripheral nervous disorder?

Ans. Lead poisoning causes central and peripheral nervous disorder. This chemical pollutant is found in drinking water. The pollutant is derived from industrial and agricultural waste.

Q. 13. What is the reason for fluorosis?

Ans. Industrial effluents and surface run off from the farm land contaminate the surface and ground water with many heavy metals like fluoride which cause flourosis.

Q. 14. What are the long term effects of the accidents?

Ans. (i) The blood of the victims in the tragedy had permanently got toxified leading to the damage of brain, kidney, lungs, muscles and gastro-intestinal system, etc.

(ii) MIC (methyl isocyanate) caused chromosomal aberration.

Q. 15. State any two methods of controlling air pollution.

Ans. The two methods of controlling air pollution are:

(i) Use of devices for the removal of dust and smoke, such as cyclone separator, setting chamber, fabric filter, wet scrubber, Electrostatic precipitator.

(ii) Control of gaseous pollutants by using catalytic converters in car engines, restrict use of low grade coal and oil, ensure complete burning of fuel, avoid open fins and use smokeless fuels.

Q. 16. State any three ways of treating polluted water.

Ans. (i) Treatment of marine water pollutants by collecting the oil off the water surface by using surface pumps, using chemicals to disperse or sink the oil.

(ii) Bioremediation is a natural process by which bacteria and other micro organisms alter and break down the complex organic compounds into substance like carbon dioxide.

(iii) Industrial effluents and domestic sewage must not be discharged into water bodies. The factory effluents and domestic sewage must be treated in the treatment plants.

Q. 17. (i) How are industries responsible for creating water pollution? **[November, 2019]**

(ii) What is Eutrophication?

Ans. (i) 1. Industries releases untreated discharge in water bodies.

2. Industry causes water pollution by contributing in acidifying rain.

(ii) Eutrophication means excessive collection of nutrients in water bodies like lakes, which causes dense growth of plant life and spoils the complete aquatic ecosystem.

Q. 18. (i) Why is 'No smoking zone' essential in public places? **[November, 2019]**

(ii) How is excessive use of fossil fuel harmful?

(iii) What is the impact of sound pollution on human beings?

Ans. (i) No smoking zone is essential in public places because smoking harms more to passive smokers than active smokers and ultimately it will increases the number of lung patients.

(ii) Fossil fuels take thousands of years to form, which means once they are used they will never be regained. Moreover, fossil fuels cause pollution to environment like burning of coal. So, excessive use of fossil fuel is harmful.

(iii) Noise or sound pollution cause loss of hearing. Regular exposure to high sounds may cause hypertension, stress or various disorders.

Q. 19. (i) What are the sources of radioactive pollution? **[February, 2020]**

(ii) How does radioactive pollution harm the environment?

Ans. (i) The sources of radioactive pollution are—nuclear waste, nuclear accidents, nuclear tests or radioactive ore processing.

(ii) Nuclear or radioactive wastes are hazardous for environment because it stays in the soil for long period and keep emitting dangerous rays. Nuclear waste is also hazardous for flora and fauna.

Q. 20. (i) Mention any two processes utilise by organic farming. **[February, 2020]**

(ii) Give two points why organic farming is important.

Ans. (i) The two process utilise by organic farming are use of biological materials and avoiding synthetic substances to maintain soil fertility.

(ii) 1. Organic farming is good for the health of soil.

2. Organic farming is sustainable farming; it is helpful for our future generations to feed on this soil.

Chapter 16. Natural Regions of the World

Q. 1. Why are these forests mostly impenetrable?

Ans. The forest is so dense that the leaves of tall trees do not allow the sun light to reach the ground. Wet ground with dense under growth hinders the construction of roads. So the forests one impenetrable.

Q. 2. Where do the tropical grassland occur? Which are the main areas of tropical grasslands?

Ans. Tropical grasslands occurs between the equatorial region and the tropical desert. The belt boarders has dry climate in the west and the wet monsoon climates in the east.

The main areas are:

(i) In Africa: Sudan, Uganda, Angola, Rhodesia, Tanzania, Kenya, Togo, Ghana, Mali, Niger, Senegal, Guinea and Chad.

(ii) In South America: Brazilian highlands, Bolivia, Paraguay.

(iii) In Central America: Cuba, Jamaica.

(iv) In Australia: Queensland.

Q. 3. Which are the typical tree species?

Ans. The tropical wet and dry climate is called savanna after its vegetation. i.e. grassland especially elephant grass that grow upto five metres. Deciduous trees are found near the equator, Trees diminish towards the deserts acacias, palm, baobad are most commonly found.

Q. 4. What are the adaptive features of the trees?

Ans. The trees shed their leaves in cool dry season. The trees are adapted to strong winds and drought so they have flattened crowns and deep roots. Baobad trees can store a lot of water to survive the drought condition. It has few leaves to prevent the loss of water through transpiration.

Q. 5. Give the location of the tropical monsoon land?

Ans. Tropical monsoon land spreads over the Indian sub-continent, northeastern Australia. northeastern part of South America. It is confined to a belt of 10° N to 30° N and along the eastern margins of the continent of the same belt in the Southern Hemisphere.

Q. 6. What kind of vegetation do we find here?

Ans. Tropical deciduous trees are the mainly found in the region. Inportant trees are sal, shishma, mango, neem, sandalwood and teak. In the drier parts, thorny bushes are found.

Q. 7. State in brief a few important features of the tropical monsoon climate?

Ans. (i) Seasonal reversal of winds is the chief features.

(ii) Temperature ranges from 15° C in the cool season to 32° C in the hot season.

(iii) Once the monsoon sets in during summer, it rains for four months from June to September with alternate dry and wet season in the Northern Hemisphere.

(iv) Mostly rainfall is of orographic in nature.

Q. 8. Point out the location of the hot desert region of the world naming the area and the continents.

Ans. Most of the world's hot deserts lies between 15° N and 35° N and 15° S to 35° S latitude.

(i) Sahara desert – North Africa.

(ii) Great Australian desert – West Australia

(iii) Arabian desert
(iv) Iranian desert
(v) Thar desert
} Asia

(vi) Kalahari desert
(vii) Namib desert
} Africa

(viii) Mexican desert North America

(ix) Atacama desert South America

Q. 9. Which areas outside the mediterranean belt experience mediterranean type of climate?

Ans. It is found between 30° and 40° north and south latitudes on the western side of the continents. Areas out side the mediterranean sea are Central California, South West Africa, Central Chile and South west and southern Australia (Adelaide to Melbourne).

Q. 10. What are the climatic features of Mediterranean region?

Ans. The region comes under sub-tropical high pressure belt during the summer season. So high temperature, clear sky and no rain are the main characteristics of the region. During winter the region comes under the influence of westerlies which causes moderate rainfall.

Q. 11. What are the main charactreristics of mediterranean vegetation?

Ans. In order to withstand the long summer drought, the vegetation of the Mediterranean region is drought resistant, evergreen type. The plants have long root systems to tap water from great depths or they store water in roots. Trees have thick woody stem and rough barks waxy thick, small leaves to stop transpiration.

Q. 12. Where is the China type region located?

Ans. The China type region is located in the eastern margins of the continents in the warm temperate or mid-latitudes from 25° to 40° North and South latitude in both Hemispheres.

Q. 13. Describe the natural vegetation of the region. How does it is different from tropical vegetation?

Ans. Deciduous hard wood trees are the most common type of vegetation. Due to severe winter condition plants shed their leaves. Important species are oak, beech, hazel, elm in East U.S.A. Bamboos, ferms, cedar, spruce, maple are common in China. In South America quebracho and yerba mate are important trees. Magnolia, comphor, and camellia are found in Japan.

The vegetation is different from the tropical monsoon forest because the species are relatively few. Predominance of one or two species is common.

Q. 14. Why are the daily and annual ranges of temperature is great here?

Ans. Clear sky favours rapid heating of the land during the day. At night this heat is radiated and given off readily. So the daily range of temperature is high.

Being situated in the interior middle latitude the regions do not get the advantage of marine influences specially in the Northen Hemisphere, the summers are very hot and the winters are very cold.

Q. 15. Name the chief taiga areas of the world?

Ans. Coniferous forest or taiga area of the world are in North Siberia, Sakhalian islands in Asia. Tasmania is Australia and New Zealand, mountainous part of Southern Alaska in North America, parts of Norway, Sweden, Finland, Northern parts of Russia in Europe.

Q. 16. Give an account of the winter conditions in the taiga region.

Ans. Long cold winters last from October to April and temperature can fall to – 30 °C. During winter the precipitation is received in the form of snowfall. Cold polar anticyclones or Blizzards in Canada and Northern Europe and Asia blow away vast masses of powdery snow and spread over large areas.

Q. 17. (i) Mention two characteristic features of the natural vegetation found in the Kalahari Desert.

(i) Name the primitive people of the Kalahari Desert. **[November, 2019]**

Ans. (i) 1. The vegetation is desert vegetation or xerophytes plants are found.

2. Mainly the vegetation consist of grasses shrubs. The exclusive trees which are found here are camelthorn.

(ii) The most common among the primitives of Kalahari desert are San tribe, Herero and Kgalgadi tribes.

Q. 18. (i) Which Natural region is called 'The Granary of the world'? Why is it called so? **[November, 2019]**

(i) Why agriculture is not a main occupation in the Tundra region?

Ans. (i) Prairies are called as granary of the world because this region produces largest amount of wheat and have all the suitable conditions required growing wheat.

(ii) Agriculture is not a main occupation in Tundra region because Tundra region experiences extremely cold climate and most of the time remain covered with snow. Thus, these geographical conditions make this part of the world adverse for agriculture activities.

Q. 19. In which of the natural regions of the world would the following be found: **[February, 2020]**

(i) Pine trees (ii) Tall grass

(iii) Olive trees

Ans. (i) Pine trees- Taiga region

(ii) Tall grass- Tropical grasslands

(iii) Olive trees- Mediterranean region

Q. 20. (i) What is the impact of the natural vegetation of the Taiga region on the occupation of the people living in that region? **[February, 2020]**

(ii) Give a reason as to why the Savanna grasslands are found in Africa.

(iii) What type of climate is found in the Tundra region?

Ans. (i) The Taiga trees have softwood and are commercially used for making paper, matchsticks, plywood, furniture and sports good. Farming is not well practiced as the growing period is very short.

(ii) Savannah grasslands are found in Africa because savannah grasslands need hot and dry tropical land between 5° and 20° north and south. Savannah grasslands grows well in the interior of the continent. Thus, Africa is ideal location for Savannah grasslands to grow.

(iii) Climatic condition in Tundra region:

1. There is less and no insolation. Thus, the average annual temperature is – 12° C.

2. The winters are long and bitter. The summers are short for a period of 2 – 3 months only.

❐

Difference Between Questions | Set 3 |

Chapter 1. Earth As a Planet

Q. 1. Stars and Planets.

Ans.

Stars	Planets
(i) The celestial bodies which produce their own light as a result of reaction at the cores are known as stars.	(i) On the other hand, planets don't have lights of their own. They only reflect energy.
(ii) The stars provide a twinkling effect which is seen from the earth.	(ii) The planets do not twinkle.
(iii) The stars are very large in size.	(iii) The planets are smaller in size.

Q. 2. Inner planets and Outer planets.

Ans.

Inner planets	Outer planets
(i) The planets closer to the Sun in the solar system are called inner planets.	(i) The planets farther from the Sun in the solar systems are called outer planets.
(ii) The inner planets are Mercury, Venus, Earth and Mars.	(ii) The outer planets are Jupiter, Saturn, Uranus and Neptune.
(iii) The inner planets are usually made up of rocks. Rocky planets are also called as terrestrial planets.	(iii) These planets are usually gas balls and are called as Jovian planets.

Q. 3. Asteroids and Meteorites.

Ans.

Asteroids	Meteorite
(i) The large rocky bodies which rotate around the sun are called Asteroids.	(i) The planets farther from the Sun in the solar systems are called outer planets.
(ii) The inner planets are Mercury, Venus, Earth and Mars.	(ii) The outer planets are Jupiter, Saturn, Uranus and Neptune.
(iii) The inner planets are usually made up of rocks and we also call them as terrestrial planets.	(iii) These planets are usually gas balls and are called as Jovian planets.

Chapter 2. Latitudes and Longitudes

Q. 1. Latitude and Longitude.

Ans.

Latitude	Longitude
(i) It is the angular distance of a place in the north or south from the centre of the Earth.	(i) It is the angular distance of a place in the east or west from the centre of the Earth.
(ii) The latitudes are drawn with respect to equator.	(ii) The longitudes are drawn with respect to Prime Meridian.
(iii) The total number of latitudes is 180.	(iii) The total number of longitude is 360.

Q. 2. Equator and Prime Meridian.

Ans.

Equator	Prime Meridian
(i) It is the angular distance of a place in the north or south from the centre of the Earth.	(i) It is the angular distance of a place in the east or west from the centre of the Earth.
(ii) It divides the Earth into Northern and Southern Hemisphere.	(ii) It divides the Earth into Eastern and Western hemisphere.
(iii) It is used to categorise the Earth into three heat zones in north and south direction.	(iii) It is used to categorise the Earth into Time Zone in east and west direction.

Q. 3. Torrid zone and Temperate zone.

Ans.

Torrid Zone	Temperate zone
(i) The zone extends between 23.5° North to 23.5° South.	(i) The zone extends from 23.5° North to 66.5° North in both Northern and Southern Hemisphere.
(ii) This zone receives maximum heat from the Sun and experiences the hottest climate.	(ii) This zone experiences a moderate temperature as it receives comparatively lesser heat due to the slanting position of the Sun.
(iii) At least once in a year the Sun is over head.	(iii) The sun never shines overhead in any latitude.

Q. 4. Temperate Zone and Frigid Zone

Ans.

Temperate zone	Frigid zone
(i) The zone extends from 23.5° North to 66.5° North in both Northern and Southern Hemisphere.	(i) The zone extends from 66.5° North to 90° North in both Northern and Southern Hemisphere.
(ii) The zone generally experiences four kind of seasons: summer, autumn, winter and spring.	(ii) The zone usually experiences long spell of cold seasons. Even the summer is cold here.
(iii) This zone is dominated by vegetation types such as temperate grassland, tropical grassland, temperate desert, evergreen tropical rainforest.	(iii) Practically, there is no sign of vegetation in this zone.

Q. 5. Great Circle and Small Circle.

Ans.

Great Circle	Smaller Circle
(i) Great Circle is the circle drawn around the surface of the Earth with a centre that coincides with the centre.	(i) Small Circle is the circle drawn around the surface of the Earth but its centre does not coincide with the centre of the Earth.
(ii) The Equator and all the longitudes are Great Circles.	(ii) Except the Equator all the latitudes are Small Circles.
(iii) All the Great Circles have the same circumference.	(iii) The circumference of the Small Circles decreases from Equator towards pole.

Q. 6. Greenwich Mean Time (GMT) and Indian Standard Time (IST).

Ans.

GMT	IST
(i) GMT or Greenwich Mean Time is measured at the 0° longitude.	(i) IST or Indian Standard Time is measured at 82.5° E longitude.
(ii) The longitude passes through Greenwich in London.	(ii) The longitude passes through Mirzapur near Allahabad.

Q. 7. Local Time and Standard Time.

Ans.

Local Time		Standard Time	
(i)	Local time refers to the time of particular place based on the apparent movement of the Sun.	(i)	Standard Time refers to the official time of any country based of the standard meridian passing through it.
(ii)	The local time is determined by the shadow of the Sun.	(ii)	The standard Time is determined by the time zone in which the country falls.
(iii)	Places on the same longitude have same local time.	(iii)	Places of the same longitude may not have the same standard time.

Chapter 3. Rotation and Revolution

Q. 1. Summer Solstice and Winter Solstice.

Ans.

Summer Solstice		Winter Solstice	
(i)	It occurs on 21st June of every year.	(i)	It occurs on the 22nd December of every year.
(ii)	On this date the day is longest and the night is shortest in the Northern Hemisphere.	(ii)	On this date the day is shortest and the night is longest in the Northern Hemisphere.

Q. 2. Rotation and Revolution.

Ans.

Rotation		Revolution	
(i)	Rotation is the spinning of the Earth on its own axis.	(i)	Revolution is the movement of the Earth around the Sun in an elliptical path.
(ii)	It takes nearly 24 hours to complete one rotation.	(ii)	It takes nearly 365 days and five hours to complete one revolution.
(iii)	The rotation of the Earth results in the occurrence of day and night.	(iii)	The revolution of the Earth around the Sun results in the change of the season.

Chapter 4. Structure of the Earth and Internal Processes

Q. 1. Sial and Sima. **[November, 2019]**

Ans.

Sial		Sima	
(i)	The upper part of the crust called Sial.	(i)	The lower part of the crust is called Sima.
(ii)	The rocks of Sial mainly contain silicon and aluminum.	(ii)	The rocks of Sima mainly contain silicon and magnesium.
(iii)	The Sial makes the most of the continental crust.	(iii)	The Sima mostly makes the oceanic crust.
(iv)	The density is low due to the presence of lighter metal like aluminum.	(iv)	The density is high due to the presence of heavier metal like magnesium.

Q. 2. Crust and Mantle.

Ans.

Crust		Mantle	
(i)	The upper layer of the Earth is called the Crust or lithosphere.	(i)	The middle layer of the Earth is called Mantle.
(ii)	Only 0.5% of the Earth's volume is made up of the Crust.	(ii)	Around 84% of the Earth's volume is made up of Mantle.
(iii)	The Crust is spread up to a depth of 30 km in case of continent and 25 – 30 km in case of ocean.	(iii)	The Mantle is about 2900 km deep inside the Earth.

Q. 3. Mantle and Core.

Ans.

Mantle	Core
(i) The middle layer of the Earth is called Mantle.	(i) The innermost layer of the Earth is called core.
(ii) The thickness is around 2900 km.	(ii) The average thickness is about 4671 km.
(iii) The average density is around 3 – 5.5 gm/cm^3.	(iii) The average density is around 5.5 – 15 gm/cm^3.

Q. 4. Asthenosphere and Mesosphere.

Ans.

Athenosphere	Mesosphere
(i) The upper part of the Mantle is known as Athenosphere.	(i) The lower part of the Mantle is known as Mesosphere.
(ii) It is made up of molten ultrabasic rocks.	(ii) It is made up of solid ultrabasic rocks.
(iii) It extends up to a depth of 660 km.	(iii) It extends from 660-2900 km.

Chapter 5. Landforms of the Earth

Q. 1. Young fold mountain and Old fold mountain.

Ans.

Young Fold Mountain	Old Fold Mountain
(i) Young Fold Mountains were formed around 10-25 million years ago.	(i) Old Fold Mountains were formed nearly 240 million years ago.
(ii) They have steep slopes, deep valley and high mountain peak covered with snow.	(ii) As these mountains were subjected to erosion, they have gentle slopes, rounded tops and sculptured domes.
(iii) Examples of young fold mountains are Himalayan Mountains in Asia, the Alps in Europe, the Andes in South America, and the Rockies in North America.	(iii) Examples of old fold mountains are the Urals in Russia, Pennies and Welsh Highland of Britain, Harz Mountain in Germany and the Appalachians in North America and Aravallis in India.

Q. 2. Structural plains and Depositional plains.

Ans.

Structural Plains	Depositional Plains
(i) These plains are formed due to the upliftment and subsidence of continental shelves.	(i) These plains are formed by the deposition of material brought down by various agents of transportation.
(ii) These are structurally the most depressed areas of the world.	(ii) These plains are the destructional plains.

Q. 3. Intermontane Plateau and Piedmont Plateau.

Ans.

Intermontane Plateau	Piedmont Plateau
(i) When a plateau is covered by mountains from all side, it is called an intermontane plateau.	(i) When a plateau is formed between a mountain range and a coastal plain is called a piedmont plateau.
(ii) The Tibetan plateau in South-central Asia is the example of the intermontane plateau.	(ii) The plateau formed at the foothills of the Appalachian mountain and Eastern Atlantic Coast of North America is an example of the piedmont plateau.

Q. 4. Dissected Plateaus and Volcanic Plateau.

Ans.

Dissected Plateau	Volcanic Plateau
(i) These plateaus are formed due to the erosion of highlands by various agents of erosion such as rivers and wind.	(i) These plateaus are formed from the successive deposition of the solidified sheet of lava after volcanic activity.

(ii)	These are also called domed or uplifted plateau.	(ii)	These are also called plateaus of accumulation.
(iii)	The Colorado plateau are the example of a dissected plateau.	(iii)	The Deccan Trap of Maharashtra in India is the example of the volcanic plateau.

Q. 5. Continental Plateau and Fault-block Plateau.

Ans.

Continental Plateau		Fault-block Plateau	
(i)	These plateaus are formed either by extensive continental uplift from the low land or sea or deposition and solidification of sheets of lava over an extensive area.	(i)	These plateaus are formed from the horizontal movement of between blocks along with a strike-slip- fault.
(ii)	Examples of continental plateaus are plateaus in the parts of Africa, Arabia and Greenland, etc.	(ii)	Central Plateau of France is an example of Fault- block plateau.

Q. 6. Erosional Plains and Depositional Plains.

Ans.

Erosional Plains		Depositional Plains	
(i)	The plains are formed due to the denudation of elevated landforms like hills and mountains by various agents such as river, winds and glaciers, etc.	(i)	The plains are formed by the deposition of material brought down by various agents of transportation such as river, winds, waves and glaciers.
(ii)	These are also known as destructional plains.	(ii)	These are also known as constructional plains.
(iii)	The erosional plains can be categorized into various types such as peneplain, pediplain, karst plain and glacial plain.	(iii)	The depositional plains can be categorized into various types such as alluvial plains, lava plains, lacustrine plains and drift plains.

Q. 7. Fold Mountains and Block Mountains.

Ans.

Fold Mountains		Block Mountains	
(i)	Fold Mountains are formed due to the folding of the upper part of the earth's crust.	(i)	Block Mountains are formed due to the development of a crack in the earth's crust.
(ii)	These mountains are huge in terms of length and height.	(ii)	These mountains are huge in terms of width.
(iii)	These mountains have resulted from the convergence of crustal plates.	(iii)	These mountains have resulted from the divergence of crustal plates.

Q. 8. Lacustrine Plains and Loess Plains.

Ans.

Lacustrine Plains		Loess Plains	
(i)	When the lake bed is filled with silt brought by the rivers, the silts eventually settles down to form lacustrine plain.	(i)	When the silts are transported by the wind and deposited to form plains, they are called loess plain.
(ii)	The Kashmir valley of India is an example of lacustrine plains	(ii)	The plains of northwestern China and the plains of Rajasthan in India are the examples of Loess plain.

Chapter 6. Rocks

Q. 1. Rocks and Minerals.

Ans.

Rocks		Minerals	
(i)	Rocks are the combination of more than one naturally occurring minerals.	(i)	Minerals are the inorganic solid formation on the earth.

(ii)	Rocks do not have unique chemical compositions or crystalline structures.	(ii)	Minerals have their unique chemical composition and also a crystalline structure.
(iii)	They are classified into three types igneous, sedimentary and metamorphic.	(iii)	They are classified into silicates, sulphides, carbonates and metallic minerals.

Q. 2. Igneous Rocks and Sedimentary Rocks.

Ans.

	Igneous Rocks		Sedimentary Rocks
(i)	Igneous rocks are formed out of tectonic activities.	(i)	Sedimentary rocks are formed out of denudation executed by agents like river, wind and glaciers, etc.
(ii)	These rocks are formed from the cooling and solidification of molten magma.	(ii)	The rocks are formed from lithification.
(iii)	The rocks are non-porous for water.	(iii)	These rocks are porous for water.
(iv)	These rocks are harder.	(iv)	These rocks are softer.
(v)	These rocks don't have any sign of fossil.	(v)	These rocks are rich in fossils.

Q. 3. Extrusive Igneous Rocks and Intrusive igneous rocks.

Ans.

	Extrusive Igneous Rocks		Intrusive igneous rocks
(i)	The rocks which are formed when the magma cools down and solidifies on the earth surface.	(i)	The rocks are formed when magma cools down and solidifies below the surface of the earth.
(ii)	These rocks solidify at a faster rate as they are exposed to the outside atmosphere and therefore they are smooth, crystalline and finely grained.	(ii)	These rocks have course structure with large crystals, because they get enough time to get solidified within the surface of the earth.
(iii)	Basalts and dolomites are the examples of extrusive rocks.	(iii)	Lapolith and baccoliths are the example of intrusive rocks.

Q. 4. Plutonic Rocks and Hypabyssal Rocks.

Ans.

	Plutonic Rocks		Hypabyssal Rocks
(i)	Plutonic rocks are the coarse grained intrusive rocks.	(i)	Hypabyssal rocks are medium grained intrusive rocks.
(ii)	These rocks are formed deep within the earth, where the cooling and solidification process is very slow.	(ii)	These rocks are formed in the cracks just beneath the earth, where the cooling and solidification is slow.

Q. 5. Dynamic Metamorphism and Thermal Metamorphism.

Ans.

	Dynamic Metamorphism		Thermal Metamorphism
(i)	This metamorphism process involves a high temperature in which the rocks transforms into a new type of rocks.	(i)	This process of metamorphism involves tremendous pressure to transform one type of rock into another .
(ii)	For example, sandstone changes into quartzite, shale changes to slate and coal changes to graphite.	(ii)	For example, transformation of clay into schist and granite into gneiss.

Q. 6. Contact Metamorphism and Regional Metamorphism.

Ans.

	Contact Metamorphism		Regional Metamorphism
(i)	In this process existing igneous rocks come under the influence of newly released lava, the process of metamorphism starts which involves tremendous heat over a smaller areal extent.	(i)	This process of metamorphism involves a large area due to the movement of earth.

(ii)	This is a high grade metamorphism.	(ii)	This is a low grade metamorphism.

Q. 7. Detrital Sediments and Chemical Sediments.

Ans.

Detrital Sediments		Chemical Sediments	
(i)	The detrital sediments are the fragmented segments of pre-existing rocks.	(i)	These are the minerals crystals of solutions formed due to the evaporation or precipitation of water.

Q. 8. Acid Igneous Rocks and Basic Igneous Rocks.

Ans.

Acid Igneous Rocks		Basic Igneous Rocks	
(i)	These rocks have high percentage of silica and lesser percentage of basic oxides.	(i)	These rocks have lesser percentage of silica and higher percentage of basic oxides, like iron and magnesium. For example, Gabbros.
(ii)	They are coarse textured, light coloured rocks.	(ii)	They are fine-textured and smooth rocks.
(iii)	Quartz, feldspar and mica are the example of acid igneous rocks.	(iii)	Basalt is the example of basic igneous rocks.

Chapter 7. Volcanoes

Q. 1. Active Volcano and Dormant Volcano.

Ans.

Active Volcano		Dormant Volcano	
(i)	The volcanoes which still erupt lava, gases, ashes, cinder, pumice, etc. at frequent intervals or have erupted in the recent past. Mount Etna in Italy is an example of an active volcano.	(i)	These are the volcanoes that were active in the past 2000 years, but now their status is sleeping or inactive. Barren Island near the Andaman sea is an example of dormant volcanoes.

Q. 2. Acid Lava and Basic Lava.

Ans.

Acid Lava		Basic Lava	
(i)	They are rich in silica but poor in iron and magnesium.	(i)	They are rich in iron and magnesium but poor in silica.
(ii)	The viscosity of the lava is very high due to the abundance of silica in it, and thus, they flow for a short distance.	(ii)	This type of lava does not have viscosity due to the absence of silica and flows for a long distance.
(iii)	This type of lava flow results in the formation of steep-sided cones.	(iii)	This type of lava flow produces a flat shield, and eruption takes place silently.

Q. 3. Extrusive landforms and Intrusive landforms.

Ans.

Extrusive landforms		Intrusive landforms	
(i)	The landforms are created when the lava flows out of the volcanic vent and gets cooled and solidified.	(i)	The landforms are created when only a little amount of lava flows out to the surface, and the remaining large part cools down inside the earth's crust.
(ii)	The process of cooling is swift.	(ii)	The process of cooling is prolonged.
(iii)	The pyroclastic materials are thrown outside the earth and deposited around the vent.	(iii)	The magma get stuck inside the horizontal and vertical fractures and cracks inside the earth and form various landforms.

(iv)	The major extrusive landforms are cinder cones, lava shield, calderas.	(iv)	The major intrusive landforms are sills, dykes, batholiths, laccoliths, lapoliths,etc.

Q. 4. Sills and Dykes.

Ans.

	Sills		Dykes
(i)	It is the molten magma, which solidifies horizontally between the layers of sedimentary rocks.	(i)	These are formed when the lava makes its way out through cracks and fissures.
(ii)	They found along the line of bedding planes of the sedimentary rocks.	(ii)	They pierce through the bedding planes.

Q. 5. Crater and Caldera.

Ans.

	Crater		Caldera
(i)	The craters are the depression that are created in the process of a volcanic eruption.	(i)	These are the large depressions created when the summit of the volcano blows up with a great explosion.
(ii)	The size of the crater is less than 1 kilometer.	(ii)	The size of the caldera is greater than 1 kilometer.

Q. 6. Volcanic Cone and Volcanic Plateau.

Ans.

	Volcanic Cone		Volcanic Plateau
(i)	Volcanic cones are the triangle-shaped landforms formed due to the deposition of volcanic materials around the vent.	(i)	The volcanic plateaus are the result of shield erosion, where the volcanic lava spreads and forms sheet-like structure. These sheets are deposited one over the other to form plateaus.

Q. 7. Cinder Cone and Composite Cones.

Ans.

	Cinder Cone		Composite Cones
(i)	The cinder cones are created when pyroclastic materials like clinkers and ashes are thrown out to the air and deposited around the vent as a cone.	(i)	The composite cones are the aggregation of cinder cones or parasite cones, which are made up of alternating layers of lava and ash.

Q. 8. Active and Extinct Volcanoes. **[November, 2019]**

Ans. Active volcanoes are those volcanoes which errupts after a particular period of times. For e.g., Mt. Etna. On the other hand extinct volcanoes are those which were active long time back but not erupted from past many years and there is no any possibility of eruption in near future too. For e.g., Mt. Kulal in Kenya.

Chapter 8. Earthquakes

Q. 1. Richter Scale and Mercalli Scale.

Ans.

	Richter Scale		Mercalli Scale
(i)	It was invented by American Seimologist Charles Francis Richter.	(i)	It was invented by Italian Seismologist Guiseppe Mercalli.
(ii)	Richter scale measures the magnitude of the earthquake. It has a range of 0-10.	(ii)	It measures the intensity of the earthquake. It has a range 1-12.

Q. 2. Primary Waves and Secondary Waves.

Ans.

Primary Waves	Secondary Wave
(i) These waves are the fastest and usually reach first at the recording stations.	(i) S-waves travel at a slower pace than p-waves and it is re-recorded after p-waves.
(ii) P-waves can travel through solid, liquids and gases.	(ii) S-waves can only travel through solids.
(iii) These waves shake the medium in the direction in which they are propagating.	(iii) These waves shake the medium in the direction perpendicular to which they are moving.
(iv) P-waves are compression waves.	(iv) S-waves are shear waves.

Q. 3. Circum-pacific belt and Mid Atlantic belt.

Ans.

Circum-Pacific Belt	Mid Atlantic Belt
(i) This belt is also called as Pacific ring of fire. The abundance of volcanic eruptions and tectonic plate movement make this belt most vulnerable for earthquakes in the world.	(i) The mid Atlantic belt is a mid ocean ridge of divergent and constructive boundary. This belt records moderate earthquakes which are caused due to sea floor spreading and fissures.

Q. 4. Convergent Plate Boundary and Divergent Plate Boundary.

Ans.

Convergent Plate Boundary	Divergent Plate Boundary
(i) In This boundary, two plates move towards each other.	(i) In this boundary, two plates move away from each other.
(ii) This result in mountains and subduction zone.	(ii) This results in Plate margin ridges and ocean floor spreading.
(iii) For Example: Ocean trenches and Chain of volcanoes. The Andes mountain chain and Off-shore ocean trench.	(iii) For Example: The mid-Atlantic ridge.

Chapter 9. Weathering

Q. 1. Physical Weathering and Chemical Weathering.

Ans.

Physical Weathering	Chemical Weathering
(i) Physical weathering means breaking down of rocks by physical factors. It is also called as mechanical weathering.	(i) Chemical weathering means change in the chemical composition of rock through oxidation and carbonation.

Q. 2. Biological Weathering and Chemical Weathering.

Ans.

Biological Weathering	Chemical Weathering
(i) The disintegration and decomposition of rocks, that happens because of biotic factor like plants, animals and human beings is called as Biological weathering.	(i) Oxygen, water and acids react with chemical properties of rocks and cause weathering viz; solution, carbonation, hydration, oxidation and reduction.

Q. 3. Oxidation and Carbonation. **[November, 2019]**

Ans.

Oxidation	Carbonation
(i) It is a reaction in which iron in rocks react with oxygen and form iron oxide.	(i) It is a mixing of oxygen with carbon and form carbonic acid. This helps in the formation of caves.

Q. 4. Young stage and Mature stage of a river. **[November, 2019]**

Ans.

Young Stage of a River	Mature Stage of a River
(i) This is the initial stage of river course, where river does erosion and forms landforms like valley, canyons and gorges, etc.	(i) This is second stage after young stage, where the river forms depositional landforms like meanders, wide floodplains, etc.
(ii) During this course river is turbulent and it forms many erosion landforms.	(ii) During mature stage river flows through a gentle slope and deposits even the minute sediments.

Q. 5. Block Disintegration and Granular Disintegration. **[November, 2019]**

Ans.

Block Disintegration	Granular Disintegration
(i) This disintegration happens in the well-joined rocks, due to rise and fall in temperature. This leads to disintegration along the joints of the rock into large rectangular blocks.	(i) This disintegration occurs in rocks, which are composed of various minerals. Due to temperature change different minerals (like granite, mica, quartz or feldspar) reacts differently, leading to disintegration of rocks into small pieces.

Q. 6. Delta and Estuary.

Ans.

Delta	Estuary
(i) Delta is a triangular depositional landform at the mouth of a river.	(i) It is a sharp and edged mouth of a river, without any deposition.
(ii) Deltas are fertile.	(ii) Estuary is not as fertile as delta.

Q. 7. Valley and Delta.

Ans.

Valley	Delta
(i) A valley is a erosion land feature of a river associated with its young stage. When a river descends from mountains forms narrow rills called valleys.	(i) Delta is a depositional landform of a river associated with its old stage. River deposits its load before it submerges into sea. As the deposition grows, river distribution continues and form a triangular land feature called delta.

Q. 8. Solution and Hydration.

Ans.

Solution	Hydration
(i) The rainwater charges with atmospheric gases, is able to dissolve some rocks and minerals from the surface of the earth. This process is called as solution.	(i) The chemical union of water with the minerals is called as hydration.

Chapter 10. Hydrosphere

Q. 1. Warm and Cold Ocean Currents.

Ans.

Warm Ocean Current	Cold Ocean Current
(i) Warm ocean currents originates near equator and flow towards poles.	(i) Cold currents originates at high latitudes and flow toward equator.
(ii) Warm ocean current have less salinity.	(ii) Cold ocean currents have comparatively higher salinity.
(iii) Examples are Gulf Stream Current and Kuroshio Current.	(iii) Examples are Labrador Current and Oyashio current.

Q. 2. Neap Tide and Spring Tide.

Ans.

Spring Tide		Neap Tide	
(i)	Spring tide is formed when the sun moon and the earth are in the straight line.	(i)	Neap tide occur when the moon is at first quarter or at last quarter of its rotation.
(ii)	During the spring tide the difference between high and low tide is maximum.	(ii)	During neap tide the difference is least.
(iii)	Spring tide occurs when the gravity of sun and moon pulls in a same direction.	(iii)	This phenomenon occurs when the moon is at right angle to the sun.

Q. 3. Differentiate between Tide and Ocean Current.

Ans.

Tides		Ocean Currents	
(i)	Tides are periodic rise and fall of ocean water.	(i)	Currents are continuous and directed movement.
(ii)	Tides are caused due to gravitational force of moon and sun.	(ii)	Currents are formed due to winds, variation in salinity and temperature.
(iii)	Tides are the movement of ocean water which is more of up and down.	(iii)	Current is a movement of mass of water in a fixed direction.

Q. 4. Gulf Stream and Labrador Current.

Ans.

Gulf Stream		Labrador Current	
(i)	Gulf stream is a warm ocean current	(i)	Labrador current is a cold water current.
(ii)	This current originates from Gulf of Mexico about 20 degrees north.	(ii)	Labrador current originates in the arctic ocean.
(iii)	The direction of movement of gulf stream is northward.	(iii)	The Labrador current moves southward.
(iv)	The average speed of gulf stream is 33 kms per day.	(iv)	The average speed of Labrador current is 25 kms per day
(v)	The warm water of gulf stream modifies the weather condition of western coast of Europe and eastern coast of North America.	(v)	Labrador current brings huge iceberg from the arctic ocean and forms huge dense fog at New Foundland after mixing with Gulf stream.

Q. 5. Kuroshio Current and Oyashio current.

Ans.

Kuroshio Current		Oyashio current	
(i)	Kuroshio is an important warm water current of pacific ocean.	(i)	It is a cold ocean current that originates in Bering strait.
(ii)	The impact of this current is that it keeps the eastern coast of Japan warm during the coldest months.	(ii)	The impact of this current is that it carries cold water and icebergs from the arctic ocean to the coasts of Russia and Japan.

Chapter 11. Atmosphere

Q. 1. Aurora Borealis and Aurora Australis.

Ans.

Aurora Borealis		Aurora Australis	
(i)	Aurora Borealis are the polar lights that occur near the magnetic poles of Northern Hemisphere.	(i)	Aurora Australis are the polar lights that occur near the magnetic pole of Southern Hemisphere.

Q. 2. Weather and Climate.

Ans.

Weather		Climate	
(i)	Weather is day to day report of atmospheric conditions of an area.	(i)	Climate is an average of weather of a particular place for very long period of time (generally 35-40 years).

(ii)	Weather never remain static, rather it changes very frequently.	(ii)	Because climate is an average for long duration. Thus, it remains static.
(iii)	The study of weather of a place is called as Meteorology.	(iii)	The study of climate is called as Climatology.

Q. 3. Tropopause and stratopause.

Ans.

Tropopause		Stratopause	
(i)	Tropopause is the transition zone between troposphere and stratosphere.	(i)	Stratopause is the transition zone between stratosphere and mesosphere.
(ii)	Tropopause starts at an average height of 13 kms.	(ii)	Stratopause starts at an average of 50 kms above the surface.
(iii)	The average temperature at tropopause is -80°at equator and -45° C at poles.	(iii)	The average temperature at stratopause is -15° C.

Q. 4. Troposphere and Exosphere.

Ans.

Troposphere		Exosphere	
(i)	It is the lowest layer of the atmosphere.	(i)	This is the topmost layer of the atmosphere.
(ii)	The upper limit of troposphere is called as tropopause. Here temperature stops dropping with increasing height and begins increasing with increasing height.	(ii)	This layer cut as a transitional zone between the atmosphere and the inter-planetary space.

Chapter 12. Insolation

Q. 1. Convection and advection heating.

Ans.

Convection		Advection	
(i)	Convection is the process of vertical heating of earth's atmosphere.	(i)	The transfer of heat through horizontal movement of air is called as advection process of heating.
(ii)	Convection happens only in troposphere zone of our atmosphere.	(ii)	Advection occurs on all the latitudes ranging from equator to poles.

Q. 2. How Solar Radiation is different from Terrestrial Radiation?

Ans.

Solar Radiation		Terrestrial Radiation	
(i)	As its name suggest it is the radiation that earth receives from the sun. This energy is the major source of heat and light.	(i)	Terrestrial radiation is the radiation that earth emits during night time to maintain its temperature stable.
(ii)	This radiation is in the form of short waves.	(ii)	Terrestrial radiation is a long wave radiation.

Q. 3. Conduction and Radiation.

Ans.

Conduction		Radiation	
(i)	When two bodies with unequal temperature come in contact with one another, the heat flows from cooler to hotter body is called conduction.	(i)	Radiation is the transfer of energy in the form of electromagnetic waves.
(ii)	The lower layer of atmosphere gets heat up generally by conduction process.	(ii)	The radiation by the sun is in short waves, is called as solar radiation. The radiation by the earth is in long waves, and is called as Terrestrial radiation.

Q. 4. Water Body and a Landmass.

Ans.

Water Body	Landmass
(i) Water bodies use solar radiation for evaporation process.	(i) Landmass is a solid substance which does not support evaporation.
(ii) The rays of sun penetrate the water body deeply.	(ii) The sun rays cannot penetrate deep into a land mass.
(iii) Ocean currents and waves keep the water mobile in a water body.	(iii) Landmass does not experience any movement.

Q. 5. Explain the difference between Energy surplus and Energy deficient.

Ans.

Energy surplus	Energy deficient
(i) The areas of the earth where the amount of insolation exceeds the amount of terrestrial radiation. This happens at the areas below 40° latitude.	(i) The areas where the amount of terrestrial radiation is higher than amount of insolation. This happens at the areas above 40° latitude. In this area more heat is lost than received.

Chapter 13. Pressure Belts and Winds

Q. 1. Permanent and Periodic Winds. **[November, 2019]**

Ans.

Permanent Winds	Periodic Winds
(i) As the name suggests these winds move in a fixed direction throughout a a year.	(i) These winds are limited to some seasons and period of the years and often change their direction.
(ii) For e.g. Trade winds	(ii) For e.g. Monsoon winds

Q. 2. Cyclones and Anticyclones. **[November, 2019]**

Ans.

Cyclones	Anticyclones
(i) Are the wind movements which involve a low pressure center and wind move in a anti-clock wise direction.	(i) Are the wind movement when high pressure is at the center and wind move outwards in a clock wise direction.

Q. 3. Land Breeze and Sea Breeze. **[November, 2019]**

Ans.

Land Breeze	Sea Breeze
(i) This breeze generally moves during the winter season, when the land experiences low temperature and high pressure. These winds are generally dry.	(i) This breeze generally moves during the summer season from water mass to land mass and comparatively hold more moisture than land breeze.

Q. 4. Permanent Winds and Local Winds.

Ans.

Permanent Winds	Local Winds
(i) Permanent winds are those winds which have permanent direction and last for whole year. For. e.g Trade winds	(i) Local winds keep changing and last for a very short period of time. For e.g. Loo

Q. 5. Trade Winds and Anti-trade Winds.

Ans.

Trade Winds	Anti-trade Winds
(i) These winds are surface winds and move from eastern direction. These winds blow from Sub tropical high region to equatorial low pressure zone in both hemispheres.	(i) These winds move at higher elevation than trade winds and move from western direction. These winds move from Sub tropical high region to temperate low zone in both hemispheres.

Q. 6. Trade Winds and Polar Easterlies.

Ans.

Trade Winds	Polar Easterlies
(i) The winds moving permanently from the sub-tropical belts of high pressure to equatorial low pressure zone is called trade winds.	(i) These winds blow from polar belts of high pressure to sub-polar belts of low pressure.

Q. 7. Chinook and Mistral.

Ans.

Chinook	Mistral
(i) The local warm wind, descending on the eastern slope of Rockies in North America, is called as Chinook.	(i) Mistral is a local name of a cold and dry wind that blow in Rhone Valley on southern France.

Q. 8. Aneroid Barometer and Mercury Barometer.

Ans.

Aneroid Barometer	Mercury Barometer
(i) This device uses a spring that expands and contracts due to the pressure it measures.	(i) This measuring device uses mercury that is pushed up by the atmospheric pressure until the atmospheric pressure equals the force produced by the weight of the column of mercury.

Chapter 14. Precipitation

Q. 1. Cloud and Fog. **[November, 2019]**

Ans.

Cloud	Fog
(i) The cloud is a form of condensation that may happen at any level of altitude. For example it may be as high as 12 miles or as low as the ground.	(i) Fog is a form of condensation that happens only close to surface and it always touches the surface.

Q. 2. Dew and Mist.

Ans.

Dew	Mist
(i) A form of condensation that appears generally on the grass, leaves and surface.	(i) The less dense form of fog is called mist, where the visibility level is higher than fog (generally 1 to 2 kms)

Q. 3. Absolute Humidity and Relative Humidity.

Ans.

Absolute Humidity	Relative Humidity
(i) It is the amount of vapours present in a certain volume of air.	(i) Relative humidity is defined as percentage of moisture present in the atmosphere as compared to its full capacity.
(ii) Absolute humidity is expressed in grams per cubic meter (g/m^3).	(ii) Relative humidity is presented in percentage (%).

Q. 4. Evaporation and Condensation.

Ans.

Evaporation	Condensation
(i) Evaporation is the transformation of water from liquid state to gaseous state.	(i) Condensation is the transformation from gaseous state to liquid state.

Q. 5. Fog and Mist.

Ans.

Fog	Mist
(i) It is a type of condensation near the surface, in which the visibility is very less.	(i) Mist is type of condensation in which the visibility is higher than fog. Generally upto 1-2 kms.
(ii) The density of fog is high.	(ii) The density of mist is less than fog.

Q. 6. Dew and Fog.

Ans.

Dew	Fog
(i) During winters the leaves, grass or flowers become comparatively cooler because of more radiation. When cold and moist air comes in their contact condenses in form of tiny droplets.	(i) When the earth surface re-radiate more energy during winter nights than insolation become cooler than atmosphere. The moist air in its contact condenses in form of surface clouds.

Q. 7. Conventional and Orographic Rainfall.

Ans.

Conventional Rainfall	Orographic Rainfall
(i) Conventional rainfall is the result of evaporation, condensation and precipitation.	(i) Orographic rainfall is the result of air condensation due to mountain slope.
(ii) Conventional rainfall is common in equatorial region due to intense evaporation.	(ii) The basic requirement for orographic rain is obstruction of moist air by mountain range as a barrier.

Q. 8. Snow and Hail. **[November, 2019]**

Ans.

Snow	Hail
(i) Snow consists of ice crystals. It is formed due to crystallisation of water vapors.	(i) Hail consists of ice balls. It is formed due to pressing and cooled down of water drop against each other.

Chapter 15. Pollution and Environment

Q. 1. Primary and Secondary Pollutants.

Ans.

Primary Pollutants	Secondary Pollutant
(i) Primary pollutants are the air pollutants which are directly released into the air.	(i) Secondary pollutants are the pollutant which are formed due to chemical interaction between the atmospheric compound and primary pollutants.
(ii) These are less toxic.	(ii) These are more toxic.
(iii) Example smoke, dust, ash, etc.	(iii) Example: Smog, ozone, etc.

Q. 2. Natural Source and Manmade Source.

Ans.

Natural Source	Manmade Source
(i) These include pollutants generated naturally like forest fire, volcanic eruptions and dust storm.	(i) These includes pollutants generated by human activities like automobiles, industrial brick kilns, etc.
(ii) These are difficult to control by human.	(ii) These sources can be controlled and minimised by careful supervision of human activity.

Q. 3. Biodegradable and Non-biodegradable pollutants.

Ans.

Biodegradable Pollutants	Non-biodegradable Pollutants
(i) These pollutants are organic matters which can be decomposed by the activity fo microorganism.	(i) These pollutants are inorganic which cannot be decomposed.
(ii) Can be recycled naturally or by human.	(ii) These cannot be recycled naturally.
(iii) Example: Paper, Cow dung, vegetable peels.	(iii) Examples: DDT, Synthetic Plastic fibres, etc.

Q. 4. Water Pollution and Land Pollution.

Ans.

Water Pollution	Land Pollution
(i) It occurs when the hazardous material are released in the water resources like river, lakes etc by industries.	(i) It is the contamination by harmful substances on land.
(ii) It cantaminate ground water and surface water which is the essential requirement of all the living being.	(ii) Conditions like accoumulation of garbage, cutting down of trees are associated with land pollution. It also effect ground water.

Chapter 16. Natural Regions of the World

Q. 1. Warm Temperate Region and Cool Temperate Region.

Ans.

Warm Temperate Region	Cool Temperate Region
(i) It extends from 30° N to 45° N latitude in each hemisphere.	(i) It extends from 45° latitude in each hemisphere.
(ii) It includes the mediterranean type, tropical desert type and monsoon type climatic region.	(ii) It include West-Europeon type, temperate grassland, St. lawrance type and Tiga type climatic region.

Q. 2. Humid Region and Sub-humid Region.

Ans.

Humid Region	Sub-humid Region
(i) Humid region are those in which precipitation is in excess of evaporation through out the year.	(i) It is the region in which precipitation is in excess of evaporation only is short rainy season.
(ii) The equatorial region is an example of humid region.	(ii) The arid region is the example of sub-humid region.
(iii) This region face no water deficiency in the dry season.	(iii) Face water deficiency in the dry season.

Q. 3. Evergreen and Xerophytic Trees of Mediterranean Region.

Ans.

Evergreen Trees of Mediterranean Region	Xerophytic Trees of Mediterranean Region
(i) These trees has no regular season for shedding their leaves.	(i) They have adapted themseives to the dry summer season.
(ii) They have needle shaped leaves.	(ii) They have small, stiff, shiny leaves, thorn, long deep roots and waxy surface.
(iii) Pine, Firs, Cedars are the examples of main evergreen trees.	(iii) Cork, oak with thick spongy bark are the examples of the trees of this region.

Reason Based Questions

Set 4

Chapter 1. Earth As a Planet

Q. 1. Though Mercury is the nearest planet to the Sun, Venus is the hottest planet.

Ans. Mercury is the closest planet to the Sun in the Solar System, but it does not have an atmosphere to trap the heat. On the other hand, the atmosphere of Venus contains a maximum percentage of carbon dioxide which is capable of retaining maximum heat. So even if Venus is situated farther than Mercury, it is the hottest planet of the Solar System.

Q. 2. Neptune is known as the frosty planet.

Ans. Neptune is the coldest planet of the Solar system because of its distance from the Sun which is nearly 4.4772 billion kilometres. As the planet is situated at such a great distance, it is obvious that the average temperature of the planet drops down to -214° C. Such a low temperature is a good reason to make the water of the planet frozen. Thus the planet is a frosty planet.

Q. 3. The earth is a habitable planet.

Ans. The earth is only planet in the solar system which sustains life. The factors that favour life on earth sytem are ideal temperature condition due to optimum distance from the Sun, availability of atmospheric blanket, and abundance of water. Most importantly the atmosphere contains oxygen which favours all forms of life on the planet.

Q. 4. The shape of the earth is not exactly that of a sphere, give reason.

Ans. The Earth is not a perfect sphere; rather it is an oblate spheroid, which means it is flattened at the top and bulged at the equator. This type of shape is the result of the uneven distribution of mass around the globe. The greater the concentration the higher the gravitational pool of that particular region, thereby creating the bulge around the globle.

Q. 5. Why human beings weigh less on the moon than on the earth?

Ans. Human beings weigh less on the moon than on the Earth because keeping the mass constant the weight can vary between the two objects. The object with lesser weight will surely have weak gravitational strength. As the size of the moon is much smaller than the Earth, the weight is also less. Thus the gravitational pull is only one-sixth of the Earth's gravitational pull.

Chapter 2. Latitudes and Longitudes

Q. 1. We express latitude and longitude in degrees of angles.

Ans. Latitude and longitudes are the angular distance of places situated at north and south as well as east and west direction from the centre of the earth, keeping equator and Prime Meridian as their base respectively. As they both represent distance in terms of angles, we express them in degrees.

Q. 2. No latitudes are greater than 90° N and 90° S.

Ans. Latitude is a line joining the places with same angular distances keeping the equatorial plane as base. It is an arbitrary circle that runs parallel to the line of the equator. In such a situation, the poles are the extreme points on both Northern and Southern Hemisphere up to which we can draw such parallels. Maximum each pole can make an angle of 90° with the equatorial plane. Thus the highest latitude on each side of the equator will be 90° each. That means no latitudes are greater than 90° N and 90° S.

Q. 3. The time difference between GMT and IST is 5 hours and 30 minutes.

Ans. The longitudinal difference between GMT and Indian Standard Time (IST) is 82° 30′.

For covering 1° we need 4 minutes.

To cross 82° 30′or 82.5° we will require

82.5 × 4 = 330 minutes. This is equal to 5 hours and 30 minutes.

Thus the time difference between GMT nd IST is 5 hours and 30 minutes.

Q. 4. USA has six time zones.

Ans. Countries with large east to west extent have more than one time zone. USA has six time zones because the time is mostly determined by the apparent movement of sun from east to west. The time when sun is directly overhead is known to be noon and when the sun goes down, the time is known to be evening and further it is called night. If USA had a single time zone around the entire width than the time of noon and sunset would not be consistent across country. So US need multiple time zones.

Q. 5. International Date Line has a time difference of 24 hours.

Ans. While we move from Prime Meridian to the International Date Line through east we add 12 hours. On the other hand when we move from Prime Meridian to the IDL through west we subtract 12 hours. So when we start from IDL and come to it by covering the entire globe from west to east we will be gaining a day by 12+12 i.e. 24 hours. Thus International date has a time difference of 24 hours. That means crossing International Date Line from West to east will subtract a day, whereas crossing the line from east to west will add a day.

Q. 6. The International Date Line is not a straight line.

Ans. The International Date Line is also called the anti-meridian, which lies exactly on the opposite side of the Prime Meridian. It is the complementary part of Prime Meridian with respect to the formation of the Great circle. It is the 180° longitude that passes through the Pacific Ocean. But when it touches the land surface, it cuts several countries into two parts which may not be equal in size. The International Date Line is the longitude where the dates are changing. In order to eradicate the confusion of different dates in one country the line has to be distorted or follow a zigzag pattern.

Q. 7. The distance between two successive lines of latitudes remains constant.

Ans. The latitudes are the parallel circles of lines drawn from equator towards pole. As the theory of parallel line says two parallel lines never meet at a point. The distance between them will always constant. This is why the distance between two successive lines of latitudes remains constant.

Q. 8. Frigid Zones are very coldest part of the world.

Ans. Frigid Zones extend from 66½° to 90° in both the hemisphere. These are the regions which receives extremely inclined solar radiation. Thus they remain frozen and considered as the coldest part of the world.

Chapter 3. Rotation and Revolution

Q. 1. The speed of the rotation decreases from equator to pole.

Ans. The rotational speed of the Earth is a measurement of speed, distance and time. The formula that implies the relation between these three parametres can be given as

Angular speed = distance /Time.

This implies that the speed is directly proportional to distance and indirectly proportional to time.

This shows, that at equator the rotation is for a longer distance, the speed has to be more to cover up the same distance.

Q. 2. Rotation causes day and night.

Ans. The change in the day and night occurs due to the rotation of the Earth on its axis. Half of the Earth faces towards the sun and gets the heat and light and thus experience day during rotation. The other side of the Earth does not receive any heat or light and thus experiences night. If the Earth stopped rotating the cycle of day and night would not be possible.

Q. 3. The variation in length of day and night increases towards pole.

Ans. The variation in the length of day and night towards pole is the result of decreasing amount of Sun light. As a matter of fact the Earth is oblate spheroid, it receives the solar radiation unevenly. The part of near the equator receives straight and maximum sunlight throughout the day as well as year. On the other hand the poles which are far away from the equator receives least possible amount of sunrays and that is also slanting. So the length of the day as well as the night increases towards the pole.

Q. 4. Australia celebrates Christmas in summer.

Ans. Australia celebrates Christmas in summer. This occurs due the Earth's revolution. As the Earth is tilted on its axis during December the Southern Hemisphere of the Earth is closer to the Sun and thus experiences the summer. As Australia is located in the Southern Hemisphere, it celebrates Christmas during the summer.

Q. 5. Norway is the 'Land of Midnight Sun'.

Ans. The concept of midnight sun is valid for the northern most part of the Northern Hemisphere near the circle of Arctic. The unique phenomenon is experienced only during summer. The Sun is at its peak during these months and experience 24 hours of sunlight. As Norway is located in this zone it does experience the same geographical feature every year during summers. So Norway is known as the 'Land of Midnight Sun'.

Q. 6. Rotation creates standardize time zones.

Ans. The rotation of the Earth results in the occurrence of day and night which also implies the change of time. When the Earth enters the zone of illumination the day begins and night begins when it leaves the zone. If we had only one time zone, it would have resulted in morning, night, noon and even midnight at the same time. So it is practically impossible to have one time for entire globe. Thus the concept of Time zones solves purpose that no matter where we live on the planet, the noon is the middle of the day when the Sun is highest, while midnight is the middle of the night.

Q. 7. The places located on the Equator experience duration of almost constant daylight throughout the years.

Ans. The Earth's axis makes an angle of 23.5 degree with the orbital plane. During the revolution around the Sun the earth keeps changing its tilt for 22.1 degree to 24.5 degree throughout the year. Though the tilt changes, it never crosses either Tropic of Cancer or Tropic of Capricorn. That implies the places near to equator receives the constant daylight throughout the year.

Q. 8. The Equator experiences the overhead Sun twice a year.

Ans. The Earth revolves around the Sun in an elliptical orbit. Though Sun is static in its position but from the Earth it seems the Sun moves between the latitudes of 23.½ ° N to 23.½ ° S twice a year. That implies all the places between these two latitudes receive the vertical rays of the Sun twice a year. As equator is one of the important latitude of this zone, it experiences overhead Sun twice a year.

Q. 9. Beyond the Tropics, the Sun is never overhead.

Ans. The tilt of the Earth axis with the orbital plane is 23.5 degree. So during the revolution of the Earth, the Sun apparently moves from the Tropic of Cancer to Tropic of Capricorn. This implies that the apparent movement of the Sun is only limited the Tropics in both the hemisphere. This is the reason why the Sun is never overhead beyond the Tropics.

Q. 10. Give a reason for each of the following: **[November, 2019]**

(i) The speed of rotation of Earth is maximum at the Equator.

(ii) Pilots follow the great circle route.

Ans. (i) The speed of rotation is highest at equator because the equator is the farthest point from the axis. As we move away from the axis toward the equator the speed increase and towards the poles it decreases and that happens because of distance from the axis.

(ii) Pilots always follow the great circle path because it gives them true shortest distance to travel.

Chapter 4. Structure of the Earth and Internal Processes

Q. 1. Rocks are found in a molten state in the interior of the Earth.

Ans. Inside the interior of the Earth the temperature rises with increasing depth. Till the time it reaches the mantle the temperature starts varying between 700° C to 1700° C. The rocks melt at a temperature of 1100° C. This is why the rocks are found in a molten state.

Q. 2. The lithosphere or crust is a solid layer of rocks.

Ans. Among the three layers of the Earth, the lithosphere is considered to be the surface layer of the fluid part of earth's convection system, which gets cooled down and solidified over time. Thus the lithosphere or crust is a solid layer of rocks.

Q. 3. The sial float on a sea of sima.

Ans. The crust also has its subdivisions: sial and sima. As their names depict both the layer have silicate in common but the second mineral varies. In sial silicate is found with aluminum and in sima the aluminum is replaced by magnesium. The aluminum makes sial less dense than sima. This is the reason sial floats on the sea of sima.

Q. 4. The inner core is found in a solid state.

Ans. The inner core is made up of nickel and iron. The core is characterized by very high temperature as well as pressure. It is observed that certain material like nickel and iron does not change their forms in such higher temperature and pressure. They remain solid. This is the reason the core is found in the solid state.

Q. 5. The plates of our planet surface move.

Ans. The increasing temperature and pressure within the interior of the earth create the system of convection current deep inside the earth. This produces a stream of magma that rises from the centre to the surface of the earth and spread along the sides just beneath the continental crust. Thus the convection current becomes the main driving force for the movement of tectonic plates.

Chapter 5. Landforms of the Earth

Q. 1. Old fold mountains have low altitudes and gentle slopes.

Ans. Old fold mountains were formed nearly 250 million years ago. These mountains have been subjected to denudation for millions of years. Thus a large portion of these mountains have eroded by various agents like rivers, winds and glaciers, etc. thereby reducing their heights and making their slope gentle.

Q. 2. Young fold mountains have rugged relief features.

Ans. The young fold mountains are not so old. They were formed nearly 10-25 million years ago. They have been subjected to denudation process for a short period of time. Thus they have rugged relief features.

Q. 3. Plains are thickly populated.

Ans. Plains are thickly populated as they attract population because of the following facilities.

(i) Plains are made up of alluvium brought by the rivers, which make the land fertile thus facilitates agricultural productivity.

(ii) The plains are suitable for the construction of the transport network.

(iii) The transport network can be extensively used for transporting the raw materials from their sources to industries and finished products from industries to market. Thus plains are also effectively used for setting up of industries.

Q. 4. Earth's movements have modified the Earth's surface.

Ans. Earth's movements have modified the surface of the Earth as these movements result in the formation of various landforms such as mountains, plateaus and plains. For example, the crustal movement of the Earth gives rise to fold mountain when they converge towards each other. Similarly when the plates move away from each other cracks develop in the Earth's surface. Apart from these movements, the landforms are further subjected to denudation by agents like rivers, winds, and glaciers, etc. that result in the development of various erosional and depositional landforms. Thus Earth's movement plays an important role in shaping the surface of the Earth.

Q. 5. Young fold mountains are liable for earthquake and volcanic action.

Ans. The young fold mountains are formed when the crustal plates move towards each other and collide. A zone of crustal instability is created near the margins of these plates. It also causes stress in the crusts because of the weight of the overlying rocks, movement in mantle and expansion and contraction of some parts of the crust. All these above causes trigger the phenomena like earthquake and volcanic eruption. Thus Young Fold Mountains are liable to the earthquake and volcanic action.

Q. 6. Plateaus are called tableland.

Ans. Ideally, the plateaus are the highland that consists of relatively flat surfaces, usually having steep slope at least on one side which falls abruptly to the lower land. These features give a table-like appearance of the plateaus from a distance. Thus plateaus are also called Tablelands.

Q. 7. The plateaus are the storehouse of minerals.

Ans. The plateaus are composed of old crystalline, igneous and metamorphic rocks which are rich in mineral deposits such as iron ore, manganese, mica, etc. Due to the abundance of these minerals plateaus are called the storehouse of minerals.

Q. 8. Fold mountains are associated with Intermontane Plateau. **[November, 2019]**

Ans. If the syncline of Fold Mountains is gentle and the folding force at initial stage leads to the formation of inter-montane plateau.

Chapter 6. Rocks

Q. 1. Igneous rocks are also called primary rocks.

Ans. The igneous rocks are formed in the beginning stage of rock cycle which formed out of volcanic magma. These will then go through the process of denudation, transportation and deposition to form sedimentary rocks or transformed into metamorphic rocks under tremendous heat and pressure. As the other two types of rocks are formed out of igneous rocks, they are also called as primary rocks.

Q. 2. Fossils are present in sedimentary rocks.

Ans. Fossils are present in the sedimentary rocks, because these rocks are formed in a low temperature. On the other hand the igneous rocks are formed at much higher temperature and pressure that can destroy any organic compound present in the rocks. The metamorphic rocks are created under tremendous pressure and thus it will deform the fossils. So the sedimentary rocks are the only rocks which contains fossils.

Q. 3. Extrusive igneous rocks generally have small crystals.

Ans. Extrusive igneous rocks are formed when magma comes out of the volcanic craters. They cools down and solidifies very quickly as they exposed to the outside atmosphere. The cooling process is so quick that it does not allow the crystallization process to last. Thus the crystals formed in the extrusive igneous rocks are small.

Q. 4. Silicates are the most common rock forming minerals.

Ans. The silicates are found abundantly on the earth's surface. Most of the atoms are either silicon or oxygen atoms. As a result most of the rocks on the earth surface contains silicate as the major constituent. The igneous rocks which form almost 90 percent of the Earth's crust are composed of silicates.

Q. 5. Sedimentary rocks also called stratified rocks.

Ans. Sedimentary rocks are formed when the igneous and metamorphic rocks are eroded by the physical agents like rivers, wind, etc; accumulated and eventually hardened in due course of time. The deposition of sediments are arranged in layer one after another. Thus sedimentary rocks are called stratified rocks.

Q. 6. Rocks are of economic significance.

Ans. Rocks contain minerals which are useful in many ways. When the rocks break down and form soils, they facilitates agricultural production. The minerals in rocks are also used as raw material in industries like cement industries, iron and steel industries, copper industries, etc. All these factors add on to the economic growth of a region, thus rocks are economically important to us.

Q. 7. The Dead Sea abounds in chemically formed sedimentary rocks.

Ans. The Dead Sea is a hyper saline lake with significant amount of sodium chloride and other mineral rocks in it. Chemical sediments are formed due to the evaporation of water containing salts in solution. Thus the Dead Sea abounds in chemically formed sedimentary rocks.

Q. 8. Acidic igneous rocks are formed of viscous magma.

Ans. Acidic rocks such as granite, microgranite and rhyolite are rich in silica and contain the minerals quartz, feldspar and biotite among others. These rocks are originated from the magma that comes from the interior of the earth. The magma which has higher percentage of silica is more viscous and this is the reason acidic igneous rocks are formed of viscous magma.

Q. 9. Metamorphic rocks are also called altered rocks.

Ans. Metamorphic rocks are not the original rocks. The term metamorphose shows the change in form. These rocks are formed when they substantially change their form from igneous, sedimentary or old metamorphic rocks. As a complete transformation occurred in the process of development of these rocks, they are also known as altered rocks.

Q. 10. Plutonic Igneous rocks have large crystals. **[November, 2019]**

Ans. Plutonic Igneous rocks have large crystals because plutonic rocks take more time to cool down. Thus, magma crystals get enough time to grow large in size.

Chapter 7. Volcanoes

Q. 1. Some volcanoes erupt explosively. Give reasons.

Ans. The magma in the interior of the Earth is an amalgamation of gas and viscous molten rocks. The trapped gas inside the interior is always under tremendous pressure, and at a time when the magma cannot withstand the weight, it exploded. The explosion occurs mostly when the lava is acidic in nature because they are more viscous than the basic lava.

Q. 2. Hot springs are conventional in volcanic regions. Give reasons.

Ans. The hot springs are the fountains of hot water rising from underground continuously without any eruptive forces. In the areas where the hot springs have emerged, the groundwater would sink to the underground and get deposited at a place that is nearer to the magma chamber. Their temperature keeps on increasing as a result of their proximity to the magma chamber.The belt of volcanic activities and earthquakes are the same. Thus hot springs are common in volcanic regions

Q. 3. Most of the volcanoes lie in the "Ring of Fire."

Ans. The ring of fires consists of 75% of the World's active and dormant volcanoes. The massive concentration of volcanoes in this belt results from the subduction of the vast Pacific plate underneath other plates. The subduction triggers a volcanic eruption. Thus most of the volcanoes lie in the "Ring of Fire". The rocks are found in a molten state in the interior of the earth.

Q. 4. Acid lava is viscous, where basic lava is fluid.

Ans. Acid lava is rich in silica, whereas the basic lava does not have silica in it. The silica is the mineral that makes the lava viscous with its presence. Thus basic lava is not viscous, instead it is fluid in nature.

Q. 5. A crater is a common feature in cinder cone.

Ans. The cinder cones are formed by the deposition of pyroclastic material around the vent. The mouths of the cones generally have craters at their summit.

Q. 6. The Circum-Pacific belt is known as Ring of Fires.

Ans. The Circum Pacific belt is created by the subduction of Pacific Belt underneath other plates, and thus, the area is prone to a volcanic eruption. In fact, 75% of the active and dormant volcanoes of the World are found here. Therefore the region is called Ring of Fires.

Q. 7. Although temperature is extremely high, yet the core of the Earth is not in molten state.

[November, 2019]

Ans. Temperatures is extremely high yet the core of the Earth is not in a molten state because of the intensive pressure of Earth and its atmosphere does not allow the iron to melt. The pressure and the density in the deepest section is too high to convert the iron atoms in liquid state.

Chapter 8. Earthquakes

Q. 1. "Earthquakes too have positive side for mankind" give reasons.

Ans. Positive side of earthquakes:

(i) Earthquakes resulted into development of cracks and later on formation of hot water springs or natural geysers.

(ii) Earthquake waves help the geologist to study interior structure of the earth.

(iii) Earthquakes help the minerals or oil reserves to come up at shallow depth.

Q. 2. Japan experiences high number of earthquakes in a year. Give reason.

Ans. Few common reasons are:

(i) Japan lie on the meeting point of continental and oceanic belt.

(ii) Japan has high number of active volcano.

(iii) Japan also lies of Circum-Pacific belt or Pacific Ring of fire. This zone is an area where large number of earthquakes and volcano erupts.

Q. 3. 'Seismic waves helps in better understanding of interior of the Earth'.

Ans. With the help of modern instruments and devices seismic waves can be studied. For e.g. depth of focus and structure and composition of interior of earth.

Q. 4. Earthquakes are common in Himalayan region.

Ans. Himalayas are the young fold mountains. These mountains are still rising. Thus, folding of lithospheric belts causes shakes and vibrations. That is why Himalayas are at high risk of seismic activities.

Q. 5. "Volcanic activity is the major cause of earthquakes".

Ans. While volcanic eruption, violent gases try to move out of earth's surface with great force. This force create huge tremor of high magnitude resulted in the development of earthquake situation.

Chapter 9. Weathering

Q. 1. Limestone regions have prominent examples of chemical weathering.

Ans. Limestone regions have prominent examples of chemical weathering because the limestone reacts quickly with weak carbonic acid of rainwater and get dissolved more rapidly as compared to other minerals.

Q. 2. Weathering is responsible for bio-diversity on the earth.

Ans. Weathering loosens the rocks and helps agents of erosion disintegrate the rocks and transport to other place. These disintegrated rock particles (sediments) form the soil.

Q. 3. 'Wind by and large is the most effective agent of erosion in desert area' explain the statement.

Ans. This statement says that wind plays crucial role in desert area to perform erosion because deserts have scantly vegetation cover, this does not cause obstruction to wind and leaves the soil particles loose.

Q. 4. "Geomorphic process keeps the earth unstable". Explain the statement.

Ans. The geomorphic process includes endogenetic and exogenic forces. These forces causing physical and chemical actions on earth's materials and continuously changes the earth.

Q. 5. Mechanical weathering does not change composition of a rock.

Ans. Mechanical weathering means disintegration of rocks by elements like heat, rain, wind, etc. These phenomenons only change its physical structure but not its chemical composition.

Q. 6. Oxidation causes decay and degradation of rocks.

Ans. The atmospheric oxygen enters into chemical union with rock minerals and this produces a coating of iron oxide called rusting of iron. This rusting results in decay and decomposition of rocks. The color of the rock also gets changed.

Q. 7. River form V-shape valleys.

Ans. Rivers traversing through steep slopes does deepening of rills or vertical erosion. These rills after deepening are converted into V-shape valley.

Q. 8. 'Wind by and large is the most effective agent of erosion in desert area' explain the statement.

Ans. This statement says that wind plays crucial role in desert area to perform erosion because deserts have scantly vegetation cover, this does not cause obstruction to wind and leaves the soil particles loose.

Q. 9. Alluvial plains are called as 'Food bowl of India'.

Ans. Alluvial plains are formed due to deposition work of river. New alluvium is being deposited continuously, which makes these plains fertile and suitable to grow food grains like wheat and rice.

Q. 10. River meanders are formed in middle course of a river.

Ans. In its middle course, river moves with a gentle speed and is unable to do erosion. Thus rather than making its course straight, river flows in a zigzag path which is called as River meander.

Q. 11. Change of temperature leads to physical weathering.

Ans. The rocks are bad conductor of heat. Rocks expand on heating in the day and contract on cooling in the night or due to seasonal change. The continuous change of temperature peels off thin flakes from the rock. This type of weathering is a part of mechanical or physical weathering called exfoliation.

Q. 12. Climate is the most important factor of soil formation.

Ans. Climate is one of the most important factors affecting the formation of soil. Warmer temperatures and an abundance of water have a tendency to speed up the formation of soil, in some cases rather dramatically. Whereas cooler temperatures and less precipitation slow down soil formation.

Q. 13. Give a reason for each of the following: **[February, 2020]**

(i) Exfoliation is common in deserts.

(ii) V-shaped valleys are formed by rivers.

(iii) Limestone regions have prominent examples of chemical weathering.

Ans. (i) It is due the reason that in deserts the range of temperature is very high. Higher is the range of temperature higher is the impact of exfoliation.

(ii) V-shape valleys are formed in the youth stage of river. When river flows in mountainous track, it does vertical erosion and deepens the valley. This process forms the V-shape valley.

(iii) Limestone regions have prominent examples of chemical weathering because the limestone reacts quickly with weak carbonic acid of rainwater and get dissolve as compared to other minerals.

Chapter 10. Hydrosphere

Q. 1. During winters the ports of north Western Europe remain open.

Ans. Because the western coasts of continents in the Northern Hemisphere are influenced by the warm ocean currents which controls the temperature of western coast to dip down and make the ports open during the severe winters.

Q. 2. Ships prefer to sail in the same direction of ocean currents.

Ans. Ships prefer to sail in the same direction of ocean currents because ships sailing in the same direction of the ocean currents consume less fuel and take lesser time as compared to the ships sailing in the opposite direction.

Q. 3. Ocean current losses its speed with depth. Explain.

Ans. Ocean currents are strongest near the surface and may attain the speed of 5 knots. At, depth, currents are generally slower with speed less than 0.5 knots.

Q. 4. Moons gravitational pull plays bigger role in the development of tides than the Sun.

Ans. Although Sun is a bigger celestial body than moon but moon's gravitational pull plays vital role in the development of tides because the distance of moon is way lesser than the sun's distance. That is why Earth experiences greater pull by moon than the Sun.

Q. 5. The meeting point of warm and cold current is havoc for ship transportation.

Ans. Because when the warm and cold current meets they cause huge dense fog. Fog reduces the visibility of areas. Thus, transporting or navigating in that area become difficult. The example of same is New Foundland.

Q. 6. Ocean currents do not follow straight direction.

Ans. This happens generally because of Earth's rotation. When the Earth rotates from west to east it creates deflection (Coriollis effect) of currents both in Northern and Southern Hemisphere.

The other reason is the shape of the coast. The shape of coasts is not straight. Thus the moving ocean currents strike the coasts and get deflected.

Q. 7. The direction of ocean currents in northern Indian Ocean changes with season.

Ans. The currents of Indian Ocean are primarily influenced by the monsoon winds. As we know the monsoon winds change its direction twice a year. Similar impact is seen on the currents of northern Indian Ocean.

Q. 8. The speed of ocean currents varies from 2 km/h to 10 km/h.

Ans. The speed of the ocean currents pre-dominantly varies because of friction of winds, variation in temperature and salinity of ocean water.

Q. 9. Indian ocean is known as only half the ocean.

Ans. Because Indian Ocean in the Northern Hemisphere is confined to tropical zone only and is also divided into Arabian Sea and Bay of Bengal. Thus it is called as half an ocean.

Q. 10. Give a reason for each of the following: **[February, 2020]**

(i) The waters of the Oyashio current form one of the richest fishing grounds in the world.

(ii) The coast of Norway remains ice free during winter.

(iii) Warm ocean current create a milder climate.

Ans. (i) The water of the Oyashio current form one of the richest fishing grounds in the world because one part of Oyashio (cold) current merges with Kuroshio (warm) current and makes the north-eastern coast of Japan an ideal condition for the growth of plankton. Plankton attracts the fishes and makes it one of the best fishing grounds in the world.

(ii) The coast of Norway remains ice free during winter because of movement of Gulf Stream current towards the Western Europe. This warm current of Atlantic Ocean modifies the weather conditions of Western Europe including Norway and makes this region ice free during winters.

(iii) Warm currents develop over low latitude areas and move towards high latitude areas of temperate and polar region. The areas where warm current reaches modifies the climatic condition of coastal areas and strict the temperate and polar areas to get freeze down and maintain the milder climatic conditions.

Chapter 11. Atmosphere

Q. 1. 'Global warming will increase the possibility of droughts'. Give reason to support this statement.

Ans. (i) Definitely global warming leads to rise in temperature, particularly in hot and arid regions the water masses will dry up at faster speed.

(ii) Higher the temperature higher will be the transpiration and lesser vegetation in tropical region. Moreover the precipitation level will also decrease.

(iii) Gradually the movement of desert will also be boosted by rise in temperature and the hot deserts will start expanding and turning semi-arid regions into arid regions.

Q. 2. "The lower layer of atmosphere is called Homosphere" Give reasons.

Ans. The Earth's atmosphere till 80 kms from the surface is called as Homosphere. Because the composition of atmosphere is highly uniform in terms of components of gases in air.

Q. 3. 'Stratosphere is the safe zone for the aircrafts to fly". Give reasons.

Ans. Stratosphere is a safe zone for the aircrafts to fly because stratosphere has no weather phenomenon like clouds, rain, etc. Most of stratosphere experiences constant temperature too. Thus, it provides ideal conditions for the jet to fly in the atmospheric zone.

Q. 4. Although CO_2 is only 0.03% of total atmospheric composition, but we are worried about its increase. Give reasons.

Ans. CO_2 has caused the maximum heat trap and led to the global warming. CO_2 takes the longest period among other gases to leave the atmosphere. That is why after looking at its disadvantages, we are worried about its increase.

Q. 5. The mountaineers carry oxygen cylinders with them while going for high altitude trek. Give reason.

Ans. As we go to higher altitude the atmospheric pressure decreases and atmosphere become thinner. This phenomenon causes breathing problem to the mountaineers.

Q. 6. Why troposphere is the most important layer of atmosphere for biological activities?

Ans. Troposphere contains the entire weather phenomenons. Moreover, only troposphere provides ideal temperature, air composition, humidity that supports all biological activities.

Q. 7. Man is disturbing the natural composition of air in the atmosphere. Comment on this statement.

Ans. Undoubtedly man is disturbing the environment so is air composition. The air composition will never remain the same because the anthropogenic activities disturb it. With the advancement in technology and industrialization, the release of harmful gases like methane, carbon dioxide increases and with population inflation the level of oxygen decreases.

Q. 8. The global warming will adversely affect the ecosystem" Comment.

Ans. Global warming means the increase in global temperature. Because of this phenomenon (example melting of glaciers) the terrestrial ecosystems will get affected. Some species will be forced to get out of their habitat and will get extinct and some will become vulnerable.

Q. 9. The sky changes its color very frequently. Comment.

Ans. This happens because of presence of dust particles in the atmosphere. These dust particles reflect and scattered the short wave solar radiations making the sky blue and create red and orange color at sunshine and sunrise. The sky looks blue because of dust particles.

Q. 10. The height of troposphere varies from equator to poles.

Ans. The height of to troposphere varies from equator to poles because the equator is hotter than poles. The heat variation between equator and poles leads to the convection currents flow from equator to poles. As the thickness increases the height over the equator also increases.

Q. 11. As a jet plane fly in the sky, it leaves white trail behind. Give reasons to support the statement.

Ans. This happens because airplanes fly at a high altitude and at that altitude the temperature is roughly -50° C. When aircrafts fly they release water vapours and carbon dioxide. The trail is the condensed form of water vapour and carbon dioxide.

Q. 12. In the troposphere, the temperature decrease with height. Give reasons.

Ans. This happens because the troposphere is the lowest atmospheric layer and the earth surface absorbs more heat than atmosphere and thus while moving away (vertically) from the surface the temperature decreases.

Chapter 12. Insolation

Q. 1. The south facing slopes in Northern Hemisphere are warmer than north facing slopes.

Ans. The south facing slopes in Northern Hemisphere are warmer than north facing slopes because sun rays falls at a steeper angle at south slopes than north slope and vice-versa condition in Southern Hemisphere.

Q. 2. We do not get 100% of solar radiation on Earth.

Ans. This phenomenon happens because out of 100 units of solar radiation, 35 units are reflected by dust and cloud cover and 19 units and absorbed by earth's atmosphere. Thus only 51 units reached the earth's surface and warm it.

Q. 3. Poles receive minimum solar radiations.

Ans. Poles receive minimum solar radiations because as we move away from the equator the distribution of solar radiation decreases because of the Geoid shape of the Earth and Earth's tilt on its axis.

Q. 4. Earth maintains its temperature through terrestrial radiation.

Ans. After receiving solar radiation during day time, Earth itself becomes a radiating body. The temperature of heat that Earth has received during day time, Earth send it back during night time and comes at a neutral point every day.

Q. 5. Winds modify the temperature of a place.

Ans. Winds too modify the temperature of a place. The on-shore winds bring rain to the nearby areas on the other hand off-shore winds make the places dry. Similarly hot and dry winds like loo rises the temperature of a place and wind like Bora and Mistral which are cold winds make the place colder.

Q. 6. Atmosphere receives most of its heat through terrestrial radiation.

Ans. Earth is in solid state and solid absorb more heat and release it too. Thus, more than the insolation the terrestrial radiation is influencing on Earth's atmosphere.

Q. 7. Jaipur has higher range of temperature than Kochi.

Ans. Jaipur lies away from the ocean and experiences continental type of climate. Thus, the range of temperature is high. On the other hand Kochi lies on the coastal area. It experiences maritime (Sea influencing) climate which remain equitable throughout the year.

Q. 8. Nainital is way colder than Panipat, although their latitudinal position is almost equal.

Ans. Although latitudinal position plays an important role in determing the climate but in this category Nainital lie in the Himalayas and its altitude deceases its temperature. On the other hand, panipat lies in northern plains of India with low altitude.

Q. 9. 'Vertical sun rays give more heat than slanting rays'. Give a reason.

Ans. Vertical sun rays travel through a shorter distance. Higher is the distance higher is the heat loss. Moreover, the vertical sun rays have to heat up lesser area as compared to slanting one.

Q. 10. Although earth daily receives solar radiation, but its temperature remain moderate.

Ans. Because during the day time, Earth receives the solar radiation and it gets heat up. So to lose the same proportion of energy, Earth also re-radiates it back to the atmosphere. This re-radiation or terrestrial radiation keeps the earth temperature moderate.

Chapter 13. Pressure Belts and Winds

Q. 1. The winds in the Northern Hemisphere deflect to their right and left in the Southern Hemisphere.

Ans. This phenomenon happens because of the rotation of the earth. Due to earth's rotation on its axis, the wind close to the surface get deflected to its right and left in Northern and Southern Hemisphere respectively. This phenomenon is called Coriolis Effect.

Q. 2. Hot deserts are found on the western margins of the continents in sub-tropical regions..

Ans. Hot deserts are found on the western margins of the continents in the sub-tropical regions because the sub-tropical regions are dominated by easterly winds. By the time easterly winds reached the southern section of the continents it become dry and leads to formation of arid and dry conditions.

Q. 3. The winds in the Northern Hemisphere deflect to their right and left in the Southern Hemisphere.

Ans. This phenomenon happens because of the rotation of the Earth. The rotation of the Earth produces Coriollis force which tends to turn the wind in right in Northern Hemisphere and left in Southern Hemisphere.

Q. 4. Subtropical high pressure areas are also called as Horse latitude.

Ans. In good old times, ships use to carry horse to new colonies from Europe. In the sub tropical area wind is calm and dry which used to make it difficult to sail. Thus, the sailors used to throw their cargo which includes mainly horse into the sea to safeguard them.

Q. 5. The south facing slopes in Northern Hemisphere are warmer than north facing slopes.

Ans. The South facing slopes in Northern Hemisphere are warmer than north facing slopes because the sun shines at steeper angle on the south facing slopes of Northern Hemisphere and vice versa in Southern Hemisphere.

Q. 6. Atmospheric pressure is not realized by human body.

Ans. Plants, animals and human beings do not feel air pressure because the air inside our body exerts an equal amount of pressure outwards that balances the pressure of atmosphere.

Q. 7. Westerlies in Southern Hemisphere are called as roaring forties and furious fifties.

Ans. The westerlies blow with great speed in the Southern Hemisphere because of less land distribution in Southern Hemisphere, particularly between 40^{0} and 50^{0} latitudes. That is why it is named as roaring forties and furious fifties.

Q. 8. El Nino is closely associated with pressure change in Central Pacific and Australia.

Ans. El Nino is the reversal pattern of pressure system in the pacific and Australia. Due to El Nino warm ocean current of the pacific, replaces with cold Peruvian current. This creates variations in weather pattern over the world.

Q. 9. 'Tropical cyclones cause heavy damage to life and property.

Ans. Tropical cyclones causes heavy damage to life and property because tropical cyclones are calm at the centre but are surrounded by winds of great force. This force can be of 100 km/h. This causes heavy rains and strong winds of disastrous nature. This causes heavy damage to houses, wildlife, forests and human lives.

Q. 10. 'The effect of westerlies is felt in greater extent in Europe than North America.

Ans. The effect of westerlies is felt in greater extent in Europe and North America because the Rockies mountains in the western margins of the North America alter the direction of westerlies. On the other hand there is no obstruction on the western margins of Europe. Thus westerlies enter Europe without any restriction and show its impact there.

Q. 11. Give a reason for each of the following: **[November, 2019]**

(i) The Westerlies in the Southern Hemisphere blow with a greater force than those in the Northern Hemisphere.

(ii) As we go higher atmospheric pressure decreases.

(iii) Cyclones are frequent in summer in the tropical region.

Ans. (i) The westerlies in the Southern Hemisphere blow with a greater force than those in the Northern Hemisphere because the Southern Hemisphere has more of water mass and westerlies move without facing any obstruction.

(ii) As we go higher atmospheric pressure decreases because as the altitude increases, the air expands, it become less dense and resulted into lighter and less air pressure at higher altitudes.

(iii) Cyclones are frequent in summer in the tropical region because the tropical areas are warm and cyclones need high sea surface temperature to rise up the air and then sink down causing the low pressure at the center.

Chapter 14. Precipitation

Q. 1. The coastal areas receive more rainfall than interiors.

Ans. The coastal areas receive more rainfall than interiors regions because of the effect of the sea, the wind carries ample moisture to rain. Till the time winds reached the interior of the continents, they almost lack moisture.

Q. 2. The windward side of the mountains is greener than leeward side.

Ans. The windward side of mountains is greener than leeward side because windward side of mountains faces the moisture laden winds, which causes heavy rain.

Q. 3. Smog is feature of industrial areas.

Ans. Smog is the combination of smoke and fog. This phenomenon is very common in urban areas because the concentration of smoke is very high in urban areas. The tiny droplets of fog condense over smoke particles and form smog.

Q. 4. Places located far from the sea experience low rainfall.

Ans. Places which are away from the sea experience continental type of climate. In addition to this, as an air mass moves from sea side its moisture starts decreasing.

Q. 5. Conventional rainfall is common in Equatorial Zone.

Ans. Equatorial region experiences high temperature thus results in high amount of evaporation. High amount of evaporation resulted into high chances of condensation and finally causes conventional rainfall.

Q. 6. Western Ghats of India receives orographic rainfall.

Ans. The Arabian Sea branch of monsoon enters India from western coastal side. Thus resulted in orographic rain on Western Ghats.

Q. 7. Mawsynram is the wettest place on Earth.

Ans. Mawsynram lies between the windward side of Garo, khasi and Jaintia hill of Meghalaya. This region is close to Bay of Bengal and receives rain from the moisture led south western monsoon winds.

Q. 8. The cyclonic rainfall is the result of warm air mass and cold air mass meeting point.

Ans. When warm and cold air mass meets. The warm air ascends due to light in weight. As it gains the height it loses temperature and causes cyclonic rainfall.

Q. 9. The Eastern side of Western Ghats receives lesser rainfall as compared to western side of Western Ghats.

Ans. The Western Ghats receive rainfall from the winds coming from Arabian Sea branch. Thus western side that faces the wind gets windward rain and the eastern side become leeward side and remains dry.

Q. 10. Convectional rainfall happens every day in equatorial region.

Ans. Convectional rainfall happens everyday in equatorial region because the equatorial region experiences high temperature that leads to high evaporation level and followed by condensation and precipitation. Thus conventional rainfall happens every day.

Q. 11. The amount of water vapour decreases with altitude.

Ans. We know that as the altitude increases the temperature decreases. At low temperature air has less water holding capacity.

Q. 12. The amount of water vapour varies in atmosphere.

Ans. The amount of water vapours varies in atmosphere because the evaporation, distribution of water and distribution of temperature is not uniform all over the Earth.

Q. 13. Clear sky at night is the condition required for the fog.

Ans. During the clear sky at night, Earth's terrestrial radiation can easily pass and Earth becomes cooler near the surface. This process let the loss of heat and condensation near the surface.

Q. 14. Convectional rainfall is also called as 4'clock rainfall.

Ans. Conventional rainfall is related to high rate of evaporation. At mid day, the sun rays are at highest position and after that condensation takes place and rainfall generally occurs at 4'clock daily.

Q. 15. Dew occurs commonly during winter season.

Ans. Dew occurs commonly during winter season because in winters the relative humidity rises and as it reached 100%, the excess water vapour condenses on the surface as dew.

Chapter 15. Pollution and Environment

Q. 1. Oil spills is one of the most dangerous of all the water pollutants.

Ans. Oil spills from tankers at sea or leaks from underground storage tank on land are very difficult to control as oil tend to spread very fast affecting a large area in a short time. It blocks sunlight and reduce the amount of oxygen in the water resulting into the death of marine organism, which results in the destruction of the ecosystem.

Q. 2. Give reasons how CFC affect the environment and human life in general.

Ans. CFC (Chloro Floro Carbons) are released in the environment from air conditioning systems and refrigeration system. The CFC molecules react with ozone. It causes depletion of ozone. It creates a very serious problems for human being as it shields the Earth from the harmful ultraviolet rays radiated by the Sun.

Q. 3. Noise Pollution is injurious to health.

Ans. It is defined as regular exposure to elevated sound levels that may lead to adverse effects on human or other organisms. It is the unpleasant noise created by people or machine that can be annoying, distracting and physically painful. It interferes with the normal activities such as sleeping or disrupts once quality of life. It also has adverse effect on cardiovascular system.

Q. 4. Car Pooling is a ecofriendly approach.

Ans. Car Pooling is also known as car sharing. This eco-friendly approach reduces fuel consumption there by reducing the pollution as well as reduces individual cost of travel. It also reduces emission of carbon dioxide, traffic congestion on the reads and helps Muncipal Corporation in better car parking management.

Q. 5. Solar energy is a non polluting source of energy.

Ans. It is the most important source of energy which can be generated or converted in to electricity without causing any pollution. Countries like India, pakistan Bangladesh can generate solar energy in abundance due to presence of sunny weather all through out the year. It can be used in cooking, water heating, lighting and can be supplied to power grid for transmission.

Q. 6. Radioactive radiation effect human health. Comment.

Ans. (i) The exposure to high amount of radiation generates serious and cronic disease such as cancer which is most common radiation induced disease.

(ii) It causes genetic disorders which may carry on year after year for generations.

(iii) It also causes thyroid tumor due to the accumulation of radioactive iodine in the thyroid gland.

Q. 7. Give a reason for each of the following: **[February, 2020]**

(i) Vehicles are the main source of air pollution.

(ii) The use of CFCs is the main cause of the depletion of the ozone layer.

Ans. (i) Vehicles which run on fossil fuels releases harmful gases like carbon monoxide, carbon dioxide, unburnt hydro carbons, etc. These pollutants help in the formation of secondary air pollutants. So, that is why vehicles are the main source of air pollution.

(ii) Chlorofluorocarbons are light in weight and are organic chemicals. CFC's can reach upto stratosphere easily because of this CFC's are the main cause of greenhouse effect which further deplete the ozone layer in stratosphere.

Chapter 16. Natural Regions of the World

Q. 1. Why are the equatorial region sparsely populated?

Ans. The dense forest, inhospitable climate, fear of diseases like malaria, yellow fever and sleeping sickness makes the area unsuitable for settlement.

Q. 2. Tropical grassland make excellent game park.

Ans. Tropical grasslands are the natural habitat of numerous carnivorous and herbivorous animals. There are large number of reptiles in the rivers also. So the grasslands are known as game park.

Q. 3. Savanna is know as the natural cattle country.

Ans. Many of the native people are herdsmen or pastoralists as agriculture is not possible due to non-availability water for irrigation.

Q. 4. The commercial exploitation of the equatorial rain forest is very difficult.

Ans. Trees found in the rainforest are the mixed stands some varieties of trees rot is water. So having them by floating for commercial forestry is not a viable proposition.

Q. 5. Deforestation is a matter of major concern in the region of rain forest.

Ans. Due to shifting agriculture and mining, the world has already lost half of its original cover of forest. Each day mearly seventy species are being lost. The other reason is plantation agriculture, large forest area has been cleared for it.

Q. 6. The winds are cold and dry is winter and moisture laden in winter.

Ans. During winter. Northeasterly wind blow which results in high pressure conditions, Clear sky, low temperature and no rain. During summer South West wind blow across the ocean and sea, picking up moisture and brings rain. So summers are hot and wet and winter are cold and dry.

Q. 7. Monsoon lands are the most populated climatic zone on the earth.

Ans. Monsoon lands are the world's best rice growing regions for thousand years, provide employment to large number of people so it is the most populated region.

Q. 8. The trade wind belt over the tropical monsoon region shifts with the seasonal migration of the sun rays.

Ans. Due to the aperant migration of the Sun the pressure belts and the wind belts shifts north and the south of the equator.

Q. 9. Why the diurnal range of temperature is more than the annual range of temperature in the hot desert.

Ans. Absence of clouds causes temperture to rise up to 49° C during the day and radiation is rapid at night, so the temperature may fall between 15° C to 5° C. Thus the diurnal range is higher than the annual range of temperature.

Q. 10. The tropical hot deserts occur in sub-tropical high-pressure areas.

Ans. In the area of sub-tropical high pressure belt subsidence of vertical air currents and inversion of temperature prevent the occurrence of rainfall which results in the formation of deserts.

Q. 11. Mediterranean region gets winter rain.

Ans. Due to shifting of the pressure belts, the region come under the influence of westerlies. On shore westerly winds blow in the winter bringing rain.

Q. 12. Tourism is a industry in Mediterranean region.

Ans. Due to pleasant climate, and the presence of relice of the past, tourism industry is well established.

Q. 13. The extent of China type of climate is greater in the Northern Hemisphere.

Ans. The continents are narrower in the Southern Hemisphere. So the extent of this climatic type is greater in the Northern Hemisphere.

Q. 14. The Nothern Hemisphere is hit by the severe temperate cyclone.

Ans. A shift of the pressure belts in winter in the Northern Hemisphere places these areas under the influence of temperature cyclones. Warm air blows from the south, and cold air from the north creates an anti-clock-wise cyclonic circulation which ultimately develop into a temperate cyclone.

Q. 15. 'The temperate grasslands are essentially tree less.

Ans. The climatic region receives very low rainfall between 25 cm to 70 cm annually. So the vegetation is only grass.

Q. 16. "The trees are cone shaped with needle like leaves in Tiga region. Give reason.

Ans. The trees are conical shaped with needle like leaves to avoid collection of snow.

Q. 17. Tropical deserts are found on the western margins of continents. **[November, 2019]**

Ans. Tropical deserts are found on the western margins of continents because of the direction of the trade wind. The trade winds move in North Eastern and South East direction. Till the time they reach the western part of the continents they become dry and leads to the formation of deserts.

❐

Diagram Related Questions

Set 5

Chapter 1. Earth As a Planet

Q. 1. Draw a neat and labelled diagram of the water cycle.

Ans.

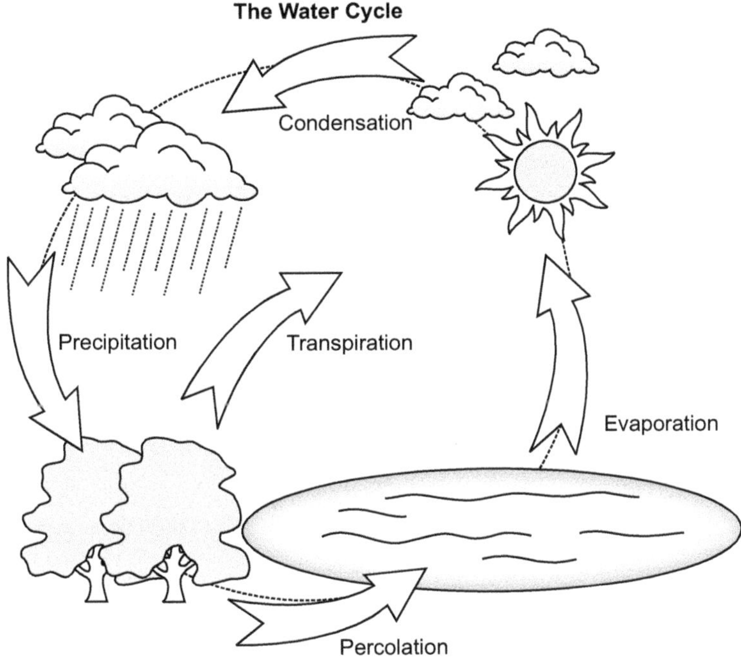

Q. 2. Draw a neat and labelled diagram of the Solar system

Ans.

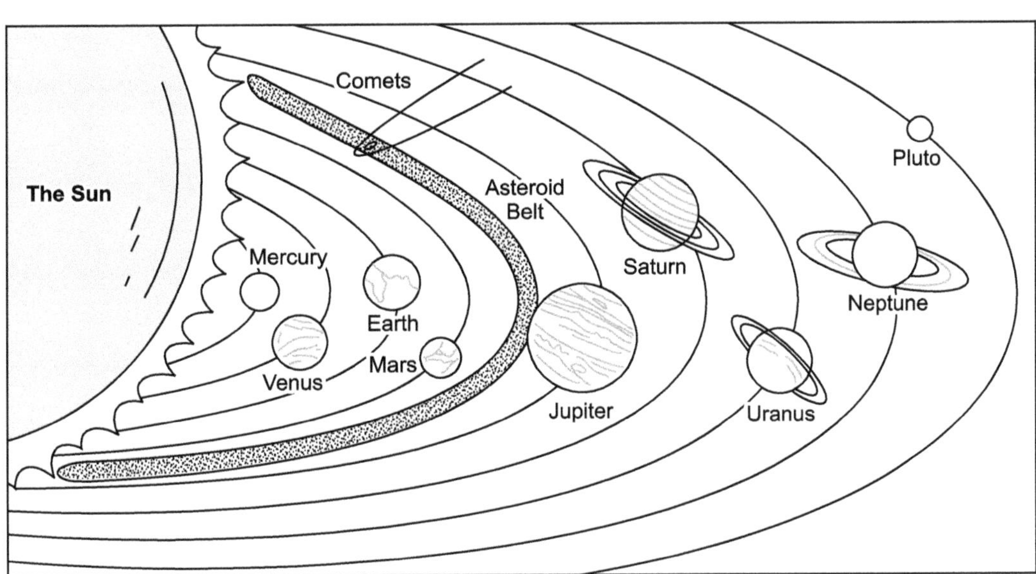

Q. 3. Look at the diagram given below and answer the questions that follow:

(a) Identify the bigger circle maked as M.

(b) Line A on Earth is not a straight line. Why and what does it signify?

(c) Earth is able to maintain fixed distance from the Sun. How?

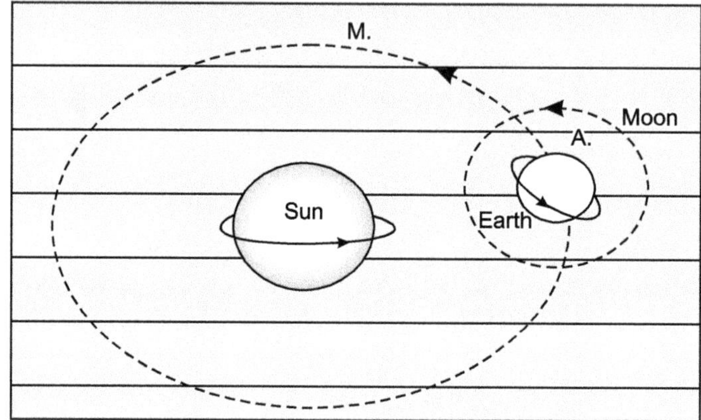

Ans. (a) The bigger circle is the imaginary path of Earth revolution.

(b) Line A is Earth's axis. It is not straight because earth is titled at a degree of 23.5°.

(c) Because Earth has its own gravitational and centrifugal force which allows the Earth to remain at a fixed distance from the Sun.

Chapter 2. Latitudes and Longitudes

Q. 1. Draw a neat and labelled diagram of the important latitudes of the Earth.

Ans.

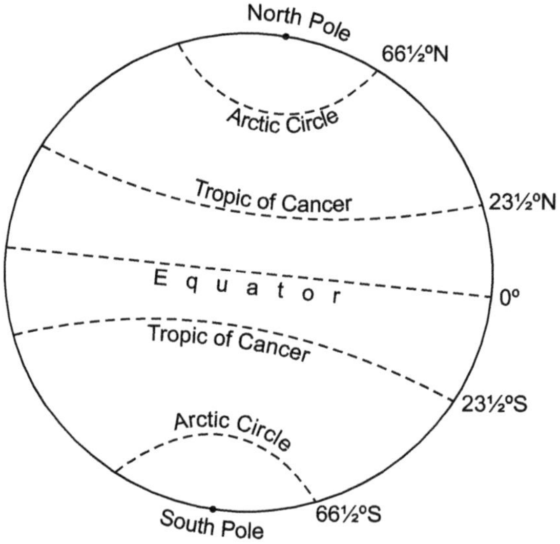

Q. 2. Draw a neat and labelled diagram of the major Heat Zones of the world.

Ans.

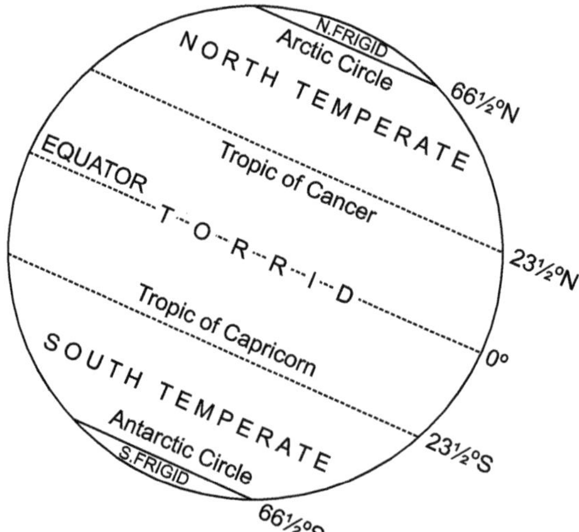

Diagram Related Questions

Q. 3. Look at the diagram given below and answer the questions that follows:

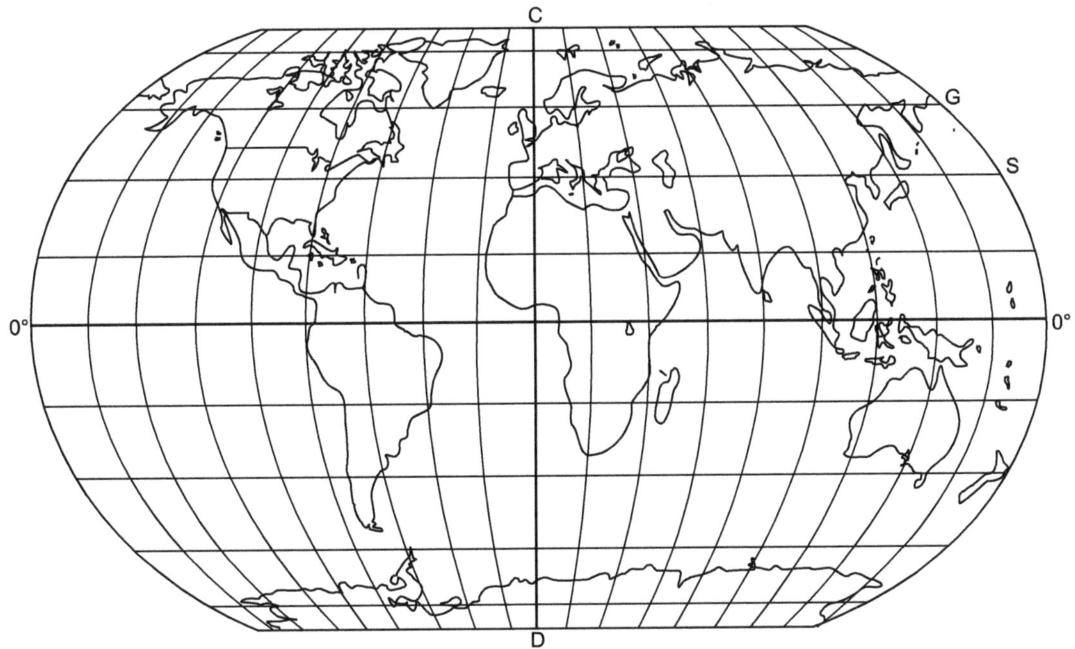

(a) Identify the line from the diagram that defines east-west location of a place on a globe.

(b) Name the two ends of the axis of the Earth marked as point C and D.

(c) Which parallel (S′ or G′) have greater length. Why this is so.

Ans. (a) 0° Longitude.

(b) Its North Pole and South Pole.

(c) Parallel 'S′ is greater in length because we know Earth is geoid in shape and as we move towards pole the size decreases.

Q. 4. Look at the diagram given below and answer the questions that follow:

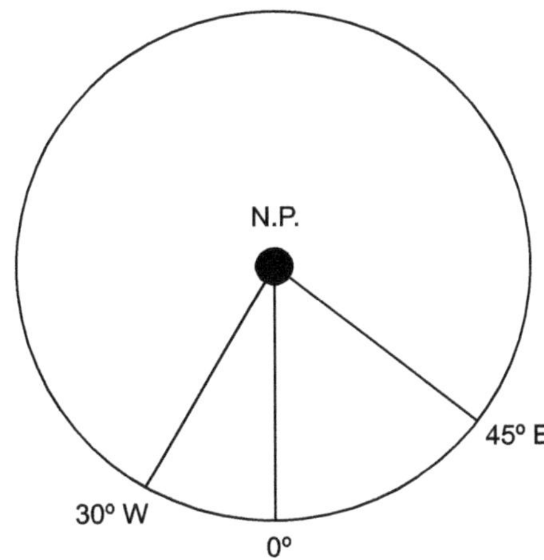

(a) Calculate the time at 45° E when the time at Johannesburg (30° W) is 2 P.M.

(b) Calculate the degree of longitude where the time is 12:00 noon.

Ans. (a) Difference in longitude: 30° W – 45° E = 75°

Difference in time = 75 × 4 = 300 minutes or 5 hours.

Local time at 45° E = 2:00 p.m. + 5 hours = 7:00 p.m.

(b) Time at 30° W is 2 p.m.

2:00 p.m. – 12:00 noon = 2 hours or 120 minutes

Longitude difference = 120/4 = 30 degree.

Thus 30 degree + 30 degree = the place where time is 12:00 noon is 60° W.

Q. 5. Study the diagram given below and answer the questions: **[November, 2019]**

(i) Calculate the time at Q when it is 7 a.m. at A.

(ii) What does IDL stand for?

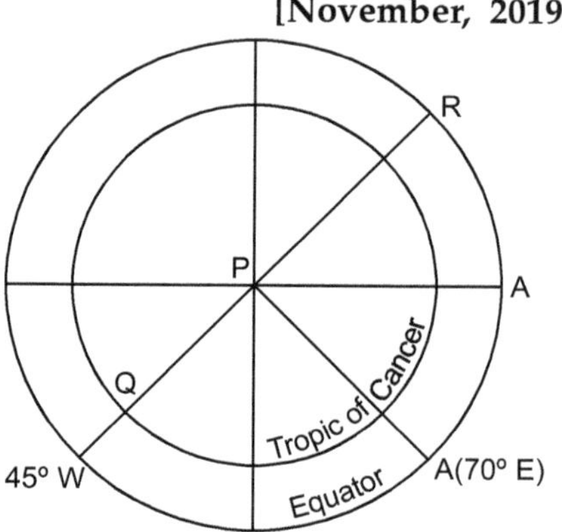

Ans. (i) Longitude difference: 115°

1° degree: 4 minutes

115° degree: 4 × 115 = 460 minutes

45° degree is in the west, thus time will be subtracted from 7:00 am (70° degree East)

Thus, the time at point Q would be 11:20 p.m.

(ii) IDL stands for International Date Line. This line is also called as 180° East or west longitude. This line counts 12 hours difference from GMT from both the sides.

Chapter 3. Rotation and Revolution

Q. 1. Draw a neat and labelled diagram showing the revolution of the Earth.

Ans.

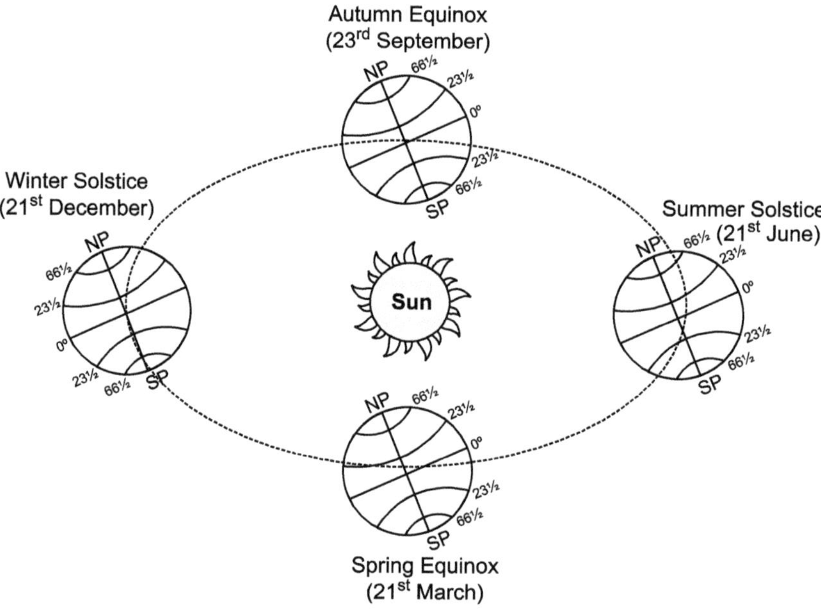

Q. 2. Draw a neat and labelled diagram showing the the process of rotation.

Ans.

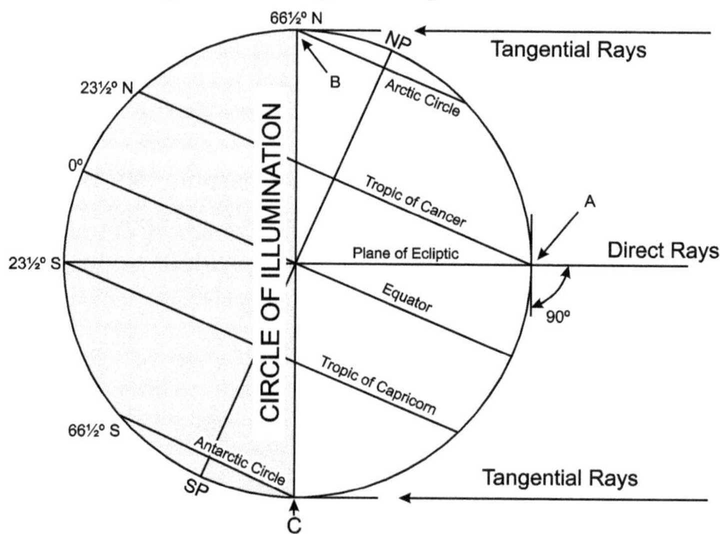

Diagram Related Questions

Q. 3. Draw a neat and labelled diagram showing the position of Aphelion and Perihelion of the Earth.

Ans.

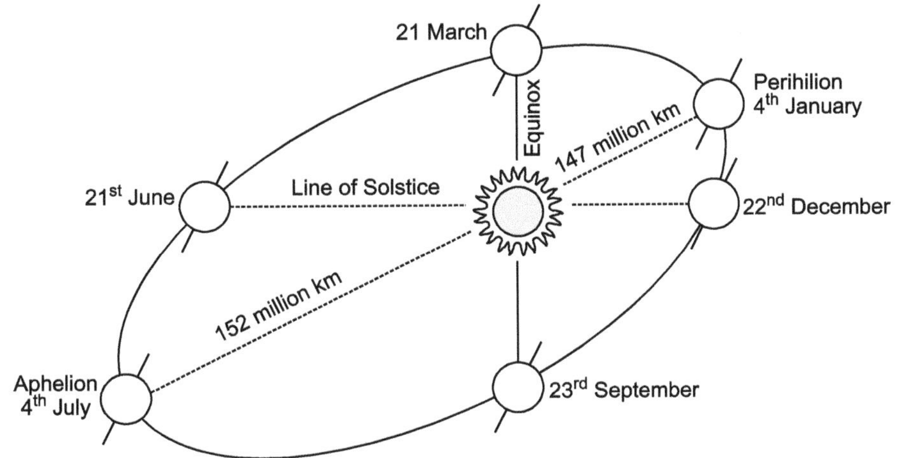

Q. 4. Draw a neat and labelled diagram showing seasons.

Ans.

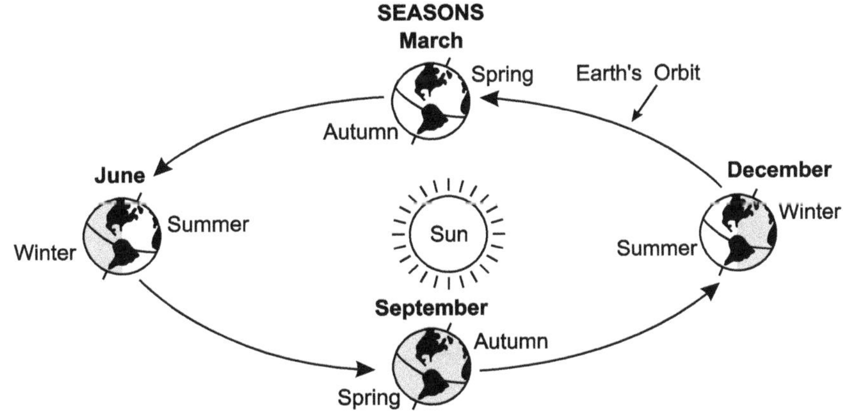

Q. 5. (a) Name the season in the Northern Hemisphere associated with picture A.

(b) Identify the movement of the earth that causes earth's position shown in picture A and B.

(c) Name the Hemisphere of the Earth that experiences summer in picture B. Why?

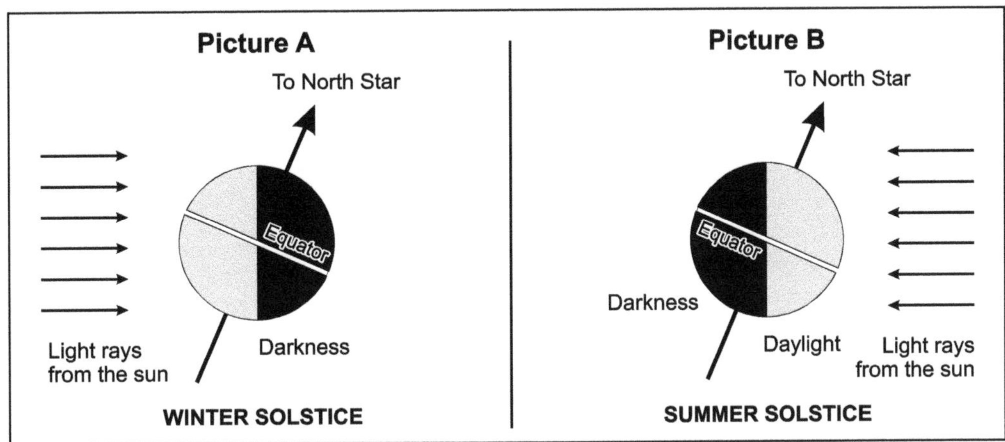

Ans. (a) Its winters in Northern Hemisphere.

(b) The revolution of Earth around the Sun.

(c) Its Northern Hemisphere because Northern Hemisphere is inclined towards the Sun and it gets vertical sun rays. Thus it experiences summer season.

Q. 6. Draw a fully labelled diagram of the position of the Earth on 22nd December.

[November, 2019]

Ans. Position of the earth during winter Solstice:

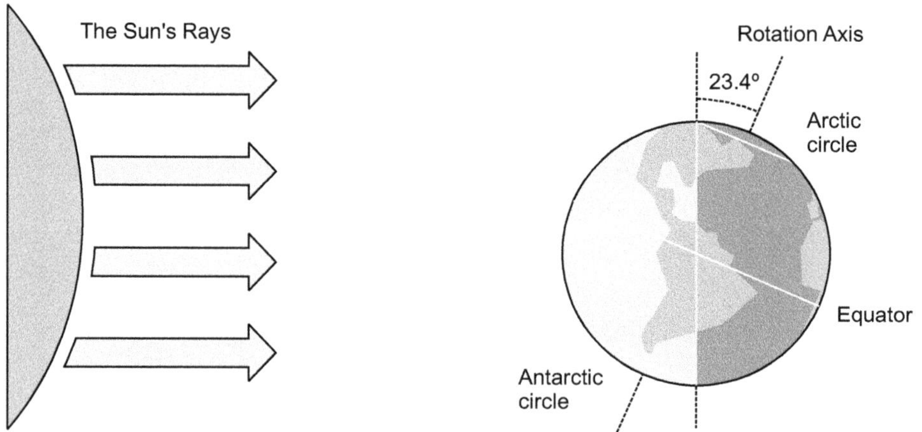

Chapter 4. Structure of the Earth and Internal Processes

Q. 1. Draw a neat and labelled diagram showing the interior of the earth.

Ans.

INTERIOR OF THE EARTH

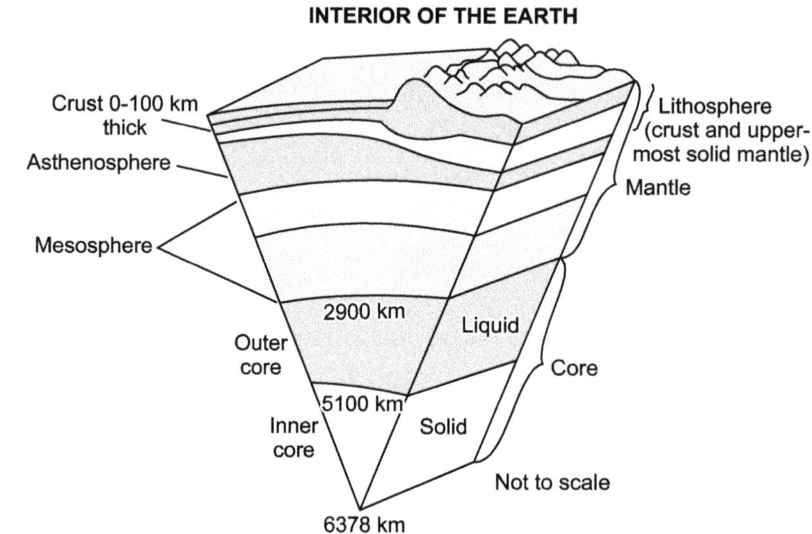

Q. 2. Draw a neat and labelled diagram showing the types of plate movement.

Ans.

TYPES OF PLATE MOVEMENT

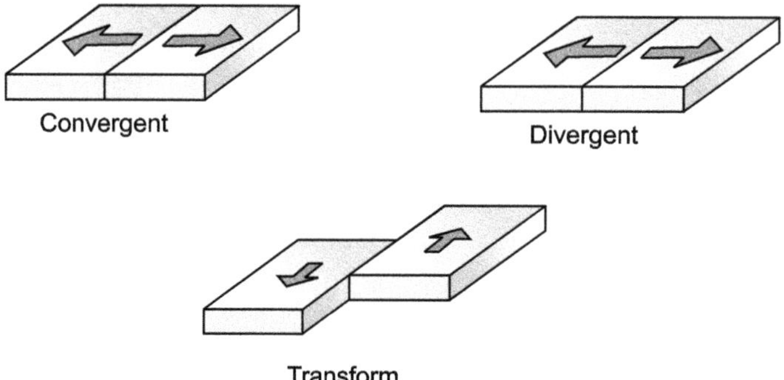

Q. 3. (a) Name the layer which supports growth of vegetation and How?

(b) Whether the layer E or F is in molten state. Given reason to your answer.

(c) Which layer out of four experiences highest temperature and Why?

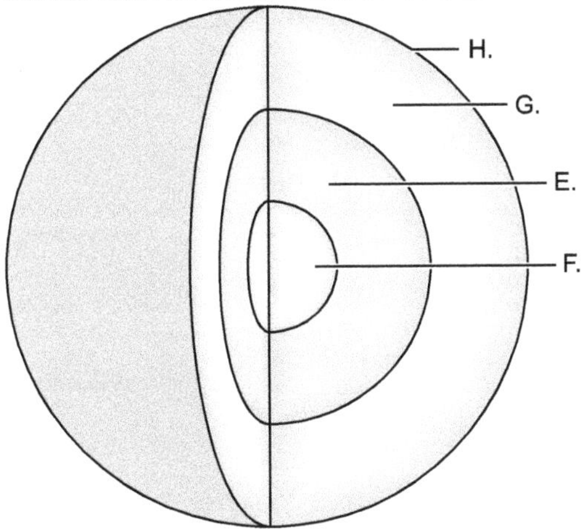

Ans. (a) Layer H or crust supports growth of vegetation, because its uppermost division (soil) is formed due to disintegration of rocks and it contains organic material, rock particles and minerals.

(b) Layer E and F is in molten form because of intense heat and pressure.

(c) Layer F experiences highest temperature because it is the deepest layer and due to extreme pressure of all the above layers, the temperature increases.

Chapter 5. Landforms of the Earth

Q. 1. Draw a neat and labelled diagram of the formation of Block Mountains.

Ans.

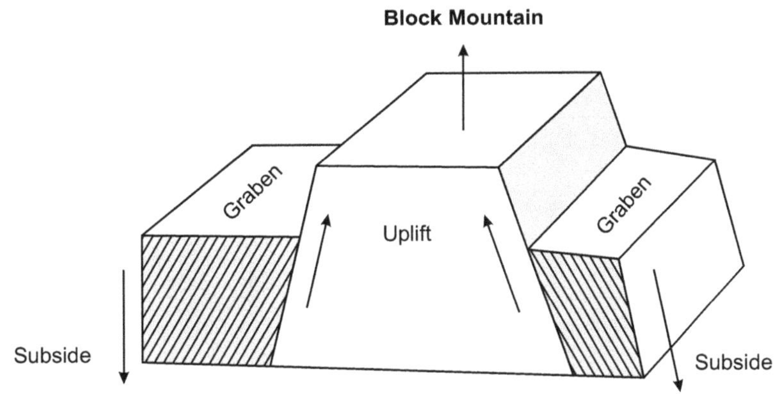

Formation of Block Mountains

Q. 2. Draw a neat and labelled diagram of the formation of volcanic mountains.

Ans.

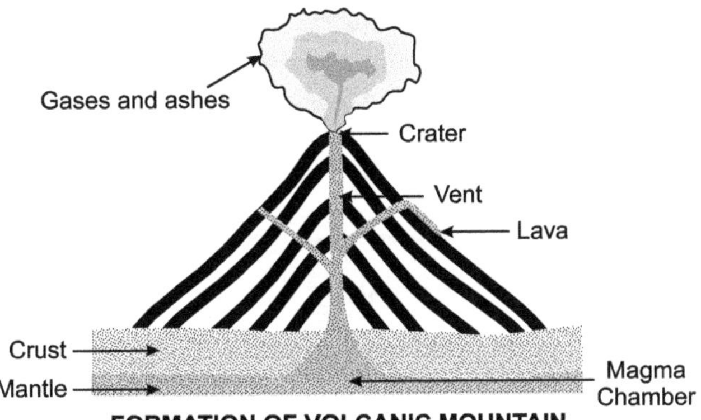

FORMATION OF VOLCANIC MOUNTAIN

Q. 3. (a) Whether movement A or B is the reason behind formation of Himalayan Mountains. Give reason.

(b) Name the types of mountain formed due to movment B.

(c) Name the movement out of three which does not contract or destruct the crust but develops cracks.

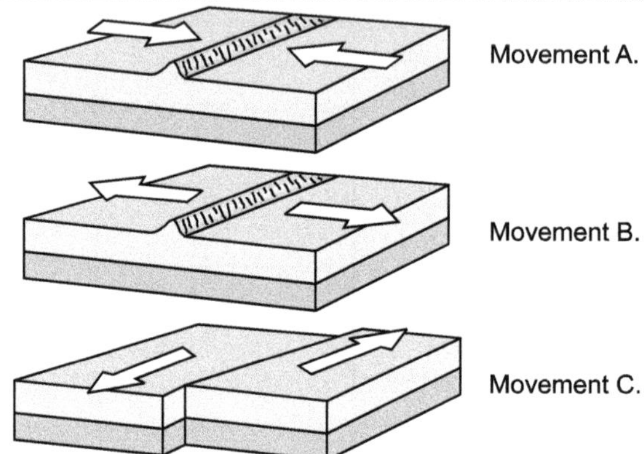

Ans. (a) Movement A or convergence movement is the reason behind formation of Himalayan mountains because Himalayas were formed due to convergence of Indo-Australian and Eurasian tectonic plate.

(b) Tectonic Movement B forms Block Mountains.

(c) Movement C or Transform movement.

Chapter 6. Rocks

Q. 1. Draw a neat and labelled diagram showing the rock cycle.

Ans.

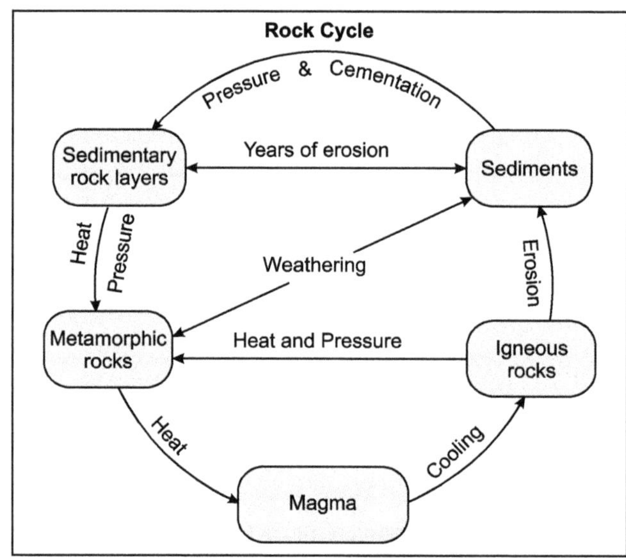

Q. 2. (a) Whether Rock type A or C. is igneous rock. Give reasons.

(b) Whether rock type B or C is metamorphic rock. Give reason.

(c) Name the natural actions behind formation of sedimentary rock.

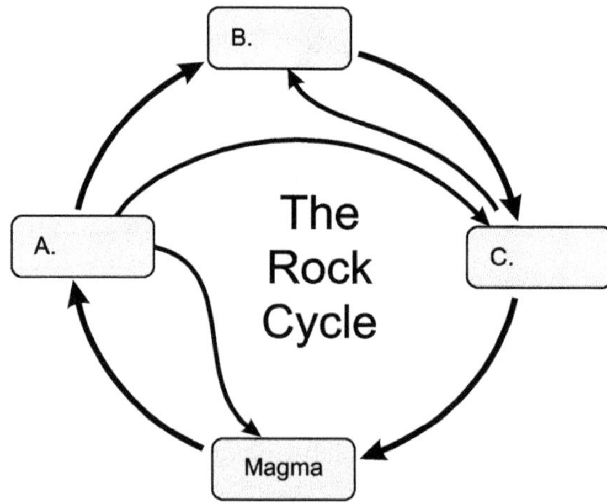

Ans. (a) Rock type A is igneous rock because it is the primary rock and is formed at the first stage after the eruption of magma.

(b) Rock type B is metamorphic rock. Metamorphic rocks are formed due to change in heat and pressure from igneous rocks.

(c) Sedimentary rocks are formed due to erosion, transportation and deposition.

Chapter 7. Volcanoes

Q. 1. Draw a neat and labelled diagram Shield volcano.

Ans.

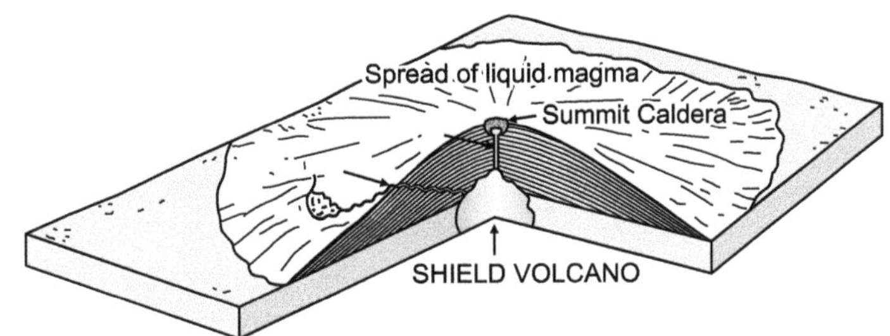

Q. 2. Draw a neat and labelled diagram and show dyke, sill, and crater.

Ans.

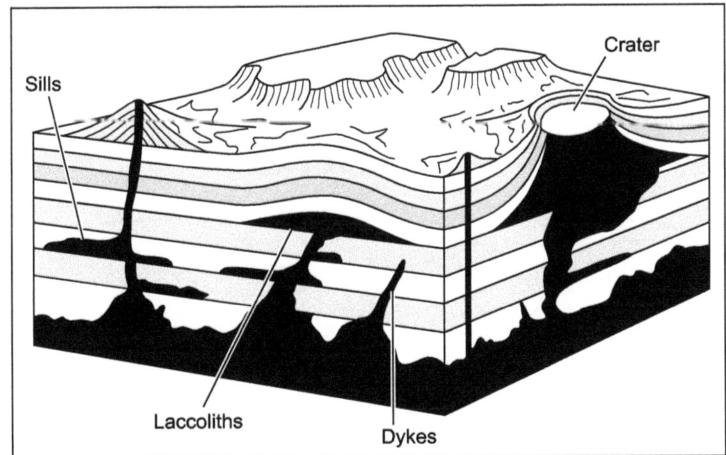

Q. 3. (a) Whether point A or B is called a vent. Give reason.

(b) Whether point E or D is a Conduit. Give reason.

(c) Identify the landform marked as C. Mention its one function.

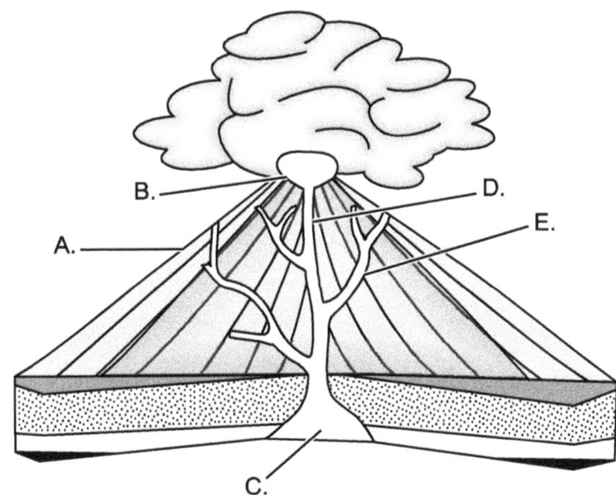

Ans. (a) Point B is vent because it is an opening for lava to come out of surface.

(b) Point D is a conduit or man pipe because it leads to crater and E is a branch pipe.

(c) Landform marked as C is Magma reservoir. It is the store house of magma which later on pushed upward to come out of surface.

Q. 4. Draw a labelled diagram of the structure of a volcano. **[Annual Examination, 2020]**

Ans. The diagram of structure of volcano:

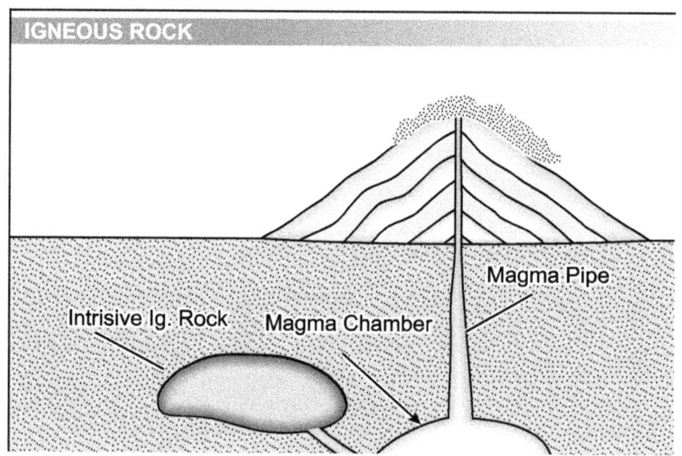

(ii) Two positive impacts of volcanoes are:

1. The volcanoes successfully bring out the minerals from the interior of the Earth to the surface.
2. Volcanoes also help in the study of interior of Earth through pyroclastic material.

Chapter 8. Earthquakes

Q. 1. 1. Draw neat and labelled diagram of seismic waves:

Ans.

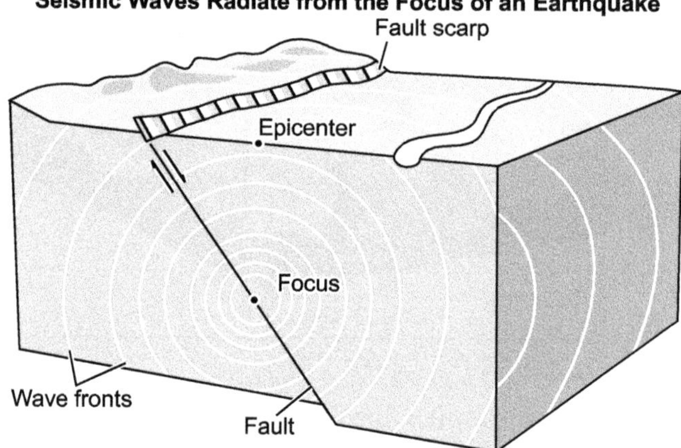

Q. 2. Study the diagram given below and answer the questions that follow :

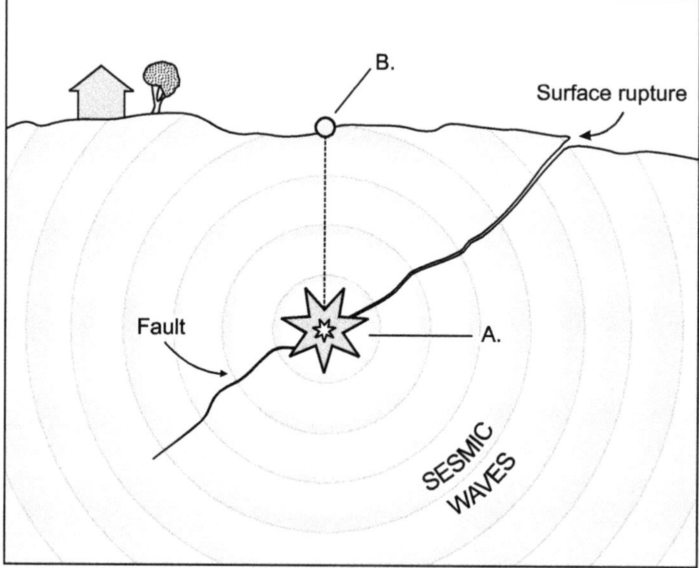

(i) Write whether point A or B is the origin point of earthquake.

(ii) Give reason to support your answer.

Ans. (i) Point A in the diagram is the origin point (focus or hypocenter) of the earthquake.

(ii) This point lies on fault line. Moreover, the intensity of the seismic waves is high around this point and travelling away from this point.

Q. 3. Draw a well labelled diagram of earthquake shadow zone.

Ans.

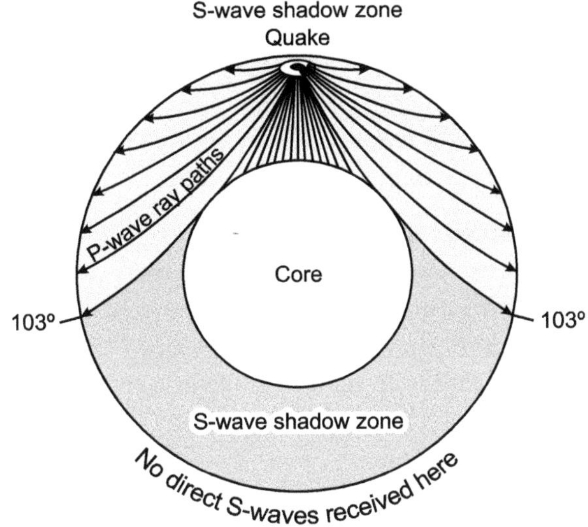

Chapter 9. Weathering

Q. 1. Draw diagram of river meander.

Ans.

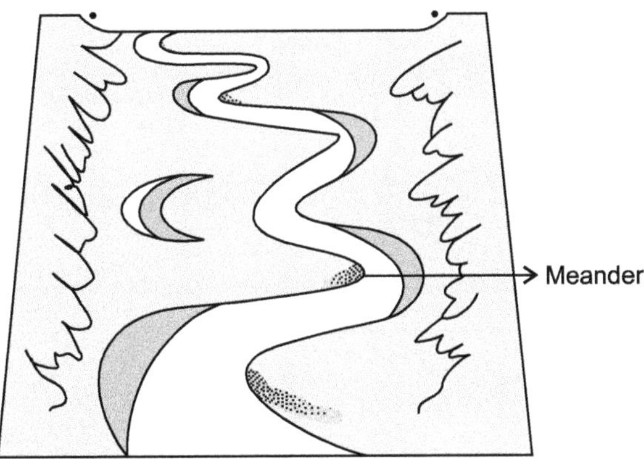

Q. 2. Draw a neat and labelled diagram of river delta.

Ans.

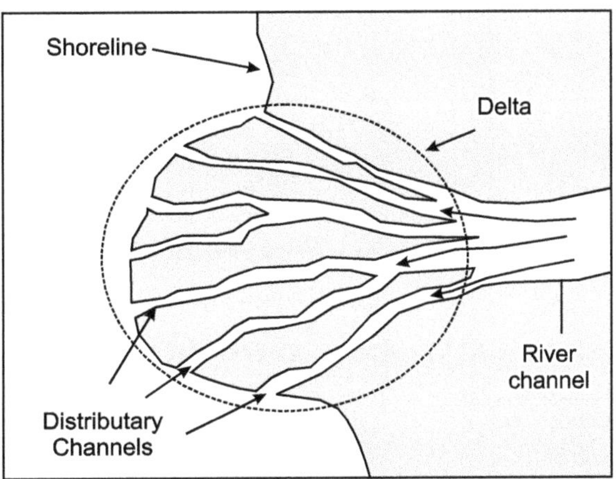

Q. 3. Study the diagram given below and answer the questions that follow:

(i) Identify the landform marked as point A and point B.
(ii) At which stage of its course, river forms this landform ?
(iii) Discuss the factors behind formation of landforms marked as point A and B.

Ans. (i) Point A is OX-bow Lake and point B is Meander loop.
(ii) This land feature is associated with mature stage of a river.
(iii) The factors are:
(a) Gradient of the land.
(b) Volume of water

Q. 4. Draw a well labelled diagram of waterfall.

Ans.

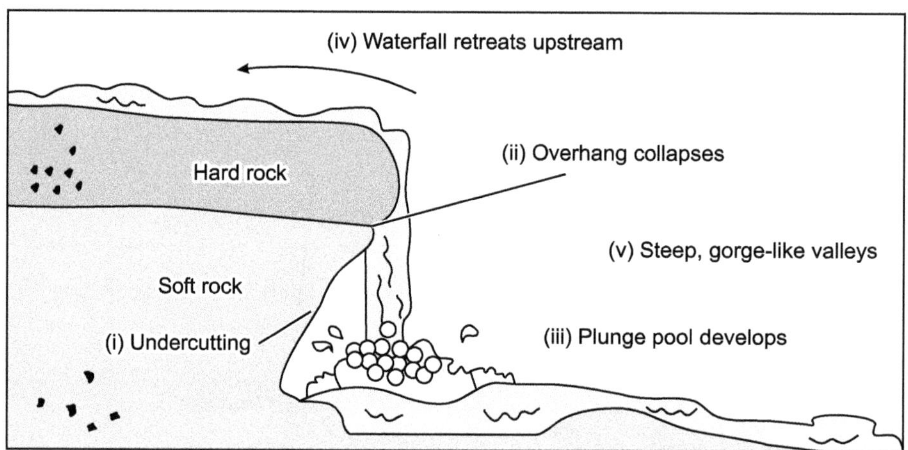

Q. 5. Draw a neat diagram of Ox-bow lake.

Ans.

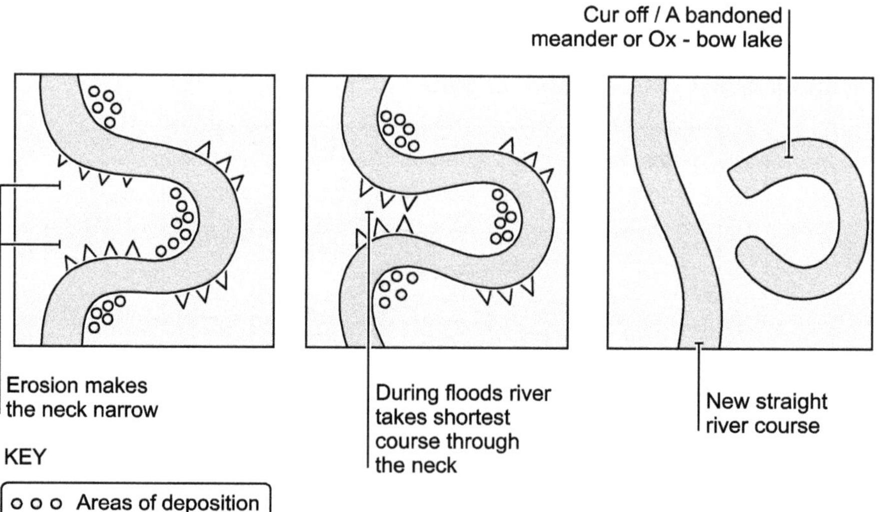

Diagram Related Questions

Q. 6. Draw a neat and labelled diagram of mushroom rock.

Ans.

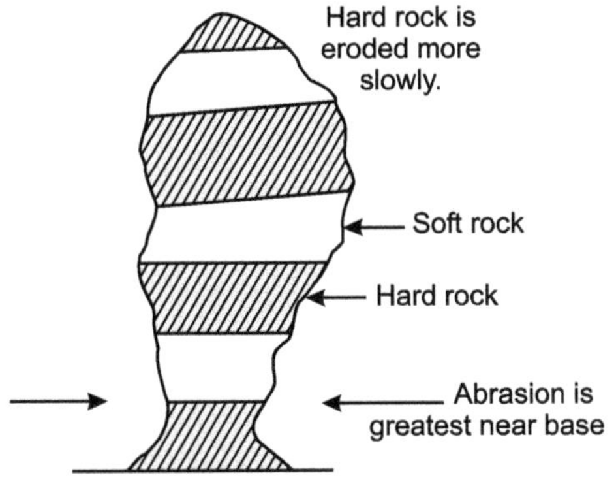

Chapter 10. Hydrosphere

Q. 1. Draw a well labelled diagram to show deflection of ocean currents in Northern Hemisphere due to coriollis effect.

Ans.

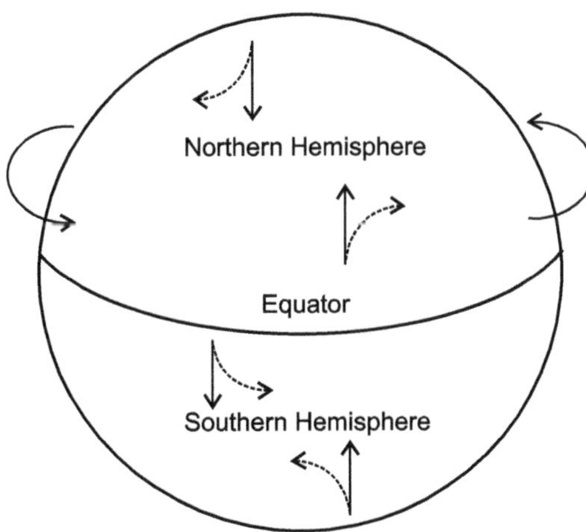

Q. 2. Draw a neat labelled diagram showing the position of the Earth during neap tide and spring tide.

Ans.

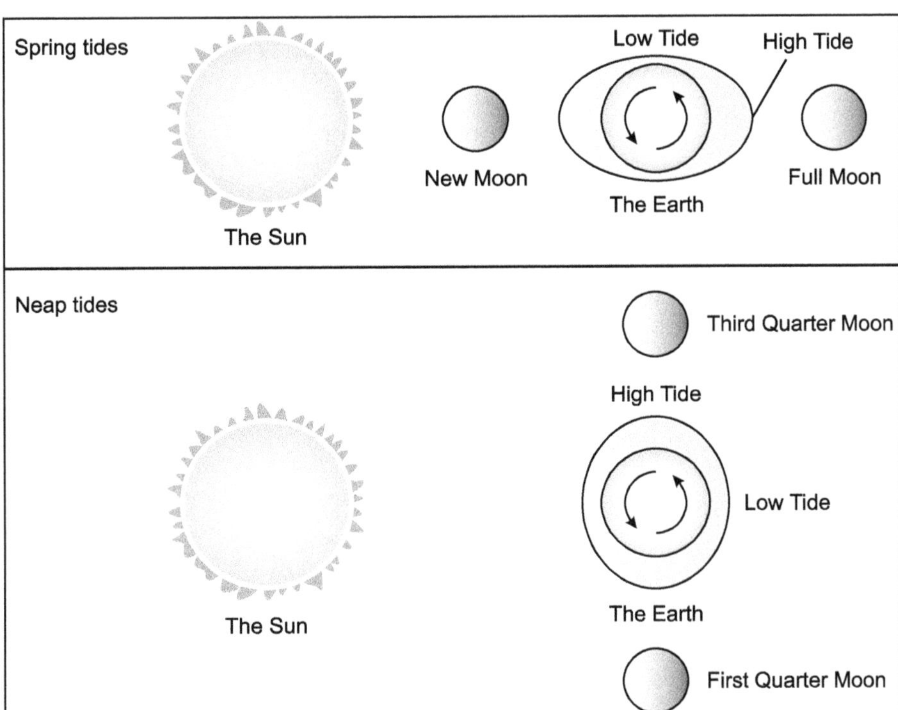

Q. 3. Draw a neat diagram of tidal range.

Ans.

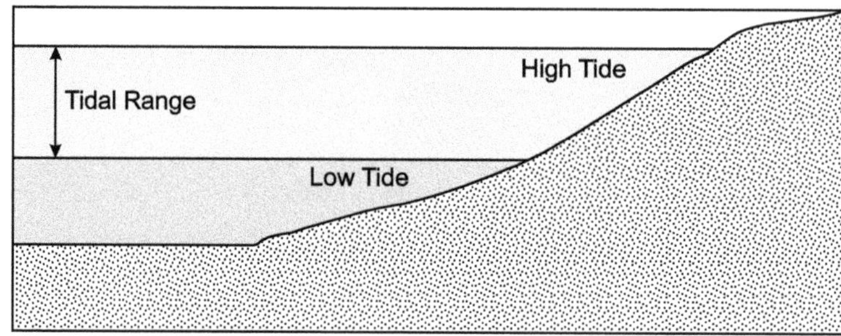

Q. 4. With the help of a pie chart, show distribution of land and water on Earth.

Ans.

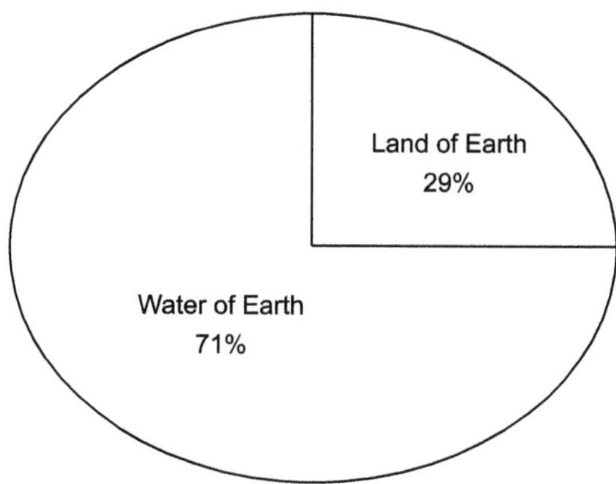

Q. 5. Draw a neat diagram to show the deflection of ocean currents in Southern Hemisphere due to coriollis effect.

Ans.

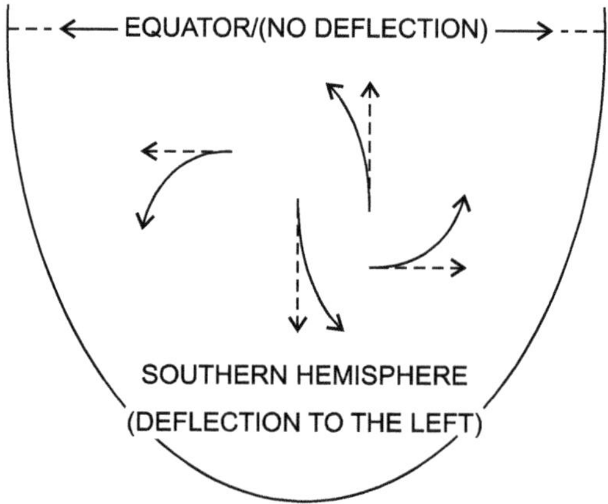

Q. 6. Study the picture given below and answer the following questions:

(i) Why do Sun, earth and moon share the different positions?

(ii) In which diagram the effect will be a high tide. Give reasons?

(iii) Which celestial body out of Sun and the moon has higher tidal producing impact on earth? Give reason.

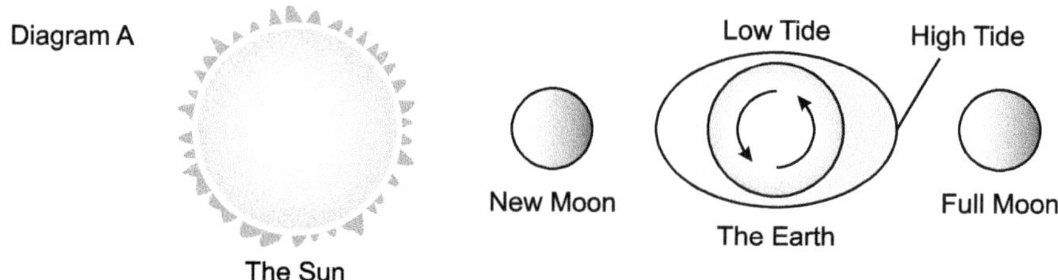

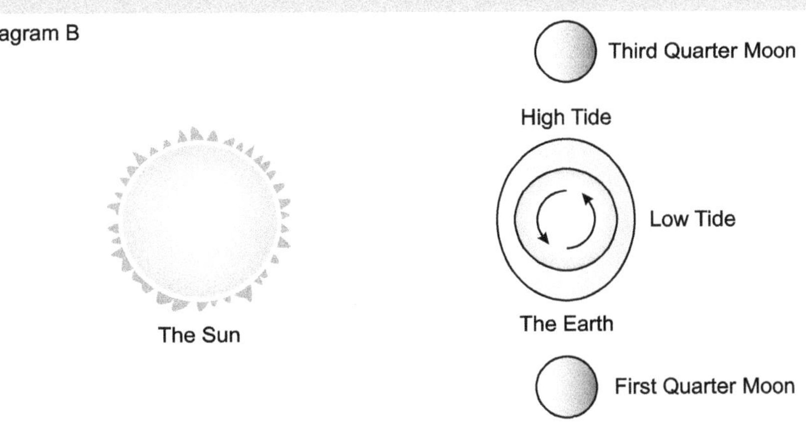

Ans. (i) This happens because of revolution of Earth and Moon.

(ii) In diagram A, because in this diagram both the Sun and the Moon pulls the Earth in a same direction. Thus higher is the gravitational pull by the Moon and the Sun results in the high tide.

(iii) Moon's tidal producting impact on the Earth is higher than the Sun. Althrough Sun is bigger than Moon but Moon is situated closer of the Earth. Thus, its impact is higher than the Sun.

Q. 7. Draw a fully labelled diagram of a Neap tide. **[November, 2019]**

Ans.

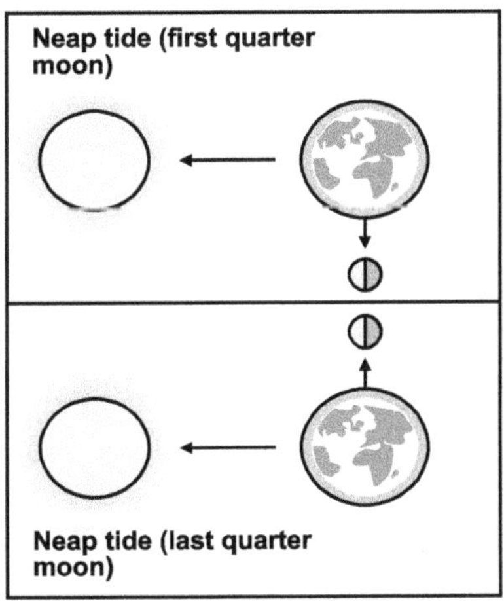

Q. 8. Draw a well labelled diagram of a spring tide. **[February, 2020]**

Ans. The diagram of Spirng Tide.

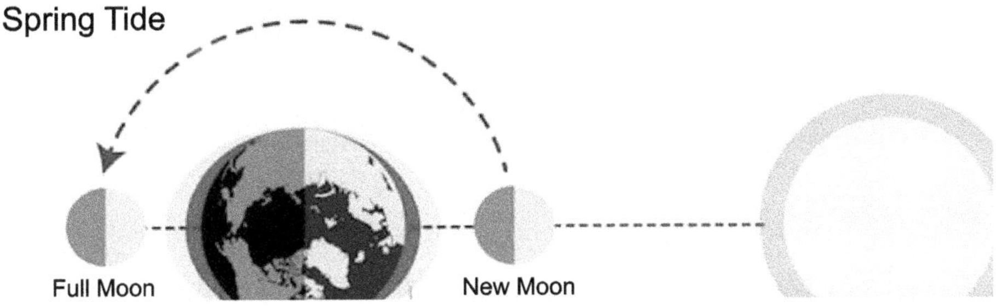

Chapter 11. Atmosphere

Q. 1. With a help of a pie chart, briefly list the composition of atmosphere.

Ans. Composition of atmosphere:

(i) Nitrogen-78%

(ii) Oxygen-20.9%

(iii) Minor gases include Argon, Carbon dioxide, Neon etc –less than 1 %

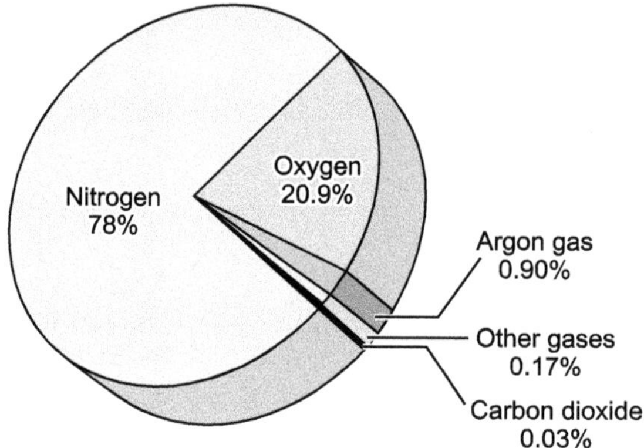

Q. 2. Draw a well labelled diagram of structure of atmosphere.

Ans.

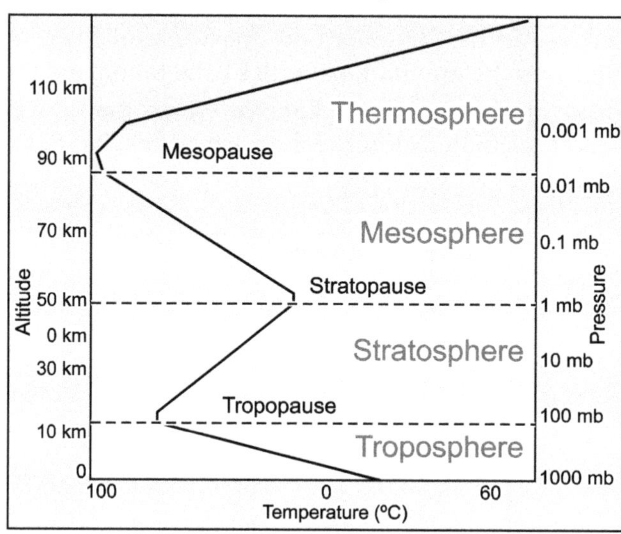

Q. 3. With the help of a diagram show the relationship between four realms of the Earth.

Ans.

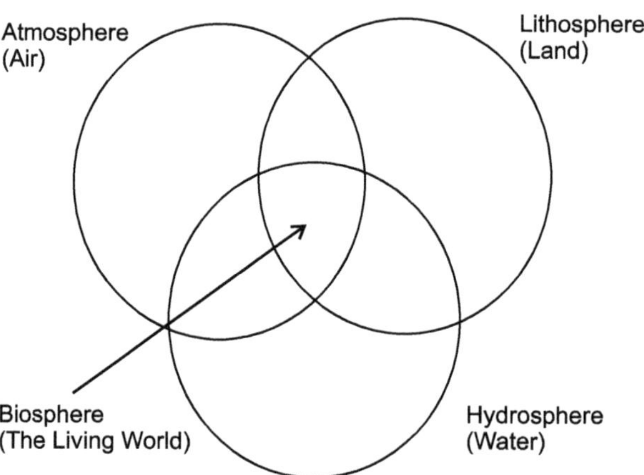

Q. 4. Draw a neat diagram of troposphere and stratosphere. Also mark the ozone layer.

Ans.

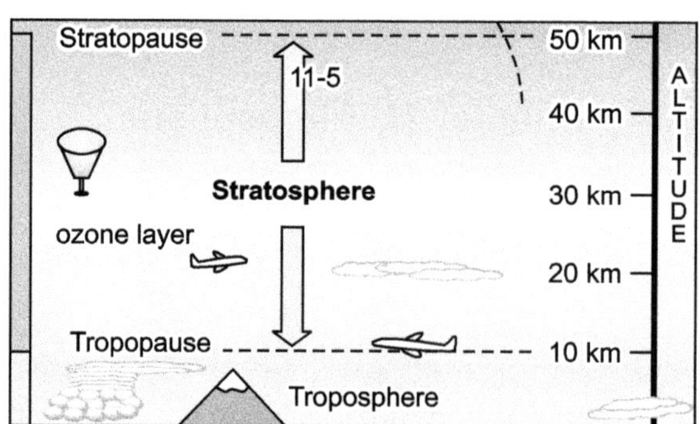

Diagram Related Questions

Q. 5. Study the picture given below and answer the following questions:

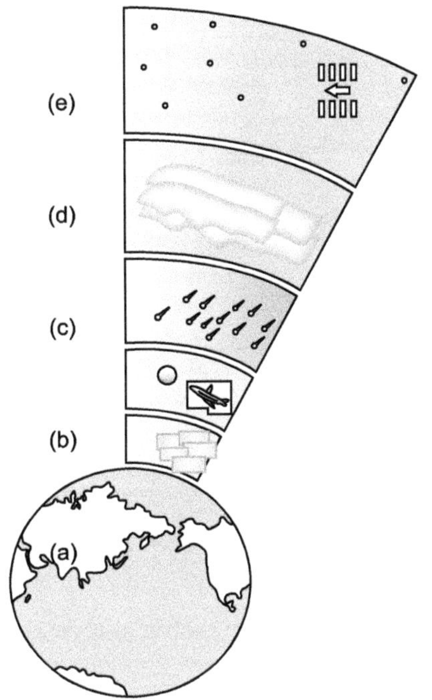

(i) Name the atmospheric layer from top to bottom.

(ii) What do the white signify in third layer? What is their function ?

(iii) In which layer aircraft fly? Give reason.

Ans. (i) (a) Exosphere (b) Thermosphere

(c) Mesosphere (d) Stratosphere

(e) Troposphere

(ii) White marks reflect presence of electrically charged ions. These ions help in radio connectivity.

(iii) Because in stratosphere there is no lapse rate, no weather phenomenons are present. Thus this atmosphere layer is highly suitable for the aircrafts of fly.

Chapter 12. Insolation

Q. 1. Draw a well labelled diagram to show heat balance on Earth.

Ans.

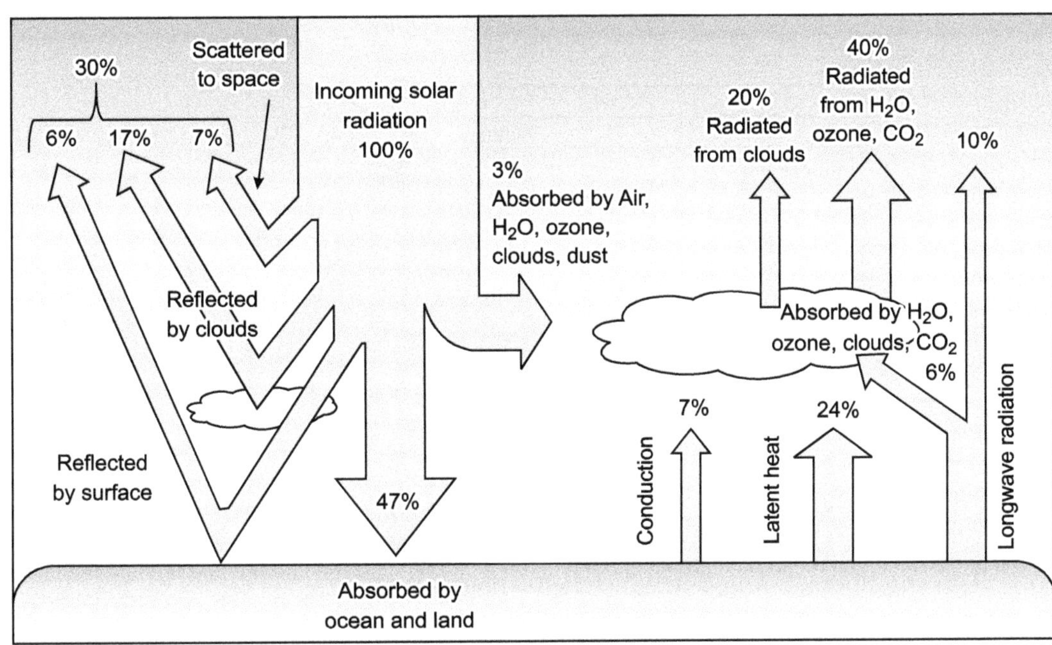

Q. 2. Draw a well labelled diagram of Heat zones of the Earth.

Ans.

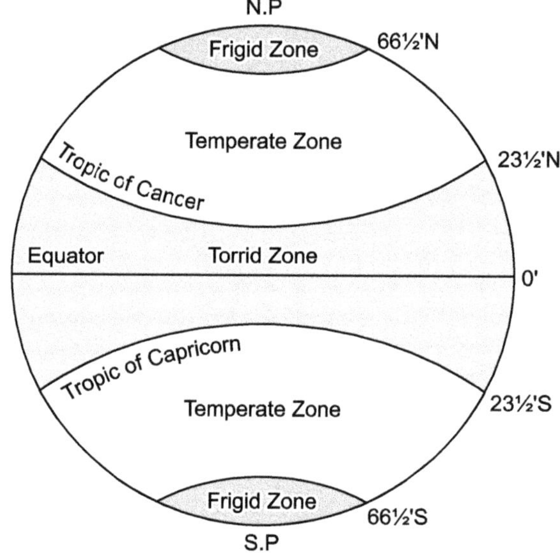

Q. 3. With the help of diagram show how the south facing slopes are warmer than north facing in Northern Hemisphere.

Ans.

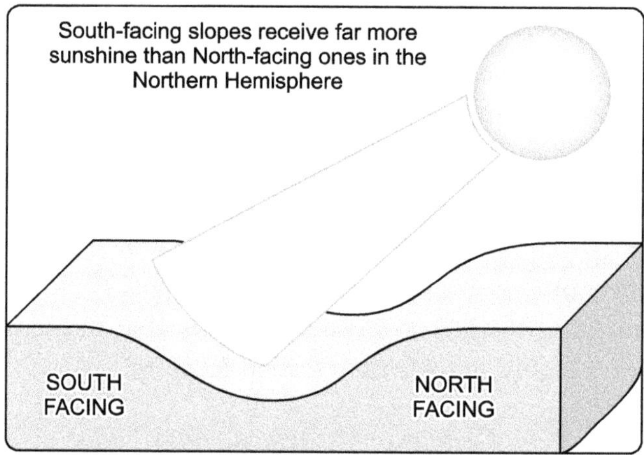

Q. 4. With the help of a neat diagram show how slanting causes less heat than vertical sun rays.

Ans.

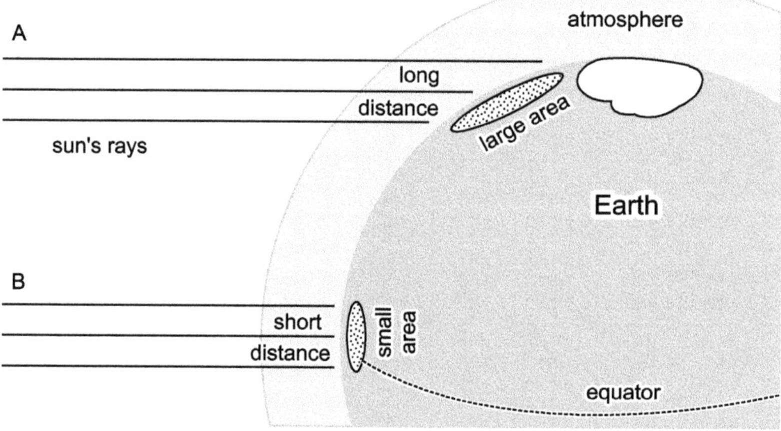

Q. 5. Study the picture given below and answer the following questions:

(i) Which slope (A or B) is warmer than the other? Why?

(ii) This conditions is found in which hemisphere. Why?

(iii) Give an example of this condition.

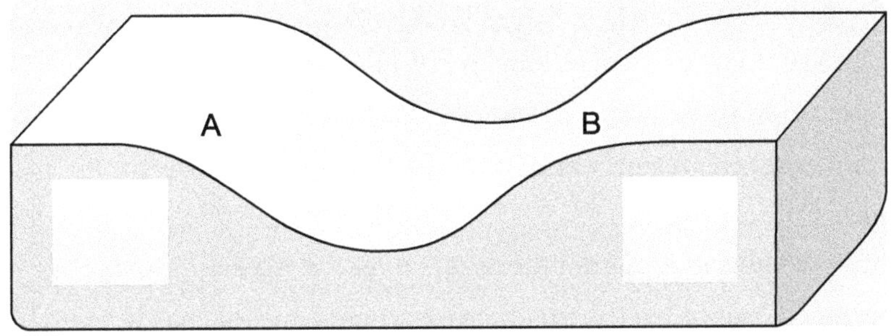

Ans. (i) Slope a is warmer than the B because the Sun rays strike on this slope and slope B is shadowed, that receives no sun rays.

(ii) This condition is found in Northern Hemisphere because Sun shine the southern slopes of mountains is exposed to sun shine at steeper angle than the northern slopes.

(iii) In India the southern slopes of Himalayas are warmer as compared to the northern slopes of Himalayas toward Tibet.

Chapter 13. Pressure Belts and Winds

Q. 1. Draw a well labelled diagram of an anticyclone in Southern Hemisphere.

Ans.

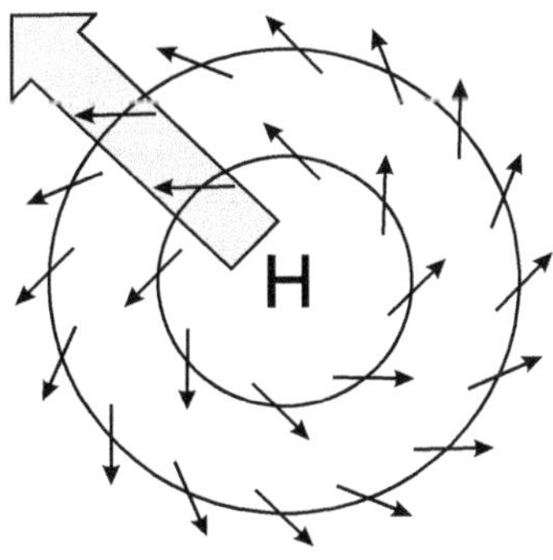

Counterclockwise outspiral

Q. 2. Study the image given below and the answer the questions that follows:

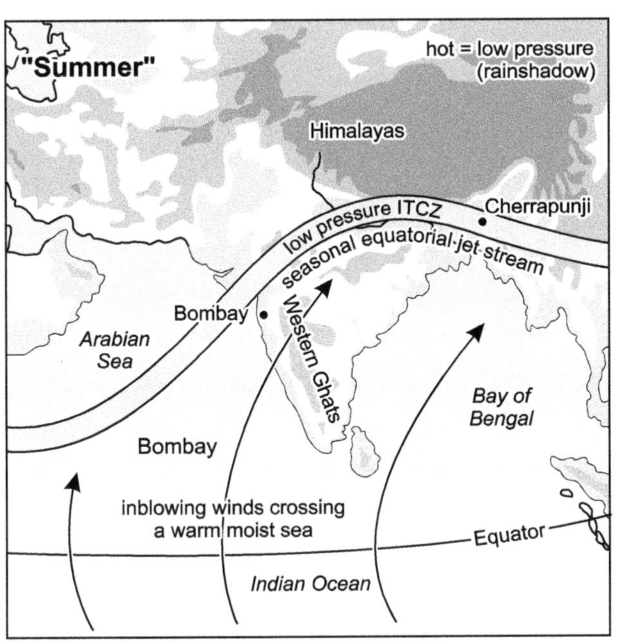

Image A

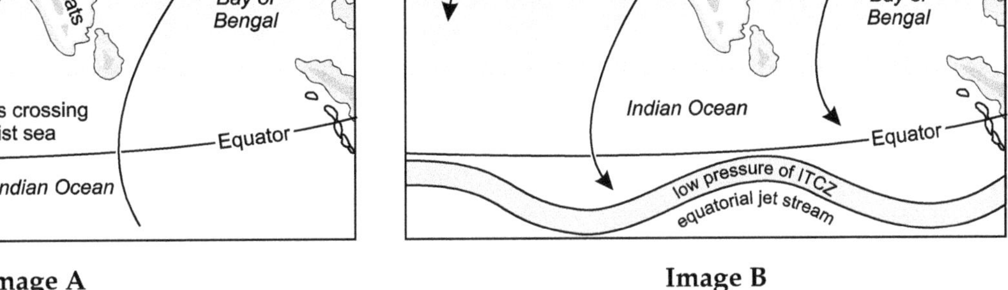

Image B

(i) Identify the direction of wind in both the images.

(ii) Why low pressure varies its positions in both the images?

(iii) In which condition India will experience more rainfall?

Ans. (i) In image A it is south-westerly and in image B it is north easterly.

(ii) It is because of the change in season. During summers the low pressure develops over the interior of the continents and in winters it develops over the oceans.

(iii) India experiences rainfall in the first picture where south-westerly wind blows. This wind moves over the ocean and carries ample moisture to rain. But in the second image the north-eastly moves over the continent and is dry in nature.

Q. 3. Study the picture given below and answer the following questions:

(i) Both the winds have opposite directions. Why this is so?

(ii) Which one of these two is helpful in bringing rainfall?

(iii) Give example of any one such variable wind.

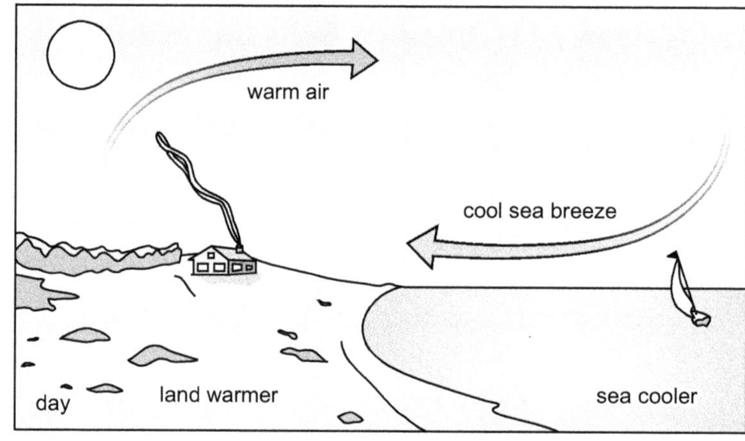

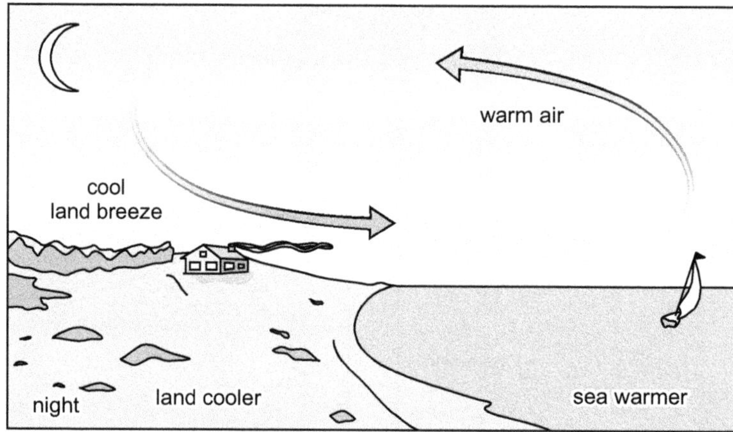

Ans. (i) Because in both the situations the pressure over land and sea varies. The wind moves from high pressure area to low pressure area. As the pressure varies, the wind changes its direction.

(ii) The wind that moves from sea to land will bring enormous rain, because while moving over the sea it will carry ample moisture and cause rain over the continents.

(iii) Monsoon wind in the south Asia is a perfect example of sea and land breeze.

Q. 4. Draw a well labelled diagram of planetary wind system showing the direction of winds.

Ans.

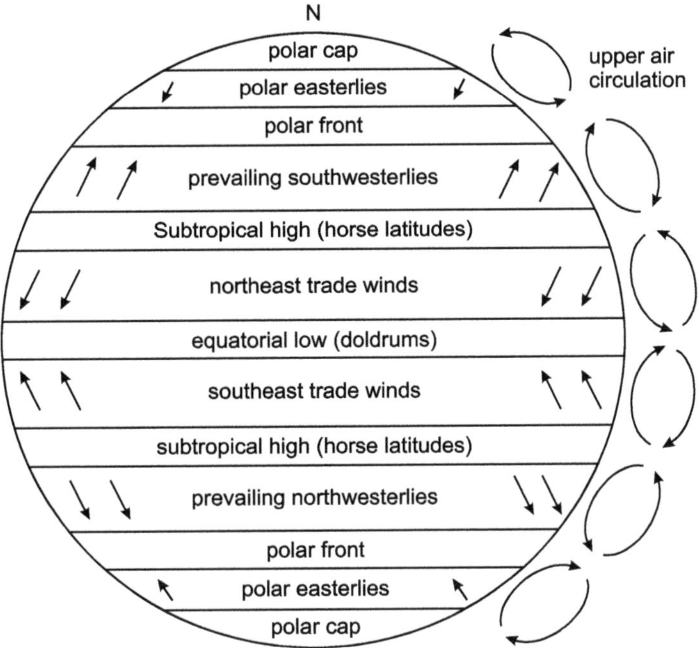

Q. 5. Draw a neat labelled diagram of major pressure belts of the world.

Ans.

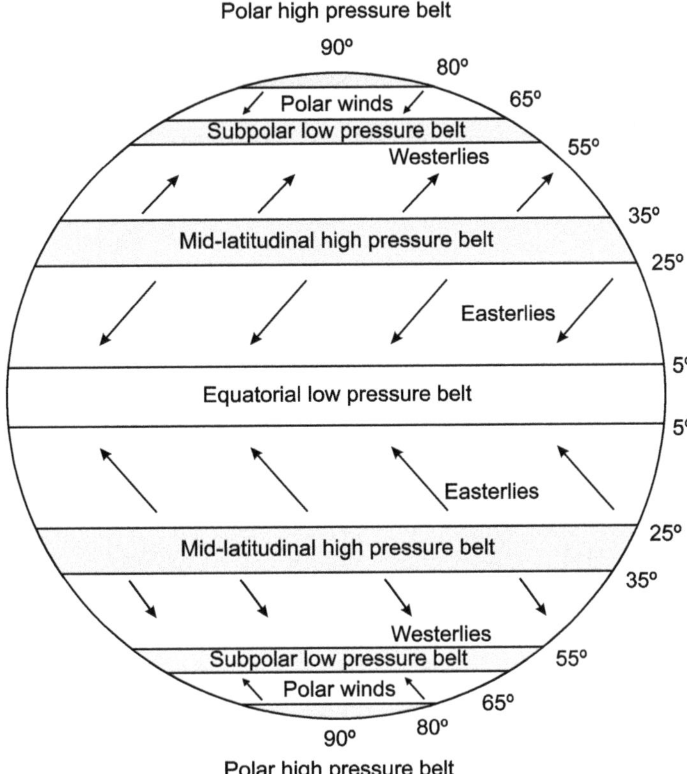

Q. 6. Draw neat and well labelled diagram of sea breeze and land breeze.

Ans.

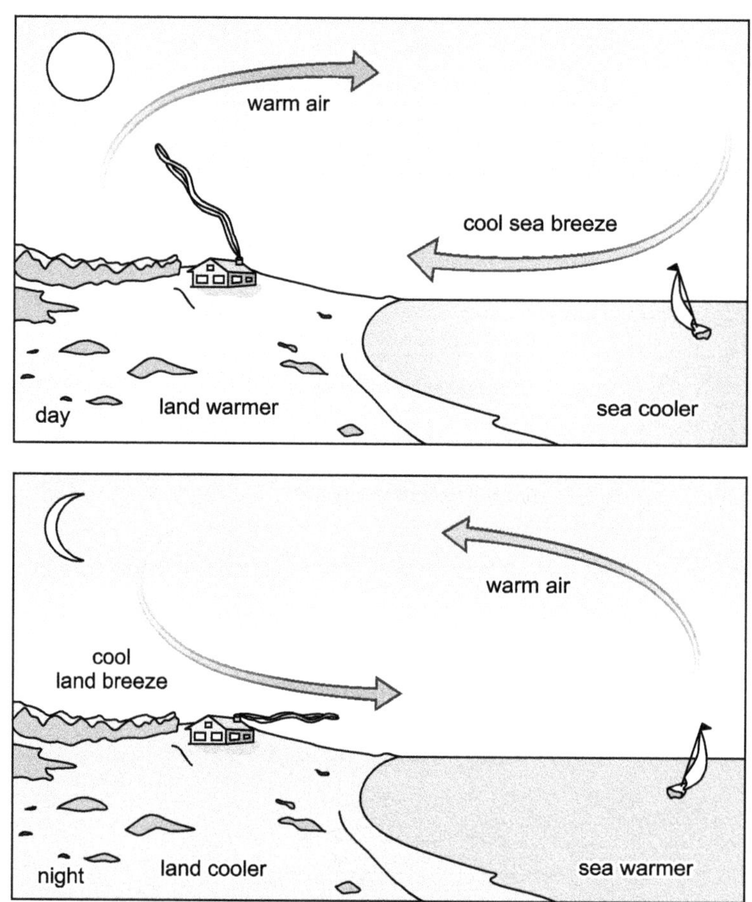

Q. 7. Draw a neat labelled diagram of cyclone and anti-cyclone to show the movement of air.

Ans.

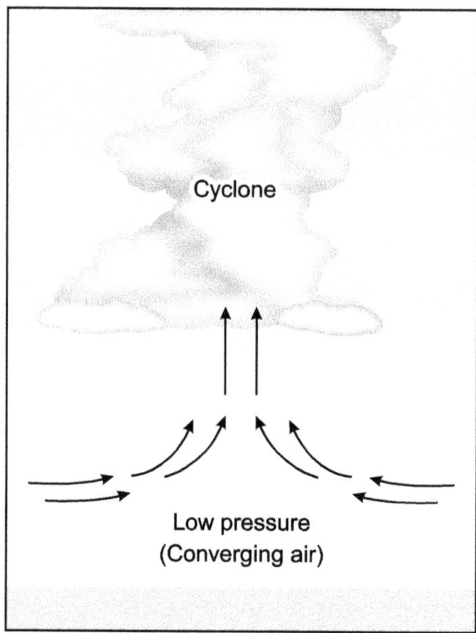

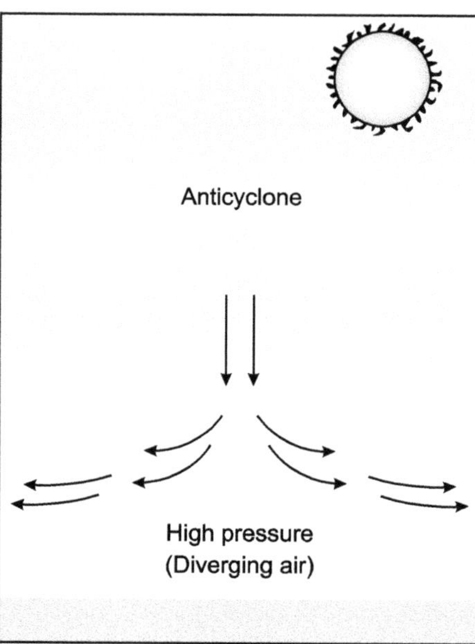

Q. 8. Draw a labelled diagram of anti-cyclone in both the hemispheres.

Ans.

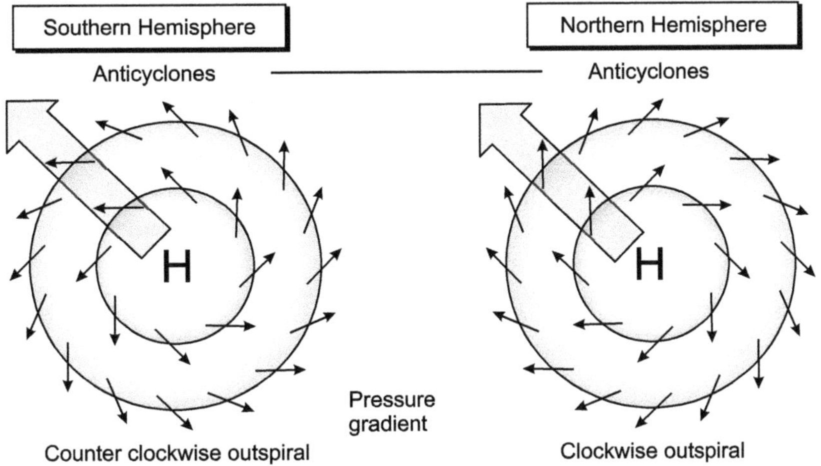

Q. 9. Draw a neat and labelled diagram of movement of trade winds in Northern and Southern Hemisphere.

Ans.

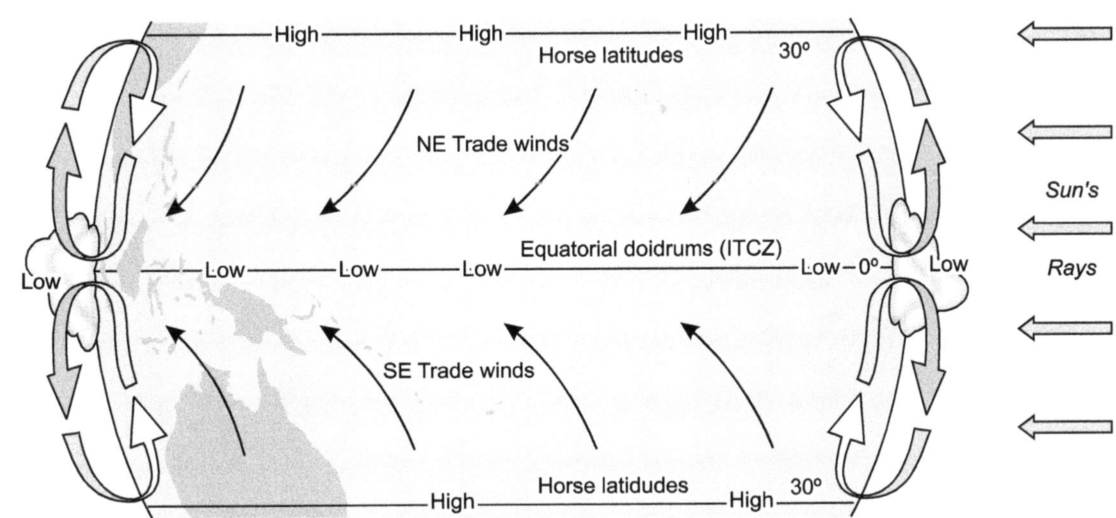

Chapter 14. Precipitation

Q. 1. Draw a diagram of frontal rainfall.

Ans.

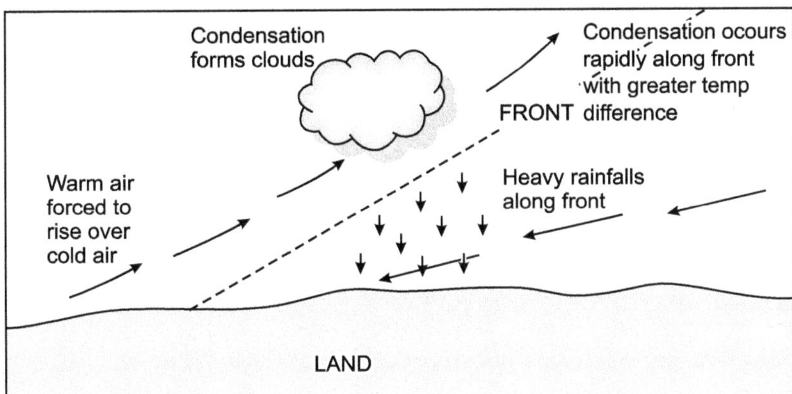

Q. 2. Draw a fully labelled diagram showing the occurrence of rainfall caused by a mountain barrier.

[Annual Examination, 2020]

Ans. The diagram of orographic rain is :

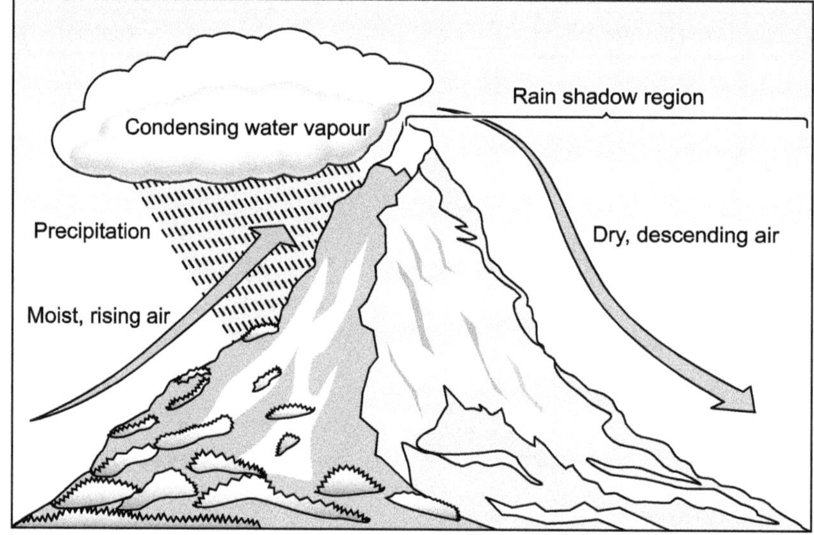

Q. 3. Draw a neat and labelled diagram of hydrological cycle.

Ans.

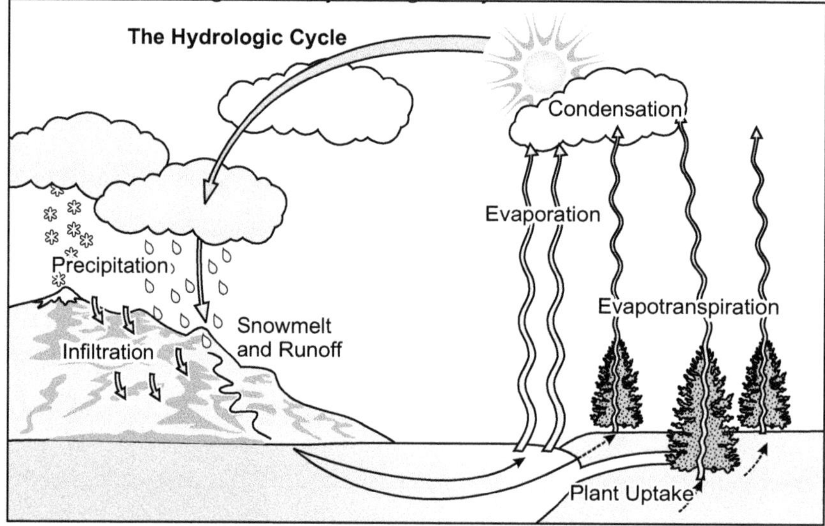

Q. 4. Draw and label the windward side of mountains.

Ans.

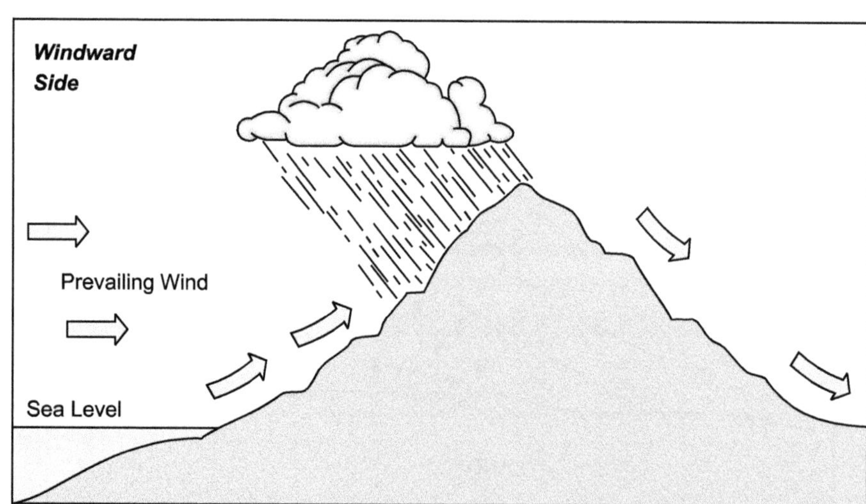

Q. 5. Draw a neat diagram of three types of rainfall.

Ans.

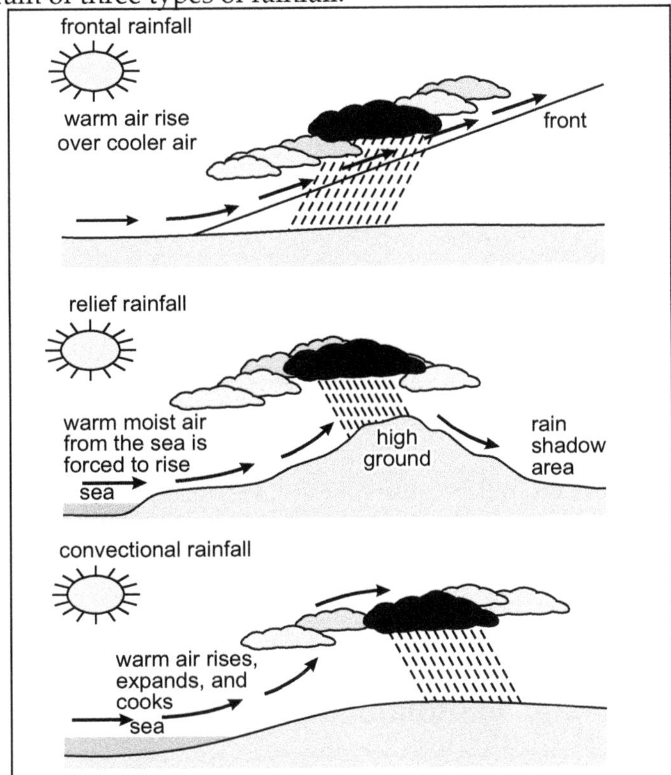

Q. 6. Study the picture given below answer the following questions:

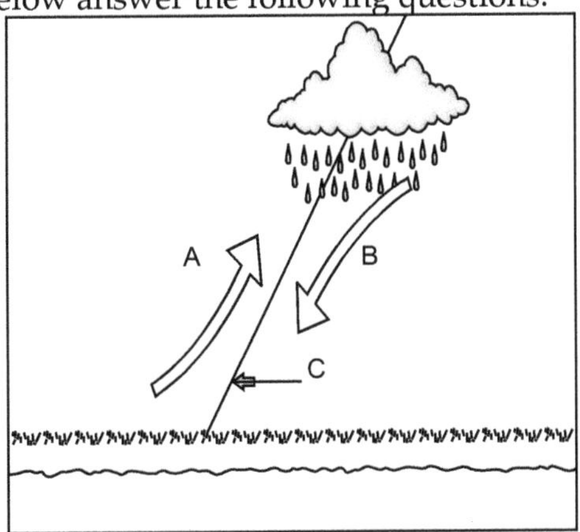

(i) What kind of air mass is A and B?

(ii) The air mass A, is ascending and air mass B is decending. Why?

(iii) What does line C signify?

Ans. (i) Air mass A, is warm air mass and B is cold air mass.

(ii) When two air mass of different heating capacity meets, the warm air mass ascends becase it is lighter in weight and on the contrary the cold air mass is heavier stays closer to the ground and pushes warm air upwards.

(iii) Line C signifies the frontal boundary. Frontal boundary is a boundary where two air masses of different heating capacity, humidity and density meet.

Q. 7. Study the diagram given below and answer the questions that follow: **[November, 2019]**

(i) Write whether place P or place Q will have less rainfall?
Give a reason for your answer.

(ii) Write whether place B or place C will have lower temperature?
Give a reason for your answer.

(iii) Between position D and E in the given diagram:

1. Which will be called windward side?
2. Which will be called rain shadow area?

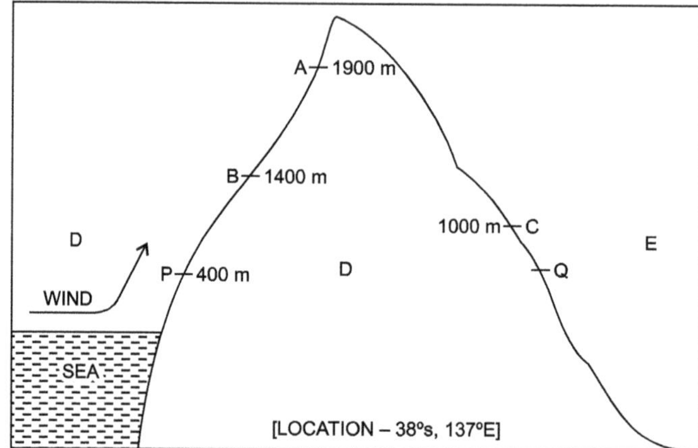

Ans. (i) Q point will have less rainfall because it lies on leeward or rain shadow zone.

(ii) Definitely place B will have less temperature because its altitude (1400 m) is higher than point C (1000 m).

(iii) 1. Position D is a windward side.

2. Position E is a rain shadow zone.

Chapter 15. Pollution and Environment

Q. 1. Draw the diagram showing the formation of acid rain?

Ans

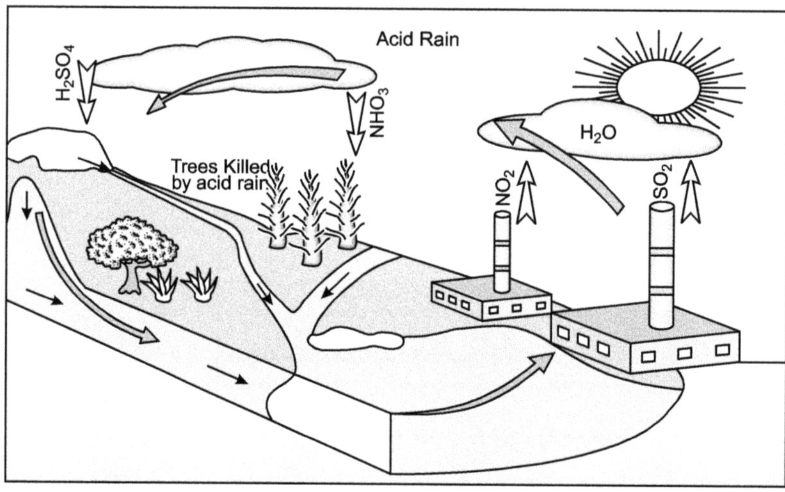

Q. 2. Draw a well labelled diagram to show the sources of air pollution.

Ans.

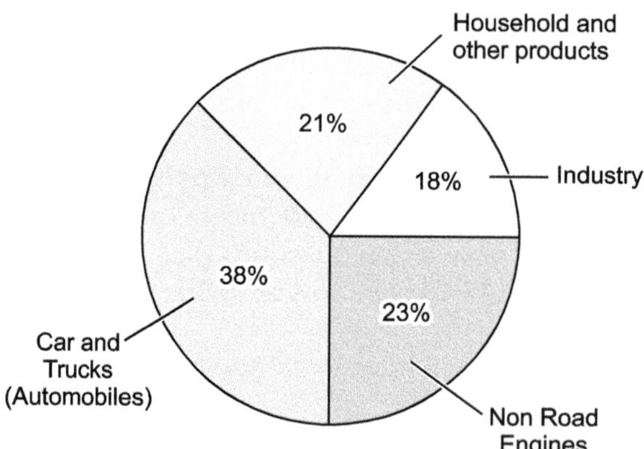

Q. 3. Study the digram of Greenhouse effect and answer the question given below.

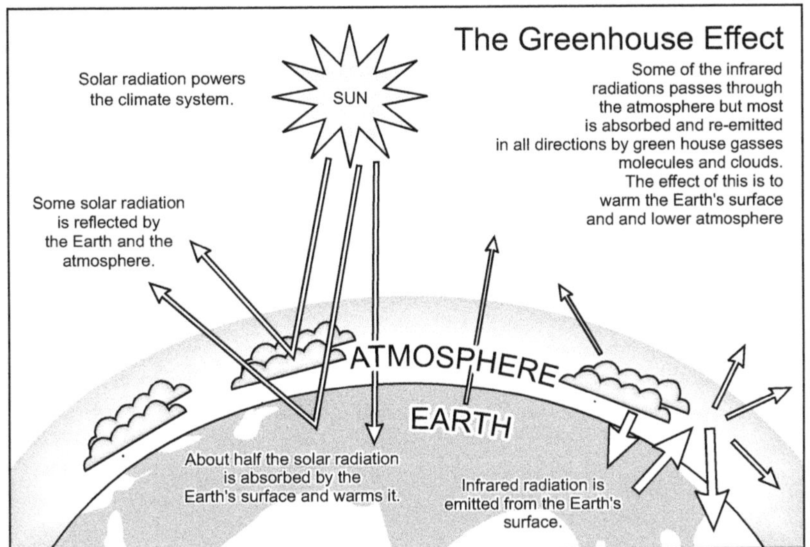

(i) What do you understand by Greenhouse effect?
(ii) What is the outcome of Greenhouse effect on the atmosphere?
(iii) Name the gases that are responsible for Greenhouse effect.

Ans. (i) The heat caused by the infrared radiations are absorbed by greenhouse gases such as water vapour, CO_2, Ozone and Methane which reduce the rate of escape from the atmosphere. This heat is re-emitted in all the directions. This is known as greenhouse effect.
(ii) The greenhouse effect results in rise in atmosphere remperature.
(iii) Carbon-di-oxide, Methane, Ozone, Water vapours.

Chapter 16. Natural Regions of the World

Q. 1. Study the diagram and answer the question given below.
(i) Identify the tree shown in the diagram.
(ii) Why the tree shown in the figure has cone shape?
(iii) The leaf of the coniferous trees are the needle shaped. What is the term used for needle shaped leaves.

Ans. (i) The tree shown in the diagram is Pine tree.
(ii) The confierous tree acquire a cone like shape by the typical dovelopment of branches stretching downward. Due to the conical shape of trees the snow slides down and does not remain suspended on tree tops or on the branches.
(iii) The needle shaped leaves are called as conifers.

Map Work

Set 6

Chapter 5. Landforms of the Earth

Q. 1. Mountains:

(1)	Rockies	(2)	Appalachian
(3)	Andes	(4)	Alps
(5)	Pyrenees	(6)	Carpathians
(7)	Scandinavia Highlands	(8)	Drakensberg
(9)	Ethiopian Highlands	(10)	Himalayas
(11)	Khinehan	(12)	Caucasus
(13)	Zagros	(14)	Tienshan
(15)	Arakan Yoma	(16)	Central Japan Aips
(17)	Atlas Mountain	(18)	Urals
(19)	Great Dividing Range		

Ans.

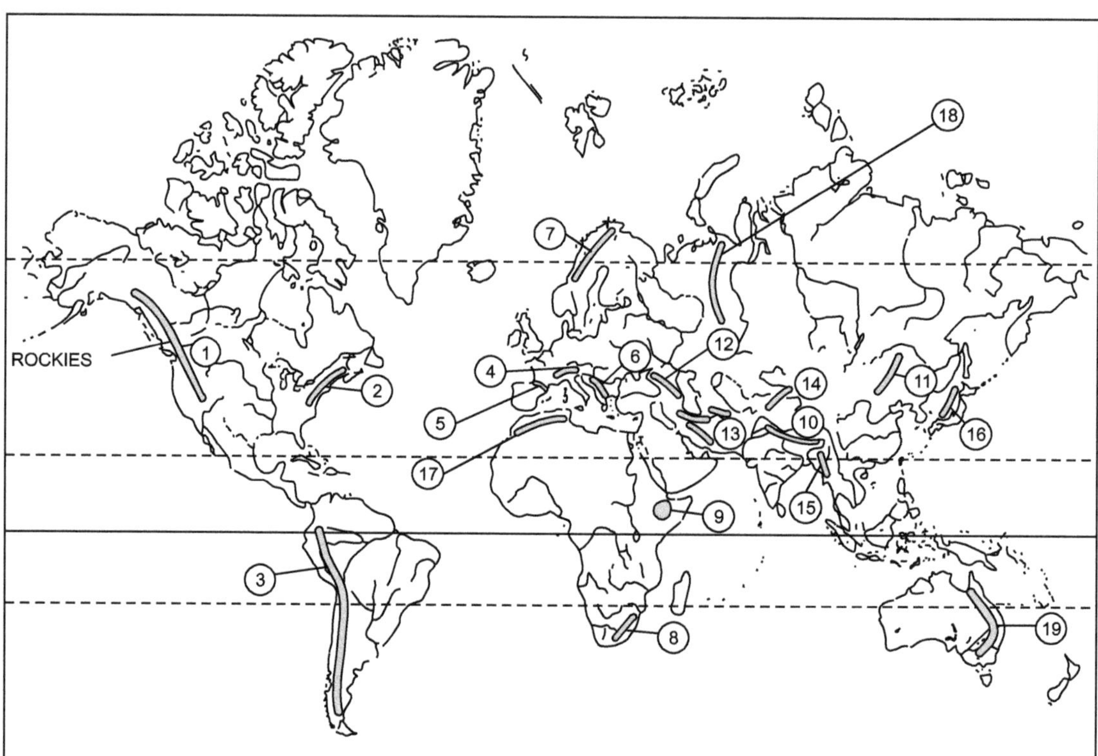

Q. 2. Plateau:

(1) Labrador Plateau

(2) Canadian Shield

(3) Brazilian Highlands

(4) Tibetan Plateau

(5) Iranian Plateau

(6) African Rift valley

(7) Patagonia Plateau
(8) Mangolian Plateau

Ans.

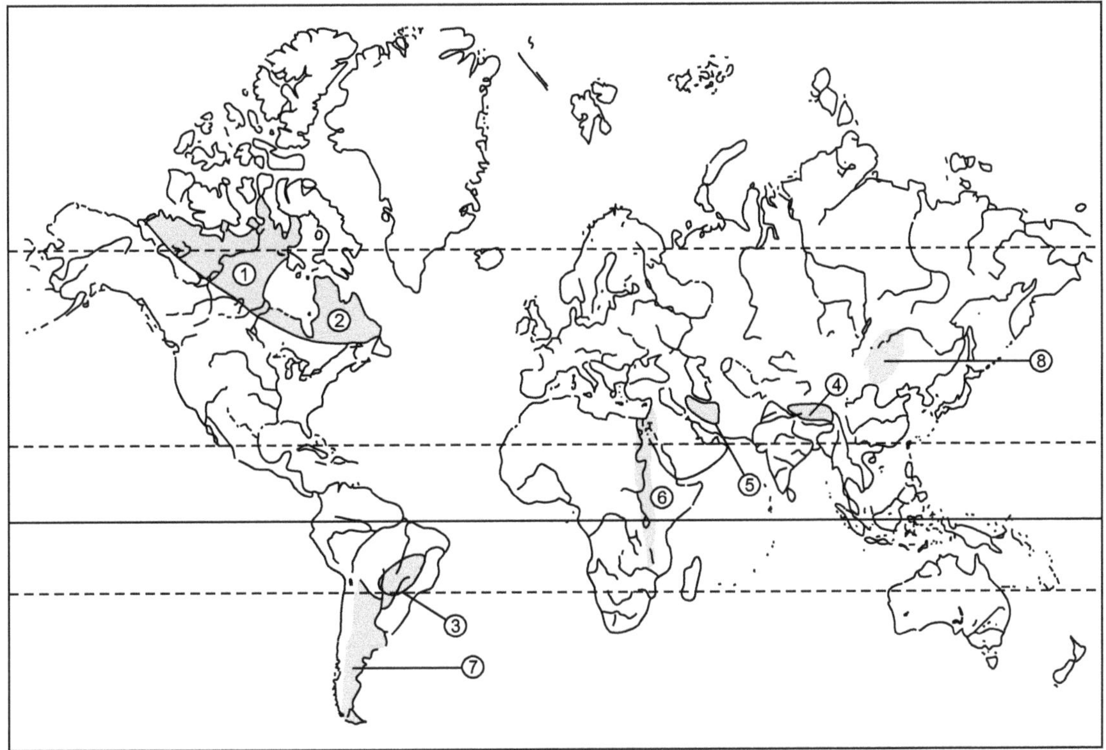

Chapter 7. Volcanoes

Q. 1. Volcanic belts of the World.

Ans.

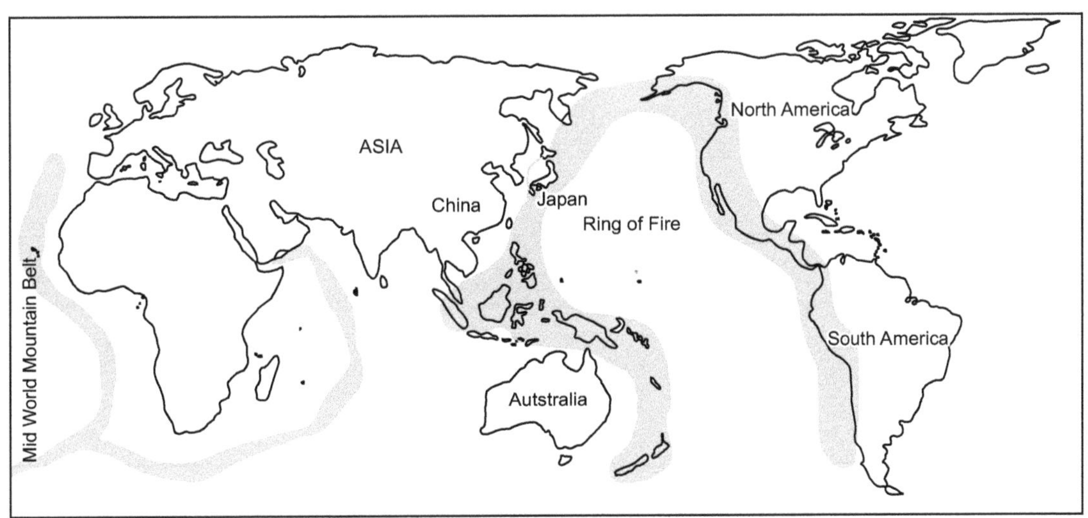

Chapter 9. Weathering

Q. 1. Rivers:

(1) Fraser
(2) St. Lawrence
(3) Mississippi
(4) Missouri
(5) Colorado
(6) Amazon
(7) Parana
(8) Paraguay
(9) Nile
(10) Zaire

(11) Niger
(12) Orange
(13) Seine
(14) Rhine
(15) Volga
(16) Danube
(17) Murray
(18) Darling
(19) Hwange ho
(20) Ganga
(21) Godavari
(22) Mekong
(23) Irrawaddi
(24) Tigris
(25) Euphrates
(26) Chang Tiang (Yangtse)
(27) Zambezi
(28) Ob river
(29) Indus

Ans.

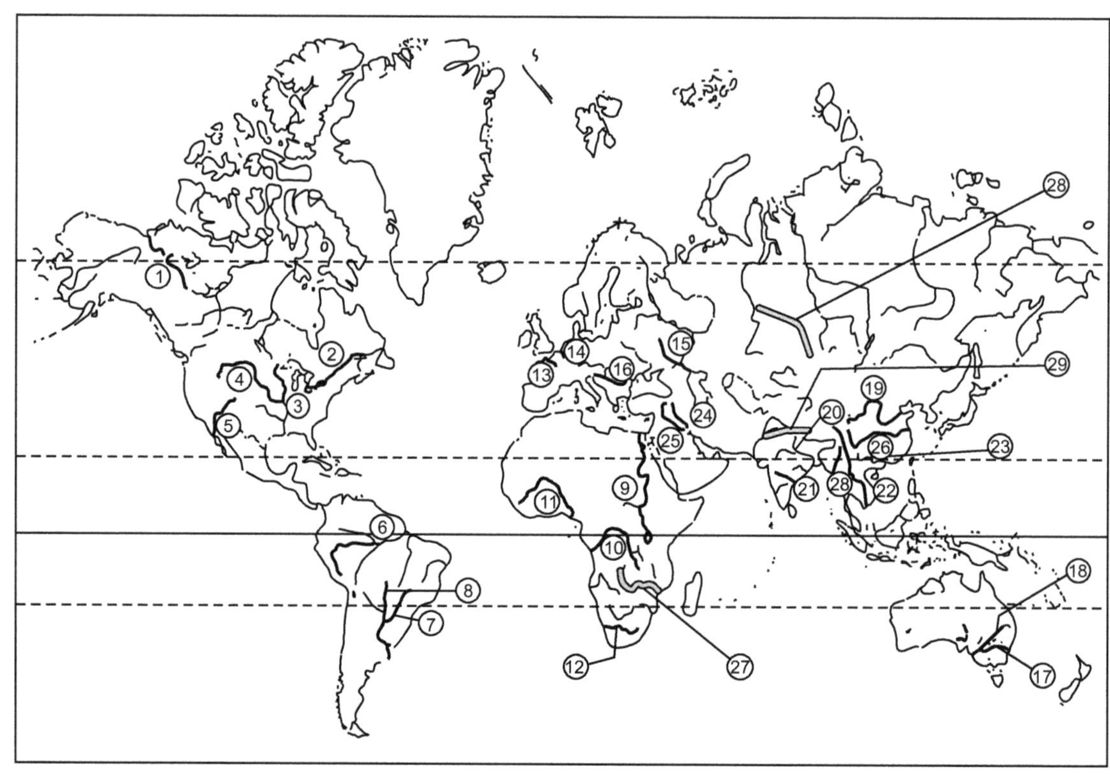

Chapter 10. Hydrosphere

Q. 1. Sea and Ocean:

(1) Caribbean Sea
(2) North Sea
(3) Caspian Sea
(4) Black Sea
(5) Baltic Sea
(6) Mediterranean Sea
(7) Pacific Ocean
(8) Atlantic Ocean
(9) Indian Ocean
(10) Artic Ocean
(11) Southern Ocean

Ans.

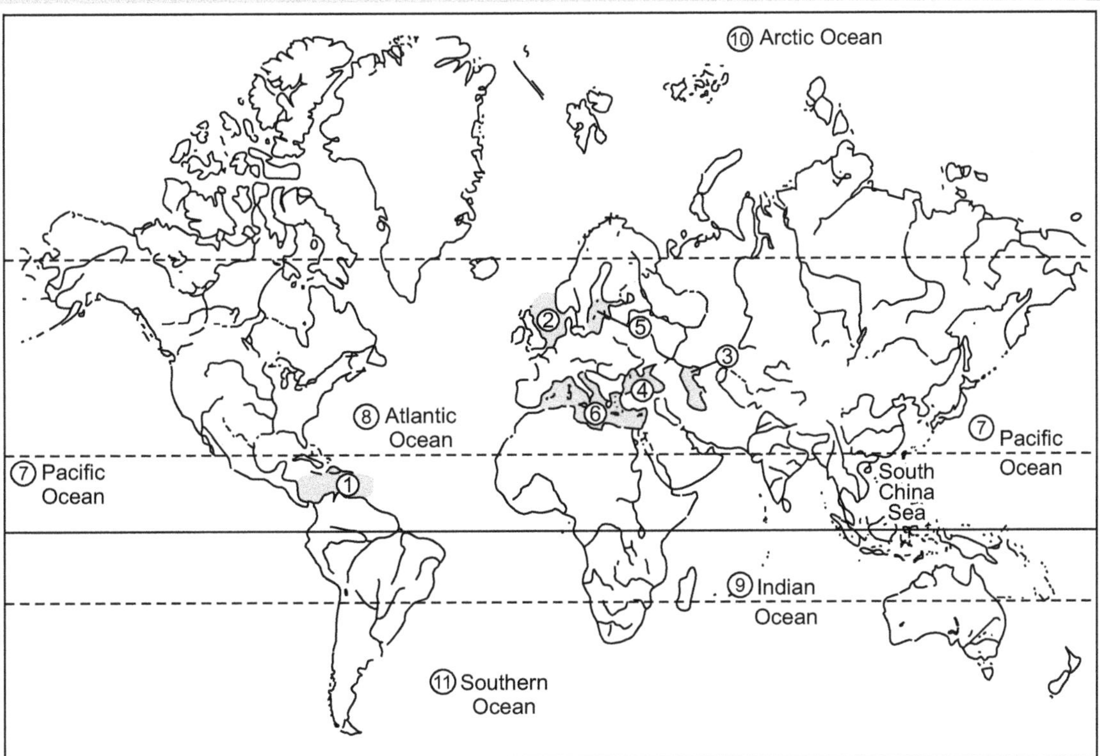

Q. 2. Gulf, Bay, Strait and Isthumus:

(1) Gulf of Alaska
(2) Hudson Bay
(3) Gulf of St. Lawrence
(4) Gulf of Mexico
(5) Gulf of Guinea
(6) Strait of Gibralter
(7) Strait of Malacca. (Longest Str)
(8) Strait of Hagellean
(9) Isthumus of Sue
(10) Gulf of Carpentaria
(11) Persian Gulf
(12) Bering Strait

Ans.

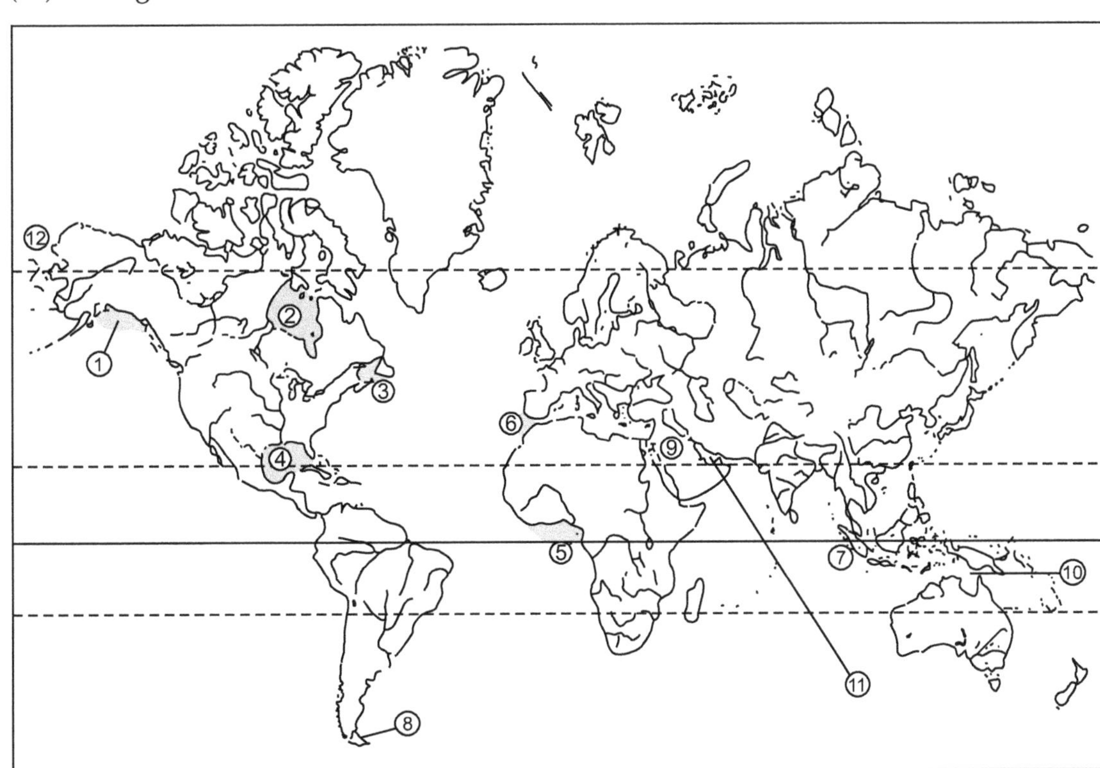

Chapter 16. Natural Regions of the World

Q. 1. Equatorial Region.

Ans.

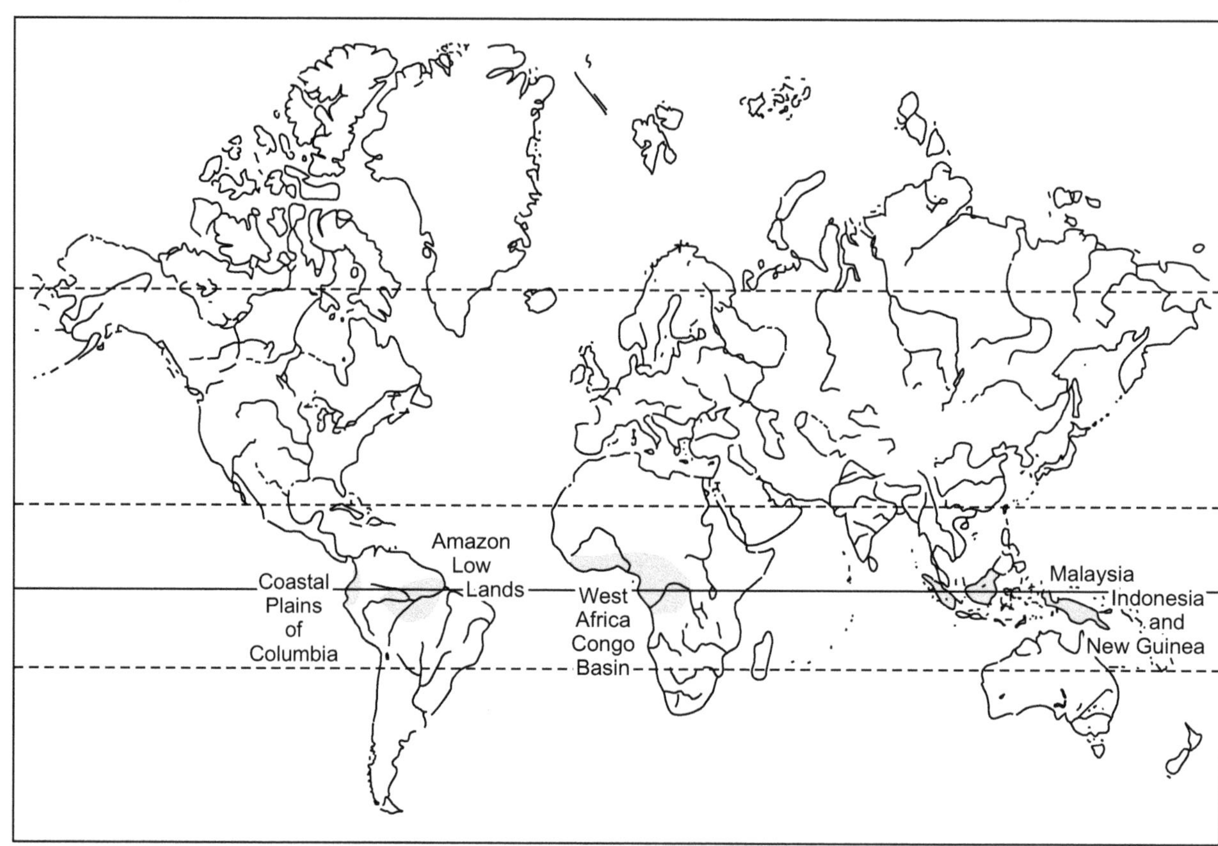

Q. 2. Tropical Monsoon Region.

Ans.

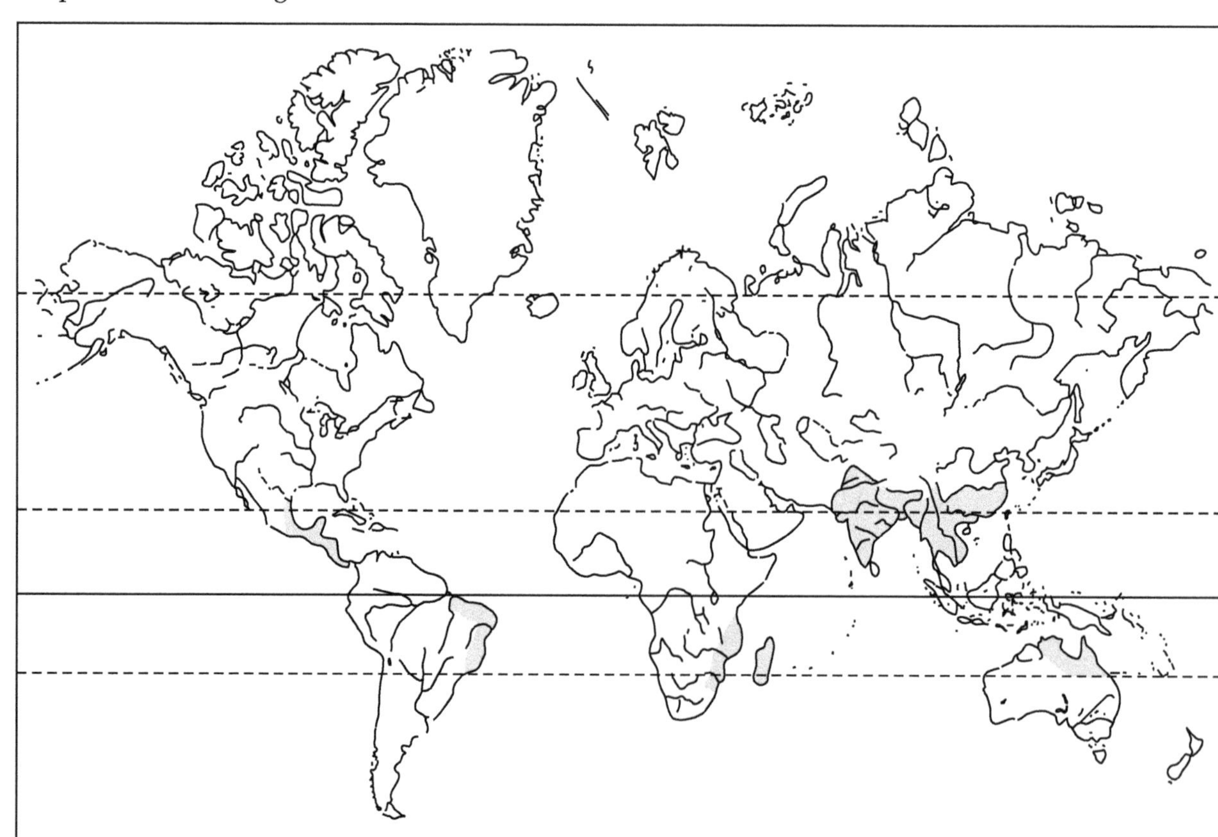

Q. 3. Tropical Hot Desert.

Ans.

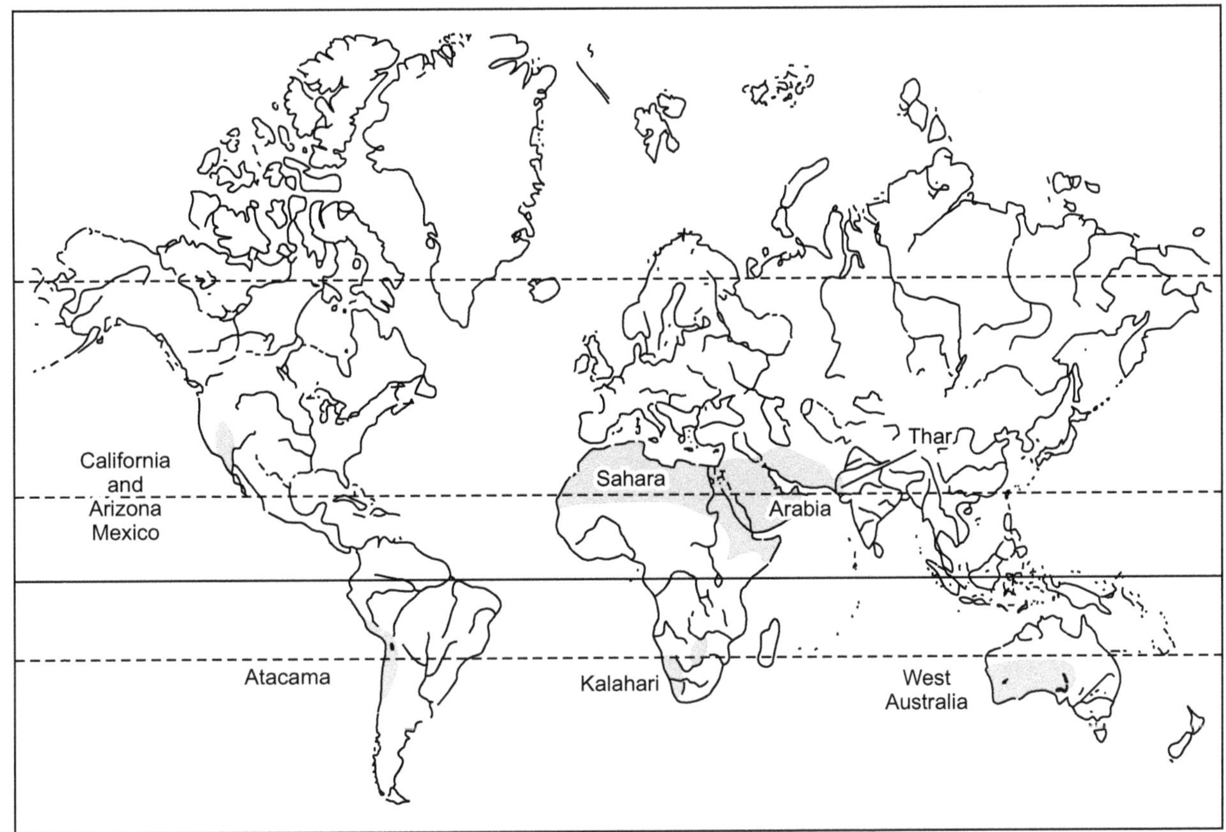

Q. 4. Mediterranean Region.

Ans.

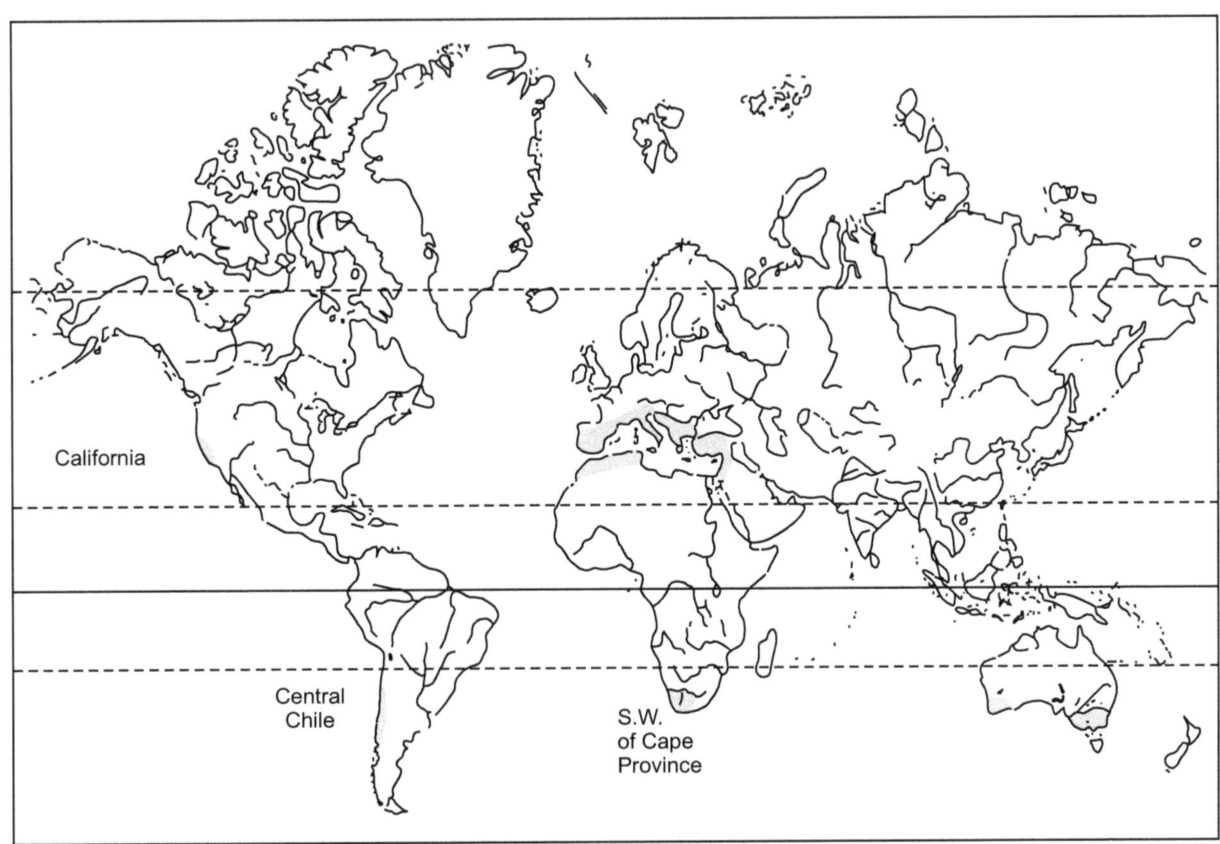

Q. 5. Cool Temperature Continental Steppe Region.

Ans.

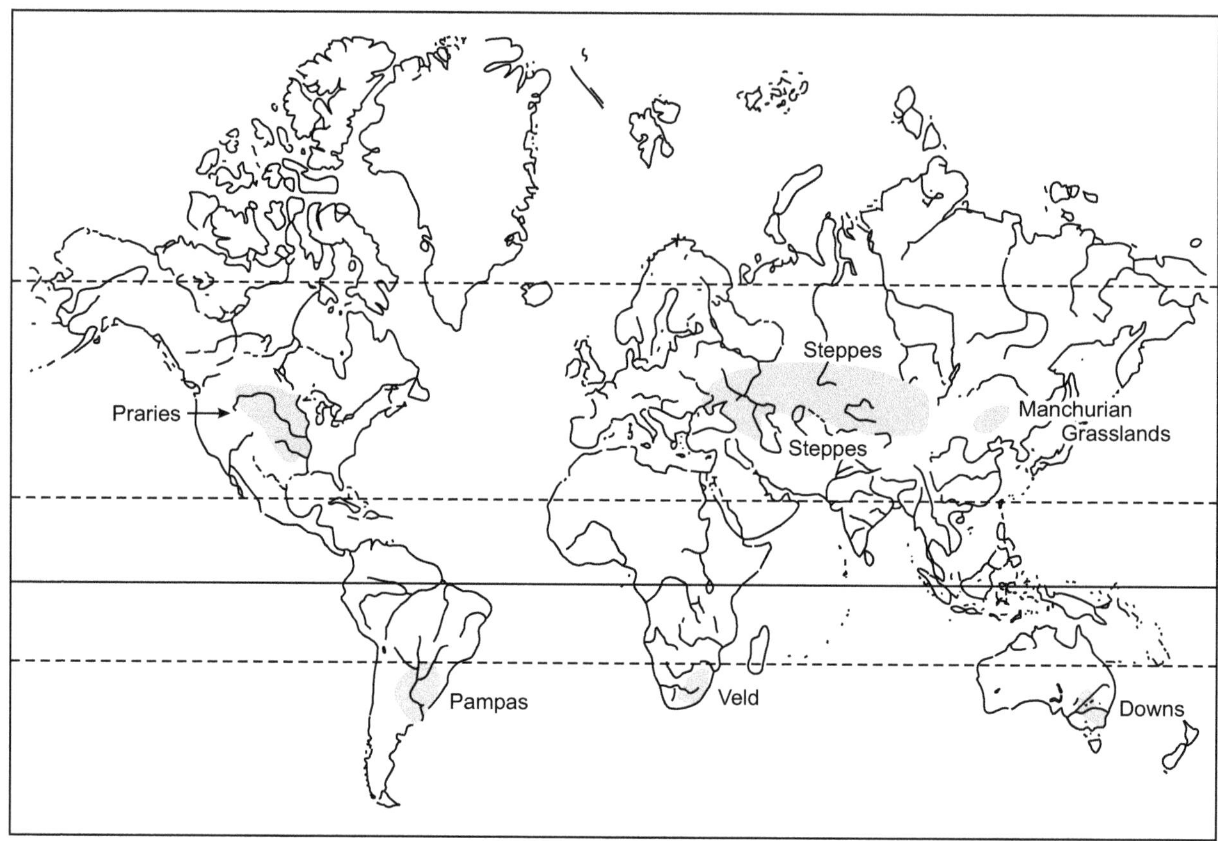

Q. 6. Cool Temperature Ocenaic China Type.

Ans.

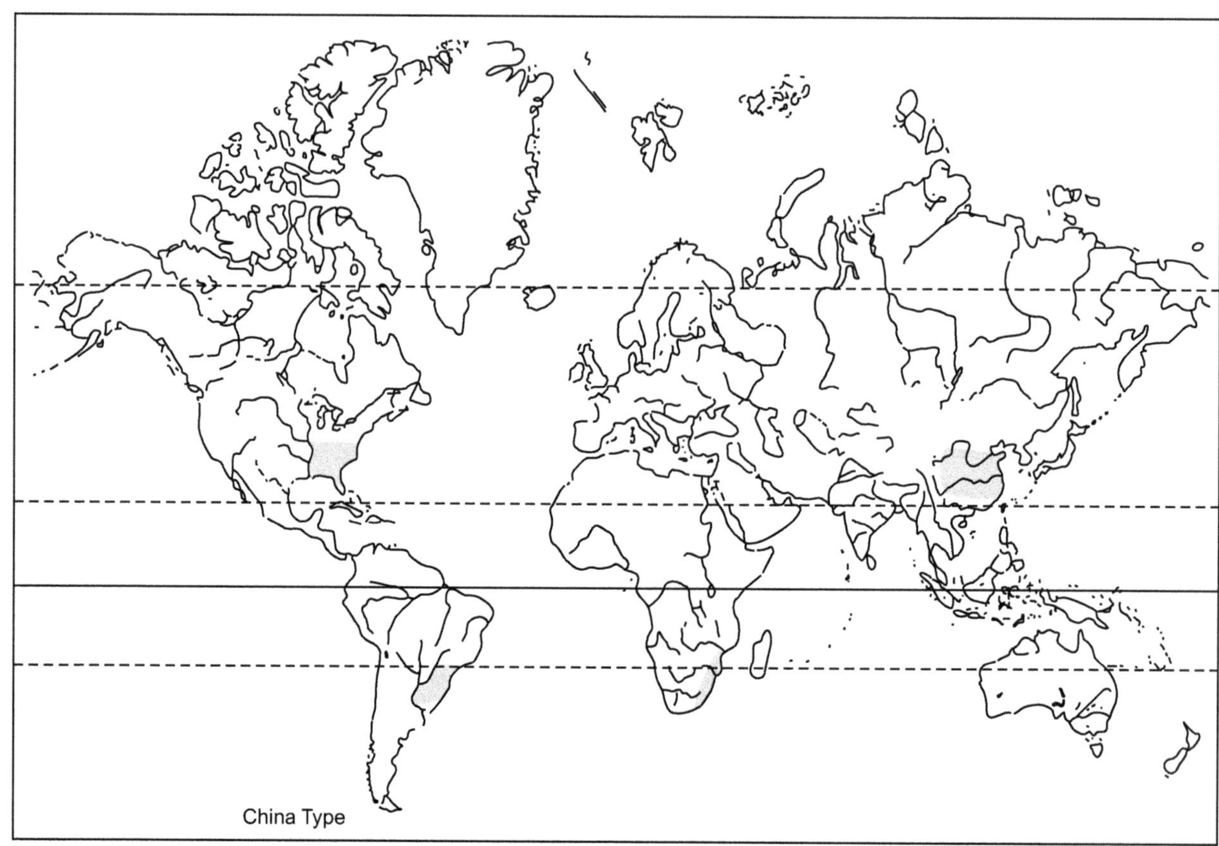

Q. 7. Temperate Grassland.

Ans.

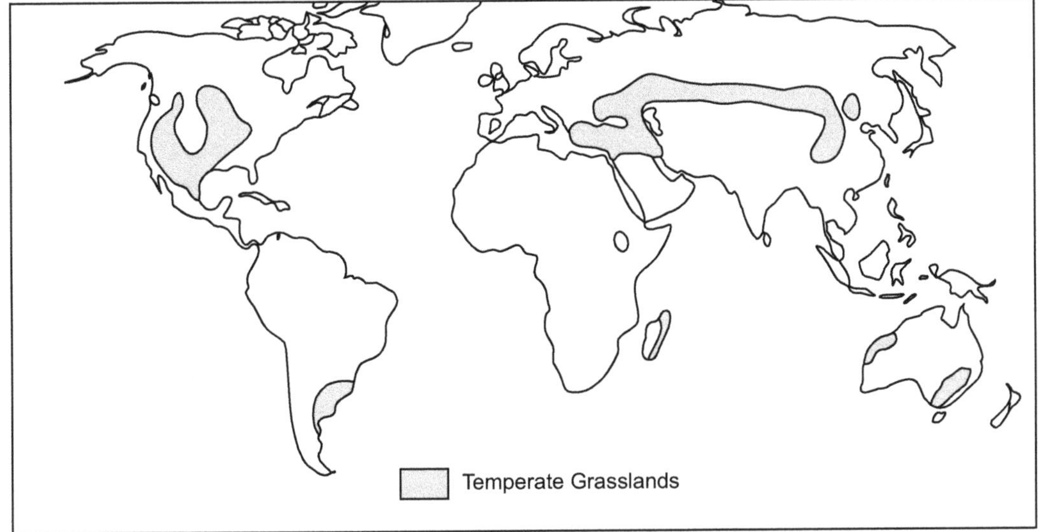

Q. 8. Tropical Grassland.

Ans.

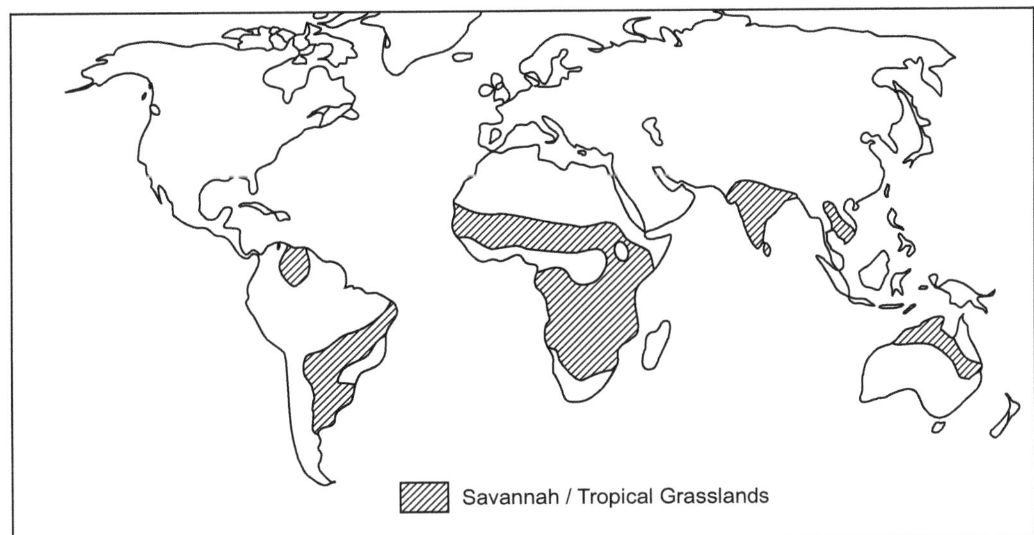

Q. 9. Tiga Region.

Ans.

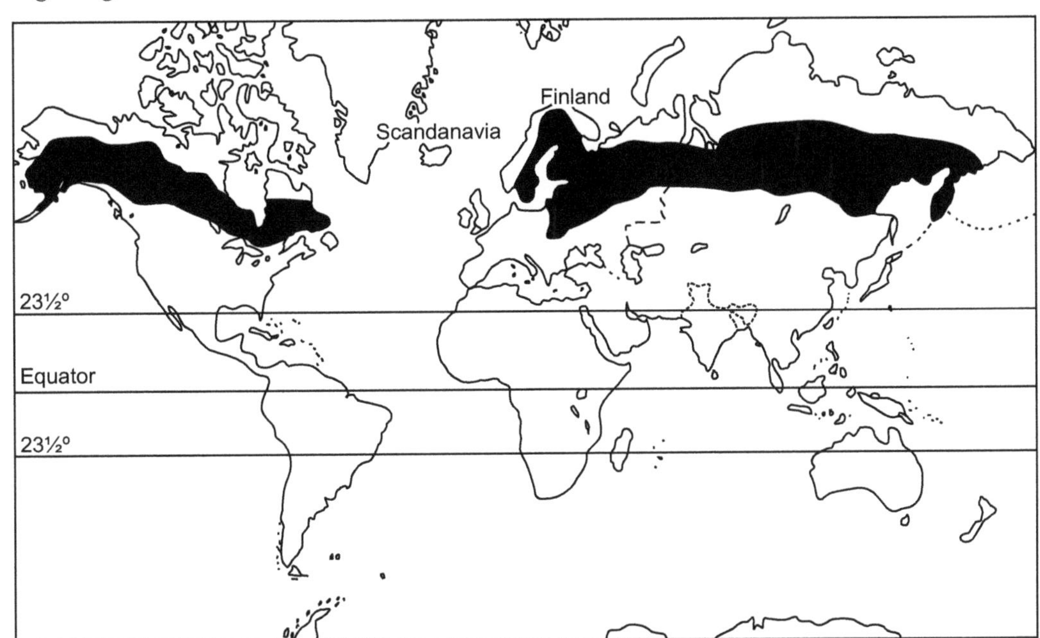

Q. 10. Tundra Region.

Ans.

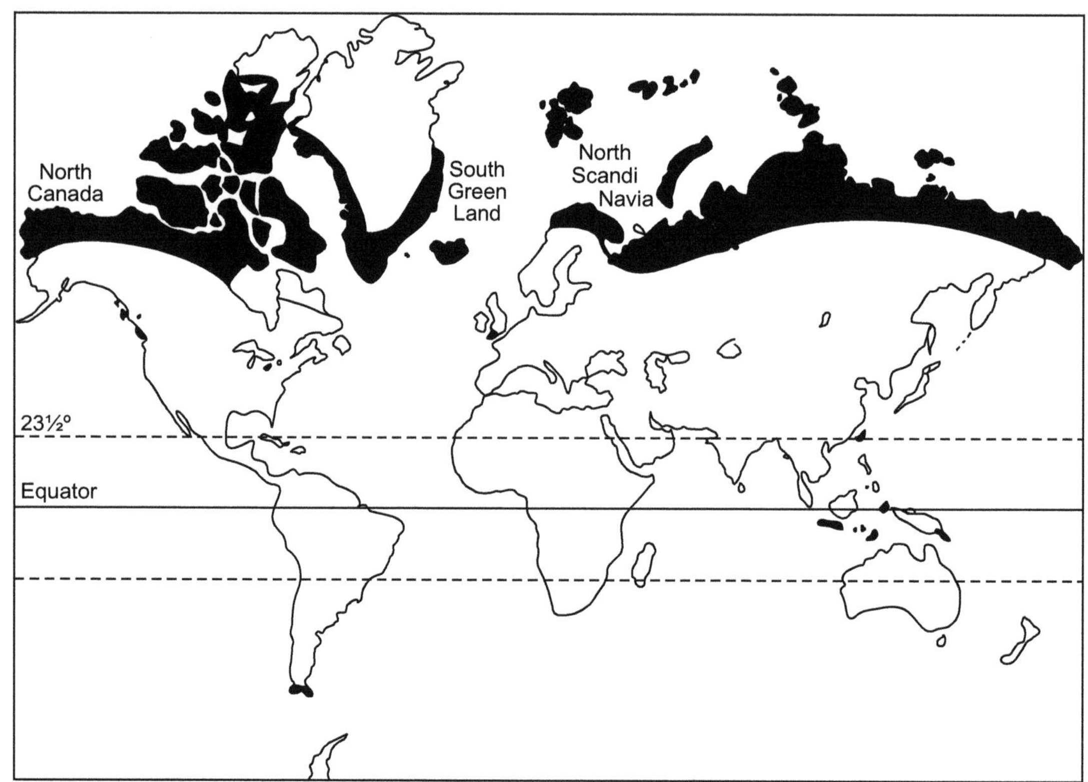

www.ingramcontent.com/pod-product-compliance
Ingram Content Group UK Ltd.
Pitfield, Milton Keynes, MK11 3LW, UK
UKHW061704190726
13853UKWH00008B/2396

9 789392 563089